JONATHAN EDWARDS

ON THE NEW BIRTH IN THE SPIRIT

The Life, Times, and Thought of America's Greatest Theologian

Peter Reese Doyle, ThD, DD

Brandon J. Cozart, MDiv, and G. Wright Doyle, PhD, Editors

Torchflame Books
An imprint of Light Messages

Published 2017, by Torchflame Books
an Imprint of Light Messages
www.lightmessages.com
Durham, NC 27713 USA
SAN: 920-9298

Paperback ISBN: 978-1-61153-246-3
E-book ISBN: 978-1-61153-249-4
Library of Congress Control Number: 2017936436

To my Joyful Life-Companion
SALLY ANN

*FOR
Cathy and Joe
with LOVE
FROM
Peter & Sally ann
1/12/21*

What Others Say

Many thanks to Peter Doyle for seeing earlier than most that the doctrine of regeneration was the heart of Edwards' ministry, pumping spiritual life blood through the rest of his body of work.

Douglas A. Sweeney
Trinity Evangelical Divinity School

In this readable, well-written work, Peter Doyle has provided a convincing synthesis of Edwards' ideas. ... Doyle's contribution will remain relevant and useful for students and scholars of Edwards' thought.

John Cunningham
Providence Christian College

I recommend this book to anyone wanting to learn from Edwards why the miracle of holy love is what happens in heart of all those who are truly born of God. That this miracle occurred in the heart of Dr. Doyle is evident by all who have known and been loved by him.

C.H. Rhyne III
Auburn, Alabama

If John the Apostle was likened to an eagle who could look directly into the brightness of the sun, Edwards gave to the eighteenth century all that John saw. Peter Doyle has looked into Edwards and brought to us the insights, the correctives, and the brilliance of that great mind, so clearly illumined by his love of the excellent beauty of God and His revelation of Jesus Christ in the Bible. ... Edwards in the hand of Peter Doyle comes alive with his elegant writing, clarity in conveying ideas, and love for the subject.

The Very Rev. E.A. (Tad) deBordenave, III
Richmond, Virginia

This book will be of interest to Edwards scholars. Among other things, it is proof that Karl Barth in his later years became aware of the intricacies of Edwards's theology. ... For all those interested in Edwards's writings on assurance, informed by scholarship before the 1980s, this work will be of help.

Gerald R. McDermott
Beeson Divinity School

One does not have to be an "Edwards scholar" to profit from this book. Peter has presented Edward's life and teachings in a very readable yet profound way. ... Reading this book has made me want to clear my shelves of many of my books and concentrate on the Holy Scriptures and Peter's book on Edwards. This book is a grand gift to the Church!

Betty Thomas
Opelika, AL

Editors' Introduction

The Author

Peter Reese Doyle possesses unusual qualifications for writing a book on Jonathan Edwards' teaching on the role of the Holy Spirit in regeneration.

After graduating from Washington and Lee University, with a major in Humanities and a strong emphasis on philosophy, he attended the Virginia (Episcopal) Theological Seminary and then Seabury - Western Seminary, where he received solid instruction in theology. He was ordained to the ministry of the Protestant Episcopal Church in 1957 and served as a pastor in rural Virginia for almost a year until he was forced to leave for expressing public opposition to racial segregation in Christian churches. He was accepted as a missionary of the Episcopal Church in 1958, when he and his wife Sally Ann moved to Cuttington College and Seminary in Libera, West Africa, where he taught courses in Systematic Theology and Church History for two years.

He was urged by his bishop to pursue doctoral studies and chose to study under Professor Karl Barth in Basel, Switzerland. He was one of Barth's last students before retirement. For two years Doyle sat under the superb teaching of Karl Barth and other eminent professors of historical and systematic theology. After two years in Basel, he returned with his family to the United States, where he became Rector of St. James Episcopal Church in Leesburg, Virginia.

Not long after he moved to Leesburg, what became known as the Renewal Movement in mainline churches broke out. He had an early experience of physical and inner healing through the ministry of Agnes Sanford. His congregation included several people who would now be considered Pentecostal in their theology and practice. Suddenly, Doyle found himself praying with others for people with seemingly incurable injuries and illnesses and seeing them miraculously healed. Manifestations of spiritual gifts, such as speaking in tongues, occurred.

So also did negative reaction from some church members and authorities, who considered claims to "know God," much less to seeing God work miracles of healing through prayer or to speak in tongues, to be conclusive proof of insanity. On the other side, he had to deal with zealous souls who, thrilled by the miracles they witnessed and the immediate experiences of the fullness of the Holy Spirit, spread the view that all such phenomena were from God and that everyone who is a true Christian should speak in tongues.

In other words, he found himself in a role very similar to that of Jonathan Edwards during the Great Awakening, when senior members of the church establishment dismissed unusual phenomena as "enthusiasm" and therefore beyond the pale of orthodoxy, and when over-eager zealots, many with little or no theological training, rushed around the countryside promoting supernatural experiences as normative for all believers.

During those years in Leesburg, Doyle had to apply what he had learned from Edwards to a variety of pastoral situations, and he found Edwards' criteria for distinguishing what were, and what were not, true signs of the work of the Holy Spirit to be extremely pertinent and practically helpful. From Edwards he also learned how to guide new believers into paths of solid Christian growth. What had begun as an academic study became a hands-on course in pastoral theology.

In 1968 he was invited to join the faculty of the Episcopal Seminary in Lexington, Kentucky. For one-and-a-half years, he lectured on Evangelical Theology, Athanasius and the Crisis of Arianism, Evangelical Theology in the Great Awakening, Modern Theology and the German Church Crisis under Hitler, Homiletics, and Ethics. In recognition of his academic training, wide knowledge, and teaching excellence, he was awarded an honorary Doctor of Divinity (D.D.) degree from the seminary.

He resigned from the Episcopal denomination in 1972 and became a Presbyterian. He was one of the founding Teaching Elders in the Presbyterian Church in America.

As an associate pastor of Briarwood Presbyterian Church in Birmingham, Alabama, he also taught for four years in the Briarwood seminary, offering courses in Systematic Theology, Calvin's *Institutes*, Church History, and New Testament.

In 1977 he accepted a call as Pastor of Covenant Presbyterian Church in Auburn, Alabama. He also enrolled in the Th.D. program at Trinity

Theological Seminary in Newburgh, Indiana. After completing a full curriculum of coursework and an examination, in 1980 he submitted this book to fulfil the final requirement for the Th.D.

He is now "honorably retired" from the Presbyterian Church in America. He serves with Reformed Ministries International, Inc., working primarily in cooperation with CRU (Campus Crusade for Christ) in Auburn, Alabama.

Scholarship since 1980

Since this book was finished in 1980, a veritable ocean of scholarship on Jonathan Edwards has appeared. Not only has the printed Yale edition of Edwards' works been completed, but all of his other writings have been digitalized and are available online, something inconceivable in the 1980s. Not only so, but many editions of individual books or collections of sermons by Edwards have been issued.

Learned monographs on aspects of Edwards' theology, or on his theology as a whole, continue to be published. There is no way to reflect either the quantity or the quality of academic publications in this introduction, or to show how they pertain to Peter Doyle's thesis.

Still, we shall attempt to take note of a few books that seem to be relevant to this volume, and then point out the special contribution that Doyle has made to the understanding of Edwards, even though he wrote more than three decades ago. Unless otherwise noted, the findings of the scholars surveyed below agree with not only the main points but many of the details, to be found in Doyle's work.

At least two major biographies of Edwards have appeared since Peter Doyle completed his dissertation: Iain Murray's *Jonathan Edwards: A New Biography*, published in 1987, and *Jonathan Edwards: A Life*, by George M. Marsden, issued in 2003. Both are excellent, but Marsden's is considered to be the more comprehensive, so we shall look at it briefly here.

Marsden naturally describes the home and church in which Edwards grew up, including his father's response to revivals, and especially his disagreement with his parents over the matter of what constituted evidence of true conversion. He does not, however, examine in any detail the formative years of Edwards' education at Yale. He does believe that Edwards read Locke, as he read all authors, including Berkeley, critically, and "was no Lockean in any strict sense."[1] He traces Edwards'

---

1   Marsden, Edwards, 63. Full publication information for this and the works

study of "natural philosophy," that is, science, but curiously asserts that Edwards "expected God to work through secondary, or natural, causes,"[2] something which Doyle vigorously denies. Marsden insists, however, upon the essentially Calvinistic nature of Edwards' thoughts about philosophy, theology, and science, and he notes Edwards' study of logic and his habit of arguing his points with ruthless rigor. Marsden also emphasizes that from his earliest oration in defense of his M.A. degree at Yale, Edwards was convinced that "Arminianism" was the chief theological foe of true orthodoxy[3] and that opposition to traditional Reformed doctrine was part of a general ascension of "modern fashion" in thought.[4]

Marsden notes the programmatic importance of the anti-Arminian lecture, "God Glorified in Man's Dependence," given in Boston, and of the sermon, "A Divine and Supernatural Light," delivered in 1734, which "related his most profound theological reflections on his understanding of true Christian experience."[5] Affections, he was convinced, lie at the heart of authentic Christian life, and must be present along with a mental knowledge of, and agreement with, biblical truth.

Marsden also stresses the centrality of love in Edwards' theology: "The Charity sermons ... stood close to the heart of Edwards theological enterprise." That is because "the very essence of reality ... was the intratrinitarian love of the Father, Son, and Holy Spirit."[6] Edwards was "thoroughly Reformed" in his view of love. Further, "God's love towards humans was essentially redemptive love."[7]

A few other key points: Marsden believes that the treatise, *The End for which God Created the World*, ... "was a sort of prolegomenon to all his work." "Few scholars have put more emphasis on the primacy of the affections." [8] "At the core of his vision of God was the beauty of God's irrepressible love manifested in Christ."[9] Edwards was "simultaneously a strict conservative and an innovator."[10]

---

quoted below can be found in the Bibliography.
2   Marsden, *Edwards*, 69.
3   See especially Marsden, *Edwards*, 138-141.
4   Marsden, *Edwards*, 139.
5   Marsden, *Edwards*, 157.
6   Marsden, *Edwards*, 191.
7   Marsden, *Edwards*, 192.
8   Marsden, *Edwards*, 254.
9   Marsden, *Edwards*, 266.
10   Marsden, Edwards, 458.

Marsden considers that the conflict between Edwards and Charles Chauncy was philosophical: Chauncey stood for the "intellectualist" and more Aristotelian (and Thomistic) tradition, which argued that the will should follow the best dictates of reason. Edwards was in the Augustinian "voluntarist" camp that viewed the whole person as guided by affections of the will.

Marsden describes the spread of "fashionable opinions" about the value of reason[11] and notes that Edwards saw himself as "an apologist for 'Calvinistic' theology versus 'the modern writers.'" [12] In this, he was prescient in his "sense of the direction that Western thought, culture, and religion were heading. ... the emphasis on the individual's wholly unfettered free will was part of what is sometimes characterized as the invention of the modern self."[13] He saw this as a part of "a trend toward what he called 'Arminianism.'"[14] The treatise on *Original Sin* can, therefore, be seen as an exposition of biblical teaching against "fashionable eighteenth-century standards of morality and justice."[15] Likewise, the *Two Dissertations* posed a direct challenge to the foundation of "modern" thought.[16]

With many others, Marsden believes that "Edwards' philosophy started with his theology."[17] *Freedom of the Will* is "a philosophical *tour de force* by someone who was, first of all, a theologian."[18] He writes, "The key to Edwards' thought is that everything is related because everything is related to God."[19] Doyle shows how this fact is seen in Edwards' teachings on regeneration. That is because Edwards held the "Christian Trinitarian conception of God as essentially interpersonal. ... God's infinite goodness is essentially the goodness of love."[20] Commenting upon Edwards' declaration, "The whole is of God, and in God, and to God; and God is the beginning, middle and end in this affair," Marsden says, "That last sentence encapsulated the central premise of his entire thought."[21]

---

11   Marsden, *Edwards*, 433.
12   Marsden, *Edwards*, 437.
13   Marsden, *Edwards*, 438.
14   Marsden, *Edwards*, 439.
15   Marsden, *Edwards*, 451.
16   Marsden, Edwards, 459-60.
17   Marsden, *Edwards*, 442.
18   Marsden, *Edwards*, 446.
19   Marsden, *Edwards*, 460.
20   Marsden, *Edwards*, 462.
21   Marsden, *Edwards*, 463.

Michael J. McClymond and Gerald R. McDermott,
The Theology of Jonathan Edwards.

When it appeared in 2012, this thick volume was praised as "compre-hensive, learned," and "an unmatched digest of [Edwards'] time and thought."[22] As such, it will serve as a representative recent treatment of Edwards' theology for our purposes and will be quoted extensively in the following pages.

The authors, like many others, observe that though Edwards assid-uously studied and interacted with the thought of a host of other thinkers, and was "deeply indebted to his theological tradition," he also examined everything from new angles, and "came up with novel, original arguments for orthodox doctrines," so that "over the course of time his entire theology acquired a distinctive character."[23] Again, in common with most other scholars, they remark on his "surprising reliance on human reasoning to support doctrines that most others had chosen to leave within the realm of mystery."[24]

At the outset, McClymond and McDermott set forth five distinctive aspects of Edwards' theology. Though the authors discern growth in Edwards' thought over the years, they comment on the remark-able organic nature of this development, using the term "evolution." They take note of his "intellectual strategies" of "concatenation and subsumption. The former refers to Edwards' search for connections among ideas that might ordinarily be thought of as disconnected." while the latter "refers to the ways in which Edwards' insights were absorbed into ever-expanding and more general categories," such as the concept of divine "communication," which features so prominently in Doyle's book.[25]

The themes are *Trinitarian communication*, a notion that "undergirds all that he had to say regarding salvation." Beauty stands at the center of God's being and is communicated to his people in the second aspect, *creaturely participation*, with God's moral beauty again central to that which is given to his people, and which they then being to reflect in their own lives.

---

22 McClymond and McDermott, *Theology*. Comments on the dust jacket by
    George Marsden, Alister McGrath, Mark Noll, and Ken Minkema.
23 McClymond and McDermott , *Theology*, 12.
24 McClymond and McDermott, *Theology*, 12.
25 McClymond and McDermott, *Theology*, 11.

Third is *necessitarian dispositionalism*, which is the essence of a thing and is indicated by our affections. This "Augustinian" facet of Edwards' thought permeates his anthropology and his soteriology and underlies not only *Religious Affections* but also *Freedom of the Will* and *Original Sin*. The fourth major theme, *theocentric voluntarism*, affirms "the divine priority in all of reality," and marks what can be called the "Calvinistic" nature of Edwards' view not only of redemption but also of creation.[26] Finally, they note Edwards' *harmonious constitutionalism*, which means that "all aspects of salvation are interrelated because all are willed together in God's eternity and according to God's degree."[27]

They find these distinctives in the late dissertations, *End of Creation* and *The Nature of True Virtue*, the *Treatise on Grace*, and *Religious Affections*. They also mine notebook entries, but also discern these recurring ideas in the early lectures, including "God Glorified in Man's Dependence on Him," "A Divine and Supernatural Light," and "Justification by Faith Alone," the last being his master's degree oration. From his earliest works to his latest, Edwards' theology is almost like a seamless garment.

The Introduction sets the stage for thirty chapters of the body of their volume, in which the authors discuss the usual *topoi* of theology, highlighting Edwards' particular contribution. Let us glance briefly at a few.

"Edwards' Intellectual Context": Edwards lived in a time of theological, intellectual, and ecclesiastical turmoil. A variety of ideas, both old and new, competed for supremacy both in the world and in the church.

The "Question of Development: Did Edwards Change?' Despite its title, this chapter, while showing how Edwards "turned" to address different problems and challenges during his theological career, that provides no evidence to refute the claim made above, that his thought evolved organically into an integrated whole.

Indeed, the next chapter, "Beauty and Aesthetics," states early that "the whole of Edwards' theology" can be interpreted "as the gradual, complex outworking of a primal vision of God's beauty that came to him in the wake of his conversion experience."[28] They even venture to say that, though "there are many reasons to regard Edwards as an orig-

---

26 *McClymond and McDermott, Theology*, 6..
27 McClymond and McDermott, *Theology*, 6.
28 McClymond and McDermott, *Theology*, 94.

inal and venturesome thinker, ... his placement of beauty at the heart of his theology may have been the boldest stroke of all."[29]

For Edwards, beauty, though consisting primarily in "proportion," was essentially moral. God's beauty, also called his "excellency," is seen in his holiness and supremely in his love, both within the Trinity and enveloping his elect people into an everlasting embrace. Edwards was consumed not only by the "objective" beauty of God, of which the world is a mirror but by a "subjective" delight that could sometimes be experienced as rapture.

Metaphysics: The authors believe that Edwards "[d]rew eclectically from Puritan authors, Cambridge Platonists, Continental metaphysicians, and Locke's empiricism, and yet he actively transmuted and refashioned nearly all of the ideas that he appropriated" from them.[30] Here the authors' aim to be comprehensive leads to an exposition that is more extensive than Doyle's, but he would agree with them on two main points: 1. Edwards built his metaphysics on the *analogia entis* – analogy of being that saw the created order as a reflection of God's own being, though without compromising divine transcendence. 2. He was always primarily a theologian, not a philosopher; his "central theme" was always "theocentrism"; and "Philosophical reasoning, for Edwards, was a means of affirming God's transcendent greatness and glory."[31]

In "Typology: Scripture, Nature, and All of Reality," McClymond and McDermott draw out the implications of Edwards' conviction that "everything is related to everything else" because everything depends on God and, in one way or another, reflects God. Edwards found justification for a typological reading of the Old Testament in the New Testament and went further than many divines had, or have since then, in identifying specific types. Because he considered the created order as a product of the effulgence of God's beauty, he found types in nature also. Likewise with both sacred and profane history: everything served as some sort of pointer to God's character and his will. The authors use not only Edwards' *Miscellanies*, but also *The End for Which God Created the World*.

"Revelation: Scripture, Reason, and Tradition": For Edwards, "the Scriptures should be 'our guide in all things, in our thoughts of reli-

---

29 McClymond and McDermott, *Theology*, 94.
30 McClymond and McDermott, *Theology*, 103.
31 McClymond and McDermott, *Theology*, 115.

gion, and of ourselves."[32] The authors emphasize Edwards' conviction that "God is a communicating being," desirous of "communicating himself" to his people, and especially to communicate "his own happiness." Edwards valued reason, and used it, but insisted that only regenerated reason, illumined by the Holy Spirit, could lead us to a saving knowledge of Christ. Theological tradition played a major role in Edwards' theology, though he felt free to depart from it if biblical revelation required a new view of things.

In their chapter on "Apologetics," McClymond and McDermott show how Edwards departed from Locke's denial of innate ideas and also combatted the Deists' reliance on unaided reason and their attempt to "distance God from the world," with "all the energy of his being," as he sought to uphold "a radically God-centered perspective."[33] They cite Edwards' sermon, "A Divine and Supernatural Light," to explain how he demonstrates that "God 'illumines' the mind of the saint, 'infuses' his grace, and 'indwells' the body of the believer through the Holy Spirit."[34]

"God as Trinity": "The Trinity was central to Edwards' theology."[35] His understanding of the Trinity informs not only Edwards' "most distinctive theological theme, the divine beauty,"[36] but also his doctrine of the work of redemption, since all three Persons participate in the salvation of men, and his view of his ethics. Edwards emphasizes the distinctive roles of the Persons, and like Augustine identifies the Holy Spirit as the Love of God and his chief effects as engendering love and joy in his people, and allowing them to "participate" in God's being and love. The "social analogy," in which the three Persons are seen as a "society of love," plays a crucial role in all of Edwards' thinking. The divine beauty mentioned above consists primarily in the harmony of mutual consent. More than any theologian before him, and more than most since, Edwards laid great stress on the person and work of the Holy Spirit. He also insisted that "there is no final disjunction between the immanent and economic Trinity. The inner life of God (*ad intra*) is replicated in and known through God's Trinitarian work for his creatures (*ad extra*)" as believers come to participate in the love and joy of the Triune God.[37]

---

32 McClymond and McDermott, *Theology*, 135.
33 McClymond and McDermott, *Theology*, 153.
34 McClymond and McDermott, *Theology*, 163.
35 McClymond and McDermott, *Theology*, 193.
36 McClymond and McDermott, *Theology*, 193.
37 McClymond and McDermott, *Theology*, 205.

"End of God in Creation": One of two major essays published after Edwards' death, this short work has been called, "the essence or wellspring of Edwards' theology." The saints who are born again are brought into fellowship with God by the Holy Spirit. They enjoy God's glory and then reflect it back to him in moral likeness and everlasting praise.

In "The Person and Work of Jesus Christ," the authors discuss Edwards' two-sided relationship with the Covenant Theology that he inherited: He accepted part of it but rejected anything that would lead to the idea that men could in any way participate in their salvation by their works. They speak, too, of Edwards' satisfaction theory of the atonement, but argue that Edwards replaced the legal metaphor for one of transaction: Christ purchased a people for himself, a people in and with whom he and they could share in the happiness of heaven. For Edwards, the atonement was a manifestation of the love, and therefore the moral beauty, of Christ.

"The Holy Spirit": The authors acknowledge that John Owen's great work, *Pneumatologia,* "anticipated Edwards' teaching by insisting on the immediate agency of the Spirit in regeneration, the Spirit's role in giving spiritual insight, and the Spirit's employments of the natural faculties." They go on to say, "Against this backdrop, Edwards developed an understanding of the Holy Spirit that was an expression of his personal experience, a response to the religious revivals of his day, and an original contribution to Christian theological reflection."[38]

What was Edwards' contribution? First, the authors observe that "the Spirit able 'to fill and satisfy the soul' was intrinsic to Edwards' experience."[39] Thus, the Spirit himself is the purchased gift that God bestows upon his people as a consequence of the redemptive work of Christ.

He extended the Augustinian idea of the Spirit as the bond of love between the Father and the Son, *ad intra,* to maintain that the Spirit also is the one in whom the love of God is poured into our hearts, *ad extra.* Furthermore, he held to Lombard's doctrine of the direct, immediate work of the Spirit in the hearts of men as uncreated grace, while also acknowledging, though to a lesser degree, the Thomistic notion that the Spirit also produces a "created grace" in the heart by bestowing a new virtuous disposition towards love. That is why the "distinguishing mark" of the saving operation of the Spirit in a person is the creation of a new love for God and for others. Lombard's idea that grace in

38 McClymond and McDermott, *Theology,* 262.
39 McClymond and McDermott, *Theology,* 262.

the soul is the Spirit himself, who works "in and through the natural faculties, and yet human beings were dependent on God's grace," is affirmed, as Edwards insists against all forms of Arminianism.[40]

At the same time, God's sovereign work of convicting of sin and convincing people of the truth of the gospel in such a way that they were persuaded does not obliterate the operation of human faculties, including the will. What happens is that what the Spirit "overcame at the time of conversion was not human nature as such but rather the disordered or corrupted nature that had imprisoned human beings in sin."[41] Finally, Edwards believed that since the Spirit is essentially the Holy Spirit, the mark of his saving influence would be greater and greater practical holiness in the lives of believers.

"The Affections and the Human Person": This chapter treats the main theme of Doyle's book: The role of the "affections" in the human person and in discerning whether the Holy Spirit has begun to transform someone. "Religious affections involve a 'fervent, vigorous engagement of the heart in religion' that displays itself in love for God with all the heart and soul." The soul is "the confluence of two faculties – the 'understanding' that perceives and judges, and the 'inclination of will' that moves the human self toward or away from things."[42] The intellectual and deciding components cannot be separated, for Edwards believed that "true religion will always have 'knowledge of the loveliness of divine things.'"[43]

"At the center of Edwards' thinking about affections and religious experience was his conviction of the unity of the human person. ... It is also apparent that his preoccupation with the mind, will and affections ... situates him in an Augustinian-voluntarist tradition that characterized the human self more in terms of its desires and choices than its thoughts and concepts."[44] Furthermore, "the godly affections were all rooted in the basic affection of love."[45]

We cannot here do justice to the wealth of information and insight in McClymond and McDermott's volume, We shall only observe that, while exploring many themes in much greater depth than Doyle does

---

40   McClymond and McDermott, *Theology*, 267.
41   McClymond and McDermott, *Theology*, 270.
42   McClymond and McDermott, *Theology*, 312.
43   McClymond and McDermott, *Theology*, 313.
44   McClymond and McDermott, *Theology*, 314.
45   McClymond and McDermott, *Theology*, 315.

in his monograph, the authors arrive at conclusions virtually identical to those of Peter Doyle.

Our brief look at more recent scholarship continues.

William J. Danaher, Jr.,
The Trinitarian Ethics of Jonathan Edwards

Though focused on Edwards' ethical teaching, this work naturally relates to various parts of Peter Doyle's study of the new birth. Danaher identifies the Trinity as a central idea for Edwards, one which permeates every other doctrine. In the first chapter, "Partakers of the Divine Nature: Trinitarian and Moral Reflection in Edwards' Psychological Analogy," Danaher traces Edwards' concept of spiritual knowledge as "nothing other than the communication of the knowledge of God's self."[46]

When the Holy Spirit takes up residence in a person, he adds something to the soul, something that produces new dispositions to love God and others, and that, in effect, replicates God's own love in the person. That is what Edwards means by "participation." It is not just resemblance, but actual repetition of God's love in the soul. In other words, we do not just know God's love or seek to imitate it, but we have something new in our inner being.

The new birth involves "the immediate 'operation or influence of God's Spirit, whence saving actions and attainments do arise in the godly.' ... The saints, unlike 'natural men,' have experienced the 'new birth,' in which the 'divine principle' produces an 'immediate' change or 'conversion' in their nature."[47] Danaher shows how Edwards' concept of the Spirit as the bond of love between the Father and the Son leads to his conviction that in giving men his Spirit, God gives them himself, and in such a way that they inevitably both (though not without making use of the means of grace) have a new sense of God's excellency and therefore love him and reproduce this love outwards toward others. Obviously, this implies that the main criterion for discerning the presence and work of the Spirit in a person is the presence or absence of love.

In later chapters, Danaher shows how all of Edwards' major works – *Religious Affections, Freedom of the Will, Original Sin, Two Dissertations* and *Charity and its Fruits* – develop from a Trinitarian core. In

---

46 Danaher, *Ethics*, 37.
47 Danaher, *Ethics*, 39.

particular, his ethical doctrine is founded upon the centrality of the intra-Trinitarian love in which the saints participate by the indwelling of the Holy Spirit, and which they replicate in their lives as the Spirit creates in them a new disposition to love both God and other people. In the *Religious Affections*, "The 'true saints' are those for whom the 'moral and spiritual excellency of the divine nature' is ... 'a beautiful good in itself' and the pattern and source of all goodness."[48] In other words, the "new sense" that the Spirit imparts to the believer causes him to delight in God, and then to reflect God's moral beauty outwards. That is why a love for God as he is, in his beauty, and especially the beauty of his grace, must be present in those who have been truly born again.

Since the Spirit of God indwells the soul of the regenerate person, "'he communicates himself in his own proper nature.' Hence, the spiritual affections themselves proceed from the 'beauty and holiness of the divine nature,' much like 'heat' proceeds from 'fire.'"[49]

Eric J. Lehner,
Marks of Saving Grace: Theological Method and the Doctrine of Assurance in Jonathan Edwards' A Treatise Concerning Religious Affections

This work is the most recent treatment of the topic of Doyle's thesis.

Lehner's book has a number of strong points:

1. He shows how the Puritan understanding of assurance before Edwards, and Edwards' own pilgrimage towards assurance, helped to shape his theology.
2. He examines the question of theological method.
3. He explores Edwards' use of contemporary philosophy and historical sources in *Religious Affections*.
4. He demonstrates the "supremacy of Scripture" in *Religious Affections*.
5. He attempts a synthesis of Edwards' theology of assurance.
6. He looks again at "Theological Method and the Doctrine of Assurance in *Religious Affections*."

We shall briefly discuss the middle three of these.

---

48 Danaher, *Ethics*, 133.
49 Danaher, Ethics, 124.

2. After surveying various models of theological method, Lehner argues for what he calls a "regulated matrix" approach, which acknowledges the contributions of philosophy, history, context, and the Scriptures to Edwards' doctrine of assurance, but which assigns greater "weight" to one of these sources, as we see later.

3. Lehner concludes that Edwards' used terms from contemporary philosophy, especially metaphysics, to make contact with his learned readers, especially the "rationalists" who opposed the revivals, and to illustrate and further explain some of his major points. Edwards did not, however, frame his theology within a particular philosophy or derive primary inspiration from philosophy.

4. He studies Edwards' view of Scripture, his use of Scripture, and the unique and supreme "significance" of biblical sources for the doctrine of assurance in *Religious Affections*. That is, Edwards clearly saw the Bible as the primary and controlling norm for evaluating all religious experiences. Doyle calls this Edwards' "exegetical intent."

For all its scope, however, Lehner's book does not include a consideration of Edward's *Treatise on Grace* as a key text for understanding his doctrine of assurance.

Douglas A. Sweeney, *Jonathan Edwards and the Ministry of the Word.*

Sweeney's volume follows Edwards' life from childhood to his early death, with an emphasis upon his exegetical and expository labors. The product is a very fine biography, filled with quotations from original sources, as well as a thorough study of Edwards as a biblical interpreter and preacher. Like all others, he emphasizes Edwards' adherence to traditional Calvinist doctrines but also points out significant developments, in particular, his teaching that regeneration by the Holy Spirit effects a fundamental change in a person. Thus, though we are justified by faith alone, our union with Christ leads God to reckon the now-imparted righteousness of Christ as our own. "What is real in the union between Christ and his people, is the foundation of what is legal."[50]

"We are saved, he taught, not merely by assenting to the gospel. ... We are saved, as well, because the Holy Spirit inhabits our bodies, reori-

---

50 Sweeney, *Edwards*, 117.

ents our souls by uniting them with Christ, lets us share in the Lord's righteousness and bears fruit in our lives."[51] What Sweeney says next sums up the core thought of Peter Doyle's book: "This teaching about the Holy Spirit's role in our salvation ... might be said, in fact, to have been the defining feature of his ministry."[52] Sweeney then shows how Edwards strove to help his people look for lasting inward change, a transformation of the "dispositions" of the heart and habits of the mind, of speech, and of action, rather than to outward manifestations of strong emotion or even inner promptings that might, or might not, come from the Holy Spirit.

Such a focus on the inner effects of the Spirit's regenerating work highlighted the entirely divine character of regeneration. It could not be "worked up" or even prepared for, but must come as a purely divine grace, though of course the usual "means of grace" must always be employed by seekers and saints alike.

In a chapter titled, "With All Thy Mind," Sweeney offers a concise and accessible summary of the great works that Edwards produced while serving as a missionary among the Indians in Stockbridge after his ejection from the pulpit in Northampton: *The Freedom of the Will*, *Original Sin*, and the *Two Dissertations*. He does so, it seems, largely to show how Edwards was a great preacher and theologian with ever-growing influence, because he "invested prayer, sweat and tears in the life of the mind."[53] In the process, however, he explains why rebirth by the Spirit is necessary for true moral renovation, and why such moral transformation is the only credible sign of the saving work of the Spirit – which is the main point of Peter Doyle's treatise.

Any Plantinga Pauw, *The Supreme Harmony of All: The Trinitarian Theology of Jonathan Edwards*.

Pauw observes that Edwards' Trinitarianism was neglected until recently, largely because (she claims) it is not "explicit" in his major published works. "In a figure as complicated as Edwards, it is unreasonable to expect to discover one interpretive window into all the facets of his life and thought. But some windows are bigger than others. I argue that Edwards' Trinitarianism provides an unusually wide view of his deepest philosophical, theological, and pastoral inclinations."[54]

---

51 Sweeney, *Edwards*, 117.
52 Sweeney, *Edwards*, 117.
53 Sweeney, *Edwards*, 164.
54 Pauw, *Harmony*, 3.

Pauw explains, "Even where the doctrine is not mentioned explicitly, Edwards' abundant use of terms like love, idea, consent, unity, and beauty in his later writings has a distinctively Trinitarian cast to it."[55] She affirms Edwards' debt to earlier Puritan theologians, including John Owen. His emphasis upon the intra-Trinitarian love counter-balances his assertion of divine sovereignty and power in anti-Arminian works and forms a bridge between his metaphysics and his ethics, which makes replication of the love of the Persons of the Trinity for each other the source and pattern of Christian love for God and for other people.

In another example of Edwards' independence as a thinker, he refused to choose between either a model of the Trinity that emphasized the unity, such as the Son and Spirit as the Wisdom and Love of the Father, or social analogies. He alternated between these two or combined them. Each image was "indispensable for telling the story of God's great work of redemption through Christ."[56]

"Edwards' identification of the Holy Spirit with the immanent divine love was profoundly correlated with the Spirit's economic work as aimed at loving union among the saints and with God. "'Tis in our partaking of the Holy Ghost that we have communion with the Father and Son and with Christians: this is the common excellency and delight in which they all [are] united.'"[57]

Pauw demonstrates how Edwards was both an heir of Reformed and Puritan thought on the Trinity and a participant in the fierce debates about the Trinity in the eighteenth century.

Also, theological knowledge is practical knowledge, meant to be applied to the Christian life. Edwards wrote, "I know by experience how useful these doctrines [including the Trinity] be."[58]

Edwards loves the term "excellency" as a description of God. This excellency is seen primarily in "relations of harmonious consent with an irreducible plurality."[59] Like many others, Pauw writes, "Beauty was irreducibly relational for Edwards. ... [it] is a matter of proportion and harmony within the thing itself, and in its relations with other objects."[60]

---

55 Pauw, *Harmony*, 5.
56 Pauw, *Harmony*, 11.
57 Pauw, *Harmony*, 13.
58 Pauw, *Harmony*, 28.
59 Pauw, *Harmony*, 80.
60 Pauw, *Harmony*, 81.

In other words, the "aesthetic dimensions of Edwards' theology derive from the more basic category of loving consent."[61]

Central for Edwards is the concept that God is a communicative being who extends, or shares, his own excellency, especially his love, to others, including the saints.

Pauw explicates Edwards' theology of the covenants in terms of his Trinitarian theology, in which the three Persons willingly assume different roles in the work of redemption without losing their fundamental equality of deity and dignity. In this scheme, the Holy Spirit's full participation in the salvation of mankind receives a new prominence.

She also shows how Edwards brought the three traditional "unions" of Christian theology (union of the Persons within the Trinity; of the two natures in Christ; and of believers with God in Christ and with each other) together in his doctrine of redemption. In particular, he highlighted the role of the Holy Spirit in effecting a union between God and the saints. "Edwards drew out 'the particular' glory of the Holy Spirit in human redemption using the motif of the emanation and remanation of God's knowledge and love" in an ever-expanding communication of love from God to creatures and of creatures to their Savior.[62] Her rich and nuanced discussion of Edwards' overall focus on union presents this concept to be "an extremely elastic and adaptable term in Christian theology."[63]

In her chapter on "the Trinity and Pastoral Perplexities," Pauw notes that, despite the lack of explicit Trinitarian language in Edwards' works on the distinguishing marks of the saving action of the Spirit, what "marks them as Trinitarian is the persistent identification of the Holy Spirit with divine love and the pervasiveness of the core trinitarian vocabulary of love, consent, and union. ... Though he used a variety of metaphors to portray the Spirit's redemptive work, love was the touchstone." Thus, love is the decisive criterion for discerning the saving presence of the Holy Spirit in a professing Christian, for the "redemptive work of the Spirit is to indwell the soul and create a new habit of love and holiness."[64]

At several points, however, Doyle would disagree with Pauw:

---

61   Pauw, *Harmony*, 82.
62   Pauw, *Harmony*, 122.
63   Pauw, *Harmony*, 149.
64   Pauw, *Harmony*, 155.

1. Accepting Ora Winslow's portrait of Edwards, she accused him of "irritability and social ineptness," whereas descriptions of his demeanor at home with his family, in his study with parishioners who sought him for pastoral guidance, and in small group meetings during the revival, he was warm, cordial, personable, and affectionate.

2. Theologically, Pauw seems to reflect the feminist and anti-authoritarian temper of our time by objecting to Edwards' view of the functional (not ontological) subordination of the Son to the Father, and of the Spirit to the Son and the Father.[65]

3. Pauw faults Edwards for not carrying his belief in the infinitely expansive love of God towards all creation to include a cosmic redemption. Instead, she says, "there is a cosmic holocaust."[66] She does not seem to understand that for Edwards the primary end of creation is the glorification of God, which required that this holiness and justice be vindicated by the eternal punishment of unrepentant sinners. Likewise, she criticizes Edwards for alternately portraying Christ as "Christ the slain Lamb" and "Christ the slayer on a white horse."[67]

4. She finds a striking disconnect between Edwards' "transactional" and "forensic" understanding of the Atonement and his greater emphasis upon union with God through Christ by the Holy Spirit. Clearly, she rejects the former in favor of the latter.

Sam Storms: *Signs of the Spirit: An Interpretation of Jonathan Edwards' Religious Affections.*

This volume consists of two parts: An "Interpretation" of Edwards' *Religious Affections* and Edwards' *Personal Narrative*. In the first part, Storms offers an abridged, edited, and modernized rendition of *Religious Affections*. In the second, he reproduces "virtually all of the *Narrative*, interspersed with brief pastoral observations that are designed to

---

65 This position, which is now being called Eternal Functional Subordination, was held by John Calvin, Charles Hodge, Philip Schaff (interpreting the "Nicene" Creed), Carl F. H. Henry, Karl Barth, Gerhardus Vos, and J.I. Packer, and has recently been affirmed by John Frame, Bruce Ware, Robert Reymond, Gordon Lewis, Bruce Demarest, and many other evangelical theologians, though criticized as "heretical" by Millard Erickson and others.

66 Pauw, *Harmony*, 132.

67 Pauw, *Harmony*, 133.

elucidate Edwards' thought and encourage us in our own pursuit of the heart of God."[68] He also includes a very detailed "Chronology of the Life, Ministry, and Writings of Jonathan Edwards" in an appendix.

Though Storms does not intend to offer an extended treatise on Edwards' theology of the spiritual life, by making these two key works more accessible and by adding his own organization and comments to the *Narrative*, he gives us the marrow of Edwards' own systematic exposition of his theology and then provides "flesh and bones" in the form of Edwards' analysis of his personal spiritual journey, along with Storms' seasoned pastoral and practical reflections on Edwards' story.

Dane C. Ortlund, *Edwards on the Christian Life: Alive to the Beauty of God.*

Ortlund opens with a defining statement: "The Christian life, [Edwards] says, is to enjoy and reflect the beauty of God."[69] In the first chapter, entitled, "Beauty," he writes, "Edwards has given us the beauty of the Christian life – first, the beauty of God, beauty that comes to tangible expression in Christ, and second, the beauty of the Christian, who participates in the triune life of divine love. Divine loveliness, enjoyed and reflected in his creatures: that is Edwards' legacy."[70] He goes on to explain that "Edwards uses beauty as a moral category," another term for it being holiness, because "supreme loveliness is found only in supreme holiness."[71] He notes that Edwards uses the "language of excellency, or beauty, in describing holiness."[72]

Ortlund is careful to say that he is not "arguing for divine beauty as a controlling theme or center to Edwards' theology as a whole, … [but] simply for beauty as a controlling theme to Edwards' theology of the Christian life."[73]

Chapter Two shows that the new birth, which he calls "the ignition of the Christian life," according to Edwards, is necessary; it changes us; is completely the work of God; does not perfect us; is the source of real joy; and is the complement of justification, which sets us right with God, through faith in the accomplished work of Christ for us on the Cross. Chapter Three states that love is "the essence of the Chris-

---

68   Storms, *Signs*, 159.
69   Ortlund, *Life*, 16.
70   Ortlund, *Life*, 23-24.
71   Ortlund, *Life*, 25.
72   Ortlund, *Life*, 25.
73   Ortlund, *Life*, 24, n. 1.

tian life," a thesis that the author then works out in great detail in the following chapters on characteristics of the Christian life, the means of grace (such as prayer and Scripture), obedience, the opposition of Satan, the centrality of the soul, and our heavenly hope.

Kyle Strobel, *Formed for the Glory of God: Learning from the Spiritual Practices of Jonathan Edwards.*

Though not claiming to be a scholarly study of Edwards' theology, and though Strobel's focus is on applying the teachings of Edwards to the spiritual growth of a Christian, the book opens with three chapters that lay the theological foundation for what follows. Strobel writes with a concise elegance that captures both the meaning and the spirit of Edwards' view of the Triune God, the goal for which he created the world and redeems his saints, and the essence of the Spirit's saving work in regeneration and sanctification. Chapter Three, "Walking in Affection," expresses the core both of Edwards' thought and of Doyle's exposition of his doctrine of the new birth so clearly and powerfully that we are tempted to quote it entirely. Instead, we refer the reader to this uniquely beautiful, practical, and powerful work on the Christian life.

Sang Hyun Lee, editor, *Jonathan Edwards: Writings on the Trinity, Grace, and Faith.*

In the *Editor's Introduction* to these writings, Lee explains what he considers to be Edwards' contribution to the doctrine of the Trinity: "Everything Edwards wrote about the Trinity expresses the intertwining connectedness of the Trinity and the Christian's experience of God as the Creator, Savior, and Sanctifier, and thus between the immanent and the economic Trinity."[74] Although Edwards remained faithful to the classical formulations of the early church councils, "remarkably, he closed the gap between trinitarian doctrine and the Christian life, thereby returning to the ancient church fathers' original desire to see the Trinity as connected with the living Christian faith."[75]

Like Pauw, Lee notes that Edwards used both the social and the psychological analogies in talking about the Trinity. He notes Edwards' acceptance of the Western insistence that the Spirit proceeds from both the Father and the Son and the Augustinian notion that the Spirit is the bond of love between Father and Son.

---

74 Lee, *Introduction*, 3.

75 Lee, *Introduction*, 4.

As Lee explains, however, Edwards made a creative and radical move when he describes the Spirit as "no longer just the bond of love but an active agent," an idea that he calls "a profound advancement over the Western church's typically underdeveloped doctrine of the agency of the Holy Spirit in the intra-trinitarian life of God."[76] This fundamental conviction comes out in Edwards' doctrine of the role of the Spirit in the new birth, in which God, in imparting the Spirit, gives himself in his very nature to the believers. Going beyond the typical Western emphasis upon the divine unity, Edwards, with a relational understanding of being and reality, stresses that the union of the three Persons is " a communion in one another." As Doyle will point out, this communion comes to include the regenerate, as they participate in the life of the triune God by the work of the indwelling Holy Spirit.

In addition to the books briefly discussed above, we have examined other volumes that relate in one way or another to Jonathan Edwards' life and theology, including his writings on the work of the Holy Spirit in the salvation of the saints. These are:

Stephen R. Holmes, *God of Grace & God of Glory: An Account of the Theology of Jonathan Edwards.*

Sang Hyun Lee, editor, *The Princeton Companion to Jonathan Edwards.*

Gerald R. McDermott, editor, *Understanding Jonathan Edwards: An Introduction to America's Theologian.*

Murray, Iain H. *Jonathan Edwards: A New Biography*

Stephen J. Nichols, *An Absolute Sort of Certainty: The Holy Spirit and the Apologetics of Jonathan Edwards.*

Mark A. Noll, *The Rise of Evangelicalism: The Age of Edwards, Whitefield, and the Wesleys.*

Paul Ramsey, editor, *Jonathan Edwards, Ethical Writings.*

Stephen J. Stein, editor, *The Cambridge Companion to Jonathan Edwards.*

Douglas A. Sweeney and Allen C. Guelzo, *The New England Theology: From Jonathan Edwards to Edwards Amasa Park.*

Though each of these volumes possesses value in itself, especially the magisterial introductions of Lee and Ramsey, none of them changes or detracts significantly from Doyle's argument. You will encounter these

---

76 Lee, *Introduction*, 19.

same core themes, as well as the extensive use of the same sources, in the following pages. As most scholars, along with Doyle, show, they are all inter-related, and they all harmonize like a symphony to produce a body of theology that possesses remarkable coherence, consistency, and elegance.

The Contribution of this Study

In light of the foregoing survey, we can say that Peter Doyle's dissertation, though composed before the vast amount of scholarship on Edwards, still possesses value for scholars and pastors today.

1. Doyle shows Jonathan Edwards' place in the flow of Reformed theology and the changes that had taken place in Puritan thought before his time. He explains how Edwards was responding to his contemporary philosophical, ecclesiastical, theological, and pastoral context. His study, therefore, is both synchronic and diachronic. In other words, he fits into the "regulated matrix" model of theological method advocated by D.A. Carson and Eric Lehner.

2. He demonstrates that Edwards, though fully conversant with, and fluent in, the vocabulary of contemporary philosophy, constructed this theology from biblical sources and used the Scriptures as the controlling principle for all his theological conclusions.

3. Along with others, especially Stephen Nicholls, he emphasizes the apologetic thrust of Edwards' theology, while at the same time showing the practical, pastoral context and purpose of his doctrine.

4. He makes use of the early lecture, "God Glorified in Man's Dependence," and the late *Treatise on Grace* in a way that illumines the consistency and coherence of Edwards' doctrine of the work of the Holy Spirit throughout his theological career. Without explicitly arguing for a "central interpretive motif" in Edwards' theology, he seems to provide support for a theocentric, and especially Trinitarian, core of all of Edwards' work.

5. Most of all, he demonstrates that his doctrine of new birth in the Spirit draws together all Edwards' main themes and central theological convictions, rather like a lens concentrating the rays of the sun in an especially powerful way. To change the metaphor, Doyle uses the doctrine of the new birth like a prism, which turns a single beam of light into a dazzling array

of colors. In doing so, he validates the judgment of Douglas Sweeney and Allen Guelzo, who wrote that from his earliest works to "his final *Dissertation on True Virtue*, Edwards devoted himself to elucidating the ways and means by which to distinguish twice-born religion from its fatal counterfeits."[77]

We would go further and say that even his great theological works on *Original Sin* and *Freedom of the Will*, as Doyle makes clear, were essential weapons in Edwards' lifelong campaign to glorify God by proclaiming the "excellencies of Him who has called [us] out of darkness into His marvelous light" (1 Peter 2:9) in magnifying the self-replicating grace of God in the regenerating work of the Holy Spirit. To put it more theologically, the doctrine of the new birth highlights what Sang Hyun Lee calls "a theological vision in which creation, by God's grace, participates in God's own life of self- communication. Though Edwards never produced a systematic theology," his writings demonstrate "the remarkable coherence and creativity of his thinking."[78]

Finally, we believe that Doyle has accomplished this task in a manner that reflects the inner coherence, consistency, and even elegance of Edwards' theological corpus. That is, the unfolding progress of his argument mirrors the organic unity of Edwards' thought, a unity that comes to brilliant expression in his doctrine of the new birth.

The result is a volume that could well serve as an introductory text on Edwards in a college or seminary course.

The Book

Doyle began this study of the theology of Jonathan Edwards under the direction of Karl Barth. He first presented to Barth the chapter on the Holy Spirit (now Chapter Four). Because, Barth said, Europeans knew little about Edwards, he asked his student to open the dissertation with introductory material that would place Edwards within the setting of his intellectual and religious environment. Such an introduction would perhaps not be required now, since so many books, theses, and articles have been produced on Edwards in the past fifty years, and especially since the manuscript was completed in 1980, that much of the contents of the first three chapters has become common knowledge

---

77 Douglas A. Sweeney and Allen C. Guelzo, editors, *The New England Theology: From Jonathan Edwards to Edwards Amasa Park (Grand Rapids, MI: Baker Academic, 2006)*, 26.

78 Lee, *Introduction*, 1.

among Edwards scholars. For that reason, the author expressed the thought that these chapters should be placed into an appendix.

Upon further reflection, however, and after reading the entire work, we believe that Doyle's treatment contains some things that are stated in a way that is fresh. He shows that Edwards' views on the work of the Holy Spirit were formed and enunciated in the context of both Reformed and early Puritan theology, the development of Puritan thinking in the New World, the Enlightenment in Europe, and the actual experiences of Christians in New England before, during, and after the awakenings that occasioned Edwards' now-classic formulations of a new understanding of "true religion." The author explains how, at almost every point, Edwards was responding to specific assumptions, concepts, and opinions held both by orthodox believers and by "rationalists." Because of the fundamental integriy and progressive development of Doyle's argument, therefore, we have retained the original order of the chapters.

The thesis of this book is that Edwards combined his thorough knowledge of the Bible and of the Reformation and Puritan thought of which he was an heir, along with his own rich and unique experience as a pastor in New England, into a new formulation of the doctrine of the Holy Spirit's operations in believers that both answered the "rationalism" and "enthusiasm" of his age and provided later generations with insights that remain as relevant as they were when he wrote them.

Doyle demonstrates the unity of Edwards thought on the work of the Holy Spirit in regeneration and sanctification by looking at the topic from different angles, but always coming back to Edwards' conviction that when God gives his Spirit, he gives himself, and that when he gives himself to a person, the result will be a love for God as he is revealed in Christ and a corresponding love for others. Since the Holy Spirit is God's Spirit, he will impart to the believers a delight in God's moral excellence and beauty, and will gradually reproduce that same moral beauty in the lives of those who are regenerated. He emphasizes Edwards' conviction that the *work* of the Spirit is inseparable from his *person* and that the effects of his work in people will reflect his moral character.

That means that the distinguishing "signs" or "marks" of the work of the Holy Spirit in a person's life will be moral in nature. That is, they will reveal the essential goodness of God as this is progressively woven into the fabric of the person who has been given a new heart by the Spirit. Sometimes, the Spirit will also produce phenomena that can be felt by a person and perhaps seen or heard by others. These, however, can also be counterfeited by our sinful flesh and by Satan. That is why Edwards was so careful to insist that many thoughts, feelings, and experiences of professing Christians do not necessarily come from God, and are therefore unreliable as evidence that such a person is born again or has been saviongly affected by the Holy Spirit.

Edwards did not, of course, deny that the operations of the Holy Spirit may lead to strong emotions, exalted thoughts, and even bodily manifestations; indeed, he shows that true religious "affections" **must** result from regeneration and ongoing sanctification. Emotions such as love, joy, peace, etc., will necessarily accompany true repentance of sin and continuing faith in God. That is where he stands solidly against the "rationalists" who denied any emotional component of the spiritual life. At the same time, Edwards strongly criticized the extravagant claims of "enthusiasts" to special spiritual experiences and decried the over-emphasis upon emotional and physical phenomena as sure indications that the Spirit had been active in a person.

Doyle thus shows how Edwards' biblical, and therefore balanced, teaching met the needs of his own time and can serve as a guide for us today.

Notes on Style

Peter Doyle composed this book more than thirty years ago. Both the canons of scholarly citation and the use of certain English words and terms have changed. For example, many academic publications do not now accept the use of "*ibid.*" and "*op. cit.*" in citations, as they did when Doyle wrote. To change these would have required more time and labor than the editors have at their disposal. We believe that most potential readers of the book will either be familiar with the former style and be able to navigate it easily, or will not care to follow the flow of the footnotes.

When Doyle wrote his dissertation, only a few volumes of the Yale edition of Edwards' works had been published. The edition he used, and the one cited most often here, is *Works of President Edwards* (a reprint of the Worcester Edition). 4 volumes. New York, NY: Leavitt & Allen, 1858). To find the corresponding volume and page in the Yale edition would have entailed, again, a prohibitive amount of time and labor. We trust that scholars will have access to that the four-volume edition, recognize the original source from their familiarity with the Yale edition, or not need to locate the exact passage from Edwards' works. We apologize for any inconvenience this will cause.

Other instances: Doyle uses the editorial "we" when he means "I." He does not avoid passive constructions, pronouns such as "this" and "it," or the use of the verb "to be."

Scholars differ on how to express the possessive of Edwards' name. With Doyle, we have chosen to use a simple apostrophe, though we have retained the spelling employed by those whom we quote.

The feminist movement has made people sensitive to the use of gender terms, so that, whenever possible, masculine pronouns and the words "man" or "men," used generically, are avoided. This was not so much the case even in the 1980s, so you will find these current standards "violated" in almost every paragraph. We have tried to substitute other terms as much as possible, but to do so throughout the document would have entailed an inordinate amount of time and effort. As all who know him would know, no offence to the feminine gender would ever be intended by the author.

Other marks of the author's distinctive manner of expressing himself also appear. Peter Doyle is a man of strong opinions and fervent convictions. In addition, he did not write as an arm-chair academic theologian, but as a pastor intimately involved in the lives of his people and the controversies and issues of his time. As a result, this book is not a dispassionate, bloodless, scholarly disquisition on certain arcane points of eighteenth-century theology, psychology, philosophy, and ecclesiastical controversy. The scholarship is there, and we believe you will find it to be precise and fair, but the tone will be anything but disinterested. Doyle believed that these issues were of paramount concern in his day, as they had been in Edwards' time, and he writes with energy and ardor. Like Edwards' own compositions, this is a work not of curious speculation or intellectual play, but a plea for a return to biblical norms in evaluating religious experiences. In other words, this is a work of advocacy as well as of scholarship.

In that way, also, the style and intent of the book correspond to the writings of Jonathan Edwards.

Brandon J. Cozart
G. Wright Doyle

Acknowledgments

I was a junior at Washington and Lee University, in Lexington, Virginia. Dr. Borden strode into the room for his class on American Literature, stepped to the podium, and without explanation or warning began calmly reading to the suddenly startled - and rapidly transfixed students - Jonathan Edwards' sermon, "Sinners in the Hands of an Angry God." We were mesmerized. I am grateful to Dr. Borden - a superb teacher - for this electrifying introduction to the great pastor and theologian whose writings became so influential and helpful in my life and ministry. I rushed to the university library when the class was over and began my study of Jonathan Edwards.

Some years later, I began graduate studies at Basel University in Switzerland. I was facing spiritual trials at the time and wished to study the Holy Spirit's work in regeneration for my guidance and assurance. Professor Karl Barth encouraged me to write my dissertation on an American theologian, and when I mentioned Edwards his face lit up with pleasure. "Excellent!" he said. "We don't know Edwards here in Europe. Give us some background on his culture and intellectual heritage. Tell me about the Puritans. Let me smell the forest and hear the war cry of the Indians! Then tell me about his theology." Excepting the forest and the Indians I did a serious study of Edwards' life and ministry and his spiritual heritage from Puritanism. (Edwards did, in fact, preach to and pastor Indians on the then Western frontier in Massachusetts.) I am grateful beyond measure also for his encouragement and guidance in the writing of the first four chapters of my dissertation. He was a gracious and kindly mentor. Like Jonathan Edwards, he was thoroughly Trinitarian in his thinking and deliberately focused on Christology.

I returned with my family to the U. S. to complete my dissertation, but medical issues interrupted my work, and I was unable to go back to Basel. Later I found an opportunity to complete my doctoral studies through Trinity Theological Seminary in Newburgh, Indiana.

Brandon Cozart, a theological student at the time, and my brother, Dr. G. Wright Doyle, encouraged me to believe that this manuscript should be published. Brandon retyped the entire manuscript and made numerous corrections. My brother followed Brandon's work and undertook intensive editing. I cannot thank these two men enough.

I am grateful to Wally Turnbull and his team for the speed and superior quality of their publication process and the splendid cover design.

Another person to thank for his major contribution to the writing of this book is Henry Coleman, the former librarian at Washington and Lee University. He gave me a four-volume set of Edwards' writings which was a huge help, especially when I was writing in Basel.

Joanne Gray Crispell typed the final draft of the original manuscript, in the day when there were no computers!

The contribution of my wife, Sally Ann, to the writing of this book, is beyond praise. I marked hundreds of passages from the four volume set of Edwards' works, in addition to passages from other books, which I asked her to type and from which I wished to write or quote. She then typed the entire manuscript. Her cheerful encouragement was constant, as it has been this past 61 years, for which I thank the Lord each day.

Errors in this work are mine, and I welcome constructive criticism and correction.

Above all, I thank the Lord God for His indescribable mercy and kindness in Christ Jesus to Sally Ann and me and to our children and theirs.

Peter Reese Doyle
Opelika, Alabama
March 10, 2017

Introduction

What do Christians mean when they say that they have been "born again?" What is the origin of this religious experience? Are there ways by which people can prepare themselves to receive it? What are the signs by which the validity of this experience can be tested? What are the consequences in the public and private lives of those who receive new birth? This matter is of vital importance to our churches today. It has been of vital importance throughout the history of the church, and it will always be so. Scripture shows quite clearly that not all those who call themselves God's people are in fact His people.[1] Multitudes have been deceived about their true state with God in past history and it is at least possible that many are as equally confused today.

Yet it is essential that Christians be able to define their relationship with God in terms that can answer the questions we have raised above. It is essential that we know what is involved when God saves sinners, and we must be able as well to let people know what to expect from the saving action of God in their lives – in their characters and in their conduct. This matter has in fact received very detailed treatment in certain periods of Christian history. In English-speaking lands, the writings of the American pastor and theologian Jonathan Edwards have been regarded as among the most important and scripturally accurate works in this field. In this book, we will examine Jonathan Edwards' writings on the subject of the new birth.

Jonathan Edwards was born in 1703 and he died in 1758. More than two centuries of cultural, religious, and linguistic development separate his age from ours. Furthermore, immense ideological changes during this period increase the difficulty of anyone in our age accurately understanding people of Edwards' time. To make matters worse, all things Puritan have been so vilified and misrepresented in American literature, historiography, and media within the last century that even greater barriers to an honest hearing of views from Puritan

---

1   See, for example, Matthew 7:21-23.

religion and culture have been raised, for Jonathan Edwards was a Puritan. He was a Puritan pastor and theologian, the son of a Puritan pastor, descended from Puritans who had migrated to the New World for the purpose of establishing a Puritan religious culture. To give a fair hearing to Edwards' views, then, and to understand the great issues that engaged his pastoral and literary attention, we shall in the early part of our study examine the historical development of New England Puritan culture. We shall then look at the major intellectual and religious movements that

were transforming the culture during Edwards' lifetime, and we shall continue to do this in each chapter of our thesis, relating these to Edwards' life-work. We shall do that because he related his ministry and writings to the culture in which he served. He was exceedingly well-informed concerning the major intellectual trends that affected eighteenth-century Anglo-Saxon thought and his publications evidence his determination to relate the gospel of Christ to the mind of his age.

Language itself poses difficulties to our study of Jonathan Edwards, because the English language has changed in many ways since he wrote and preached. We shall provide careful definition to the key terms and issues that come under our investigation, as we relate the theology of Edwards to the mindset of the time. Religious, philosophical, and scientific matters will have to be studied in this regard. Theology is not an ivory-tower enterprise. It is a science that is practiced within the life of human society, which relates to every aspect of life and thought, and that must, therefore, be related to the chief rivals for the heart of men who seek to evade the claim of the one true God.

We shall follow this procedure: In Chapter One we shall examine briefly the history of Puritanism as this affected the situation in which Edwards lived and worked. We shall study Puritan theology and the problems faced by that theology in the intellectual climate of pre-Revolutionary New England. We shall study also the Great Revival of the 1740s that was so crucial to the ministry of Edwards.

In Chapter Two we shall provide a biographical sketch of Jonathan Edwards, with a study of the formative influences in his intellectual and theological development.

In Chapter Three, we shall study his pastoral and theological ministry. Here we shall examine his theology in relation to and in divergence from Puritan theology in general, as well as in the light of the broader intellectual issues of the age, nd we shall note the distinctive character-istics of his doctrine as these affect the core of our thesis.

In Chapter Four, we shall look at Edwards' doctrine of the Person of the Holy Spirit, Who is the Author of the new birth. We shall show here how important it is to understand the *nature* of God before exam-ining in greater detail the manner of His *working*. Misunderstandings concerning God Himself were at the base of the furious controver-sies concerning His work in the Revival. We will undertake this study in conscious dialogue with leading elements of eighteenth-century philosophy, for it was these elements of philosophy that lay behind the doctrine of so many of Edwards' theological opponents.

Chapter Five is the heart of the book. Here we study specifically Edwards' doctrine of regeneration. We do so in the light of Reformed theological tradition as well as in comparison with the ideologies of his age that related to this central doctrine.

In Chapter Six we shall study Edwards' extensive efforts to describe the effects of the new birth in the lives of those who had experienced it so that Christians might know from Scripture just how to recognize the saving works of God in the souls and lives of men. A brief Conclusion ends this chapter and completes our study.

A note concerning texts: At the time of this writing, there is no satisfac-tory complete edition of the works of Jonathan Edwards.[2] There are real differences in the various editions published so far. The highly regarded Yale University Press edition of *The Works of Jonathan Edwards* will, when complete, correct this sad situation; at present only five volumes have appeared, however, and it seems that some time will thus elapse before this situation will be remedied. There are several popular editions of a large part of Edwards' works that are readily available; we have chosen to use primarily *The Works of President Edwards in Four Volumes*, with the subtitle of "A Reprint of the Worcester Edition," published by Leavitt & Allen in New York, 1858. For the crucial study of the signs of the Spirit's saving work in men, however, we have used Volume Two of the new Yale University Press edition, with the excel-lent introduction by John E. Smith, and we have used others of the Yale volumes at key parts of our study.

---

2   Since these words were written, nineteen volumes of the Yale edition of Jona-than Edwards' works have been published [Ed.].

Contents

1

The Time

New England's Fall and the Wrath of God

The Promised Land

> When England began to decline in religion, like lukewarm
> Laodicea, and instead of purging out Popery, a farther compli-
> ance was sought, not only in profaning the Sabbath and, by proc-
> lamation throughout their parish churches, exasperating lewd
> and profane persons to celebrate a Sabbath, like the heathen, to
> Venus, Bacchus, and Ceres, insomuch that the multitude of irre-
> ligious lascivious and Popish affected persons spread the whole
> land like grasshoppers – in this very time, Christ, the glorious
> king of his churches, raises an army out of our English nation,
> for freeing his people from their long servitude under usurping
> prelacy. And because every corner of England was filled with
> the fury of malignant adversaries, Christ creates a new England
> to muster up the first of his forces …[1]

So wrote Edward Johnson in his *Wonder-Working Providence of
Sion's Saviour*, published in 1654, which described to all England the
marvelous mercies of the great God who had delivered some of His
people from the sword-enforced "idolatries" of the Church of England,
to plant them in a new, "promised" land. This interpretation of the
meaning of the Puritan migrations to North America in the seventeenth-century was the basic presupposition of New England Christianity for more than a century after the founding of the Massachusetts
Colonies, and an awareness of the understanding these Puritans had of

---

1   Perry Miller, *The American Puritans*, (Garden City: Doubleday & Company,
    1956), 29.

1

themselves is essential to any appreciation of their religious and political history and the cultural forms in which that history was expressed.

The Puritan migrations to North America marked the end of one phase of the struggle of English Puritanism to reform the English National Church. (The other phase of this struggle was consummated in the civil war, the Protectorate, and, finally, in apparent failure, in the Restoration of prelacy under the Monarchy.) Those who came to New England were the heirs of a long line of Christians who from the middle of the sixteenth century onwards had struggled for greater reform in the English Church. Beginning with Henry VIII's burnings of persons for possessing Tyndale's translation of the New Testament, continuing through the frustrated hopes of many Anglican Reformers that the Geneva pattern of Church Government would utterly root out the prelacy of the National Church, and centering for a while in Essex as the disciples of Calvin and Knox, of Bucer and Bullinger, preached and wrote in favor of "thorough" reformation, what came to be known as "Puritanism" got its start and took its form.[2]

The movement was at first strictly Presbyterian in outlook. Its adherents did not quibble so much with the essential Reformation doctrine of the Anglican Church as with the un-reformed polity or structure of that church.[3] That the Lord bishops were still primarily secular officials, forced to reside in London most of the year in attendance on their governmental duties, and that their pastoral oversight of their parishioners was necessarily so slight, was a shocking offense to the Puritan doctrine of the Body of Christ and the duties of the ministry.[4] Furthermore, the function of such a monarchial episcopate, hand in hand with a predominantly secular control of the conferring of vacant parishes to those ministers pleasing to the aristocrats who owned the "livings," had no foundation in the Bible, in Puritan opinion. To Puritan eyes, the Church was not fully reformed because it was not sufficiently organized or disciplined along biblical lines. The doctrine may have been quite biblical, but the conduct of the bishops, the standards of the

---

2   William Haller's *The Rise of Puritanism* (New York: Harper & Brothers, 1957), although biased towards a strictly sociological and political interpretation of the Puritan movement, nevertheless repays study. So too does Thomas Jefferson Wertenbaker's *The Puritan Oligarchy* (New York: Crosset & Dunlap, 1947).

3   See Wertenbaker, *op. cit.*, 26.

4   The consequences of such practices of pastoral neglect are discussed by A.S. Wood in his *The Inextinguishable Blaze* (Grand Rapids: Eerdmans, 1960), 15ff.

ministry, and the discipline and common life of the parishes were not. The people called Puritans were those who wished to make it so.

Queen Elizabeth, however, was not inclined to the Presbyterianism of Geneva or Edinburgh. She was opposed to the aims of the Puritans, and she ordered her archbishops to keep them under control. In 1570 the learned Thomas Cartwright of Trinity College, Cambridge, a leading Puritan figure, was expelled from his post for preaching in favor of further reform along the Presbyterian pattern. In the same year, the Reverend Edward Dering was silenced after preaching the same message to the face of the Queen. While much agitation and preaching, publication and controversy had been going on before 1570, this date marks a turning point in the development of Puritanism. From this time on Puritans devoted themselves to the systematic implementation of their theology and church discipline *within* the bounds of the national church. Finding no possibility of help from the government of Elizabeth or of James they turned towards the development of Christian piety in those areas in which they were able to work. As most of them were allowed to take posts in the ministry of the Anglican Church, they became articulate members of a movement for reform of the congregational life of the parishes, based on the influence of dedicated and scholarly ministers and laymen who sought to guide the congregations in the life in Christ as they understood the Bible to describe that life.

Cambridge became their center, and from its colleges went out preachers and teachers filled with the love of Christ, a knowledge of Scripture unsurpassed among their contemporaries, and solid training in the theological systems then current in Calvinistic orthodoxy.[5] Since the power of the national church was withheld from their hands, their attention was directed to the development of disciplined congregational life within local parishes – a situation fraught with momentous consequences for following generations (and later one of the factors contributing to the splintering of the whole movement into various "congregationalistic" factions[6]). Common to the movement as a whole, however, were intense zeal for the congregational life of the church, love of the Bible, assurance as to its adequacy as a pattern for the current life of the Church, conviction as to the absolute necessity for the most exacting theological training of ministers, and dedicated skill in presenting the results of these studies in plain language for plain

---

5   See Haller, *op. cit.*, 19ff.
6   Ibid., 16ff.

people. Disclaiming the learned, Greek-and-Latin-studded discourses of contemporary Anglicanism, these preachers (who were masters of Greek and Latin) expounded scriptural doctrines in the simplest terms to the common people. They spoke to the heart, thus establishing a pattern of concern that became basic in the Puritan view of the role of the preacher.

Above all were the preachers to preach "practical godliness," and in an "affectionate" manner. Let us hear William Haller as he describes the preaching, and especially the writing of these Puritan preachers:

> These writers were called practical because they taught men what to believe and how to act. They were called affectionate because they appealed through the imagination to men's emotions. They were all primarily preachers who with few exceptions wrote popular sermons or works of edification directly derived from sermons. Their aim was to arouse every man to ask and then to answer for himself the ancient question ... 'Sirs, what must I do to be saved?'[7]

Their influence in England became very profound indeed: the Christian life they sought to promote gained such favor among such a large part of the people that by 1640 the nation was ripe for civil war. Many of the citizens had become disgusted with the policies of the king and of Archbishop Laud and were willing to follow the Puritan leaders in a war for reform.

For our purposes, it is sufficient to note the characteristics of this movement in the life of the congregations where they held influence: the strong foundation of biblical preaching, the strong emphasis on congregational discipline, the strong emphasis on the congregation as such (which later was to give tremendous impetus to the type of polity that became entrenched in New England), and the careful attention to "soul-care," or explicit pastoral guidance in the life in Christ.

In the first decades of the seventeenth-century, however, many of the Puritans became exceedingly discouraged. The persecution by the king and the Church, the increasing restrictions placed upon their activities in every possible way, the apparent failure to influence national policy, the seemingly impregnable position of their oppressor, Archbishop Laud: all these combined to cause many of them to seek a way of relief, a way of finding a life in which they could worship God and serve Him as they considered He wished to be worshipped and

---

7   Ibid., 25.

served. Some moved to the Low Countries, and from them came the first Puritan Colony in New England, the Plymouth Colony, begun in 1620. Others were able to organize expeditions from England. There, with strong financial backing, painstaking planning, and determined resolution, what was perhaps one of the most impressive colonizing efforts of history was organized – the Massachusetts Bay Company. The first group came to Salem, Massachusetts in 1628. In 1630 a great fleet arrived, and within a decade perhaps more than 20,000 persons followed.[8]

Once in the New World, the Puritans began to construct that state they had been unable to build in Old England. On the advice of the Reverend Francis Makemie, they organized themselves into towns, for the purpose of better structuring and regulating their religious life, as well as for the better education of their children – and, of course, for greater defensive strength against the raids of the Indians. Here the congregational emphasis of the Puritan movement found classic expression, for, contrary to the ideals of the Presbyterians, those groups that came to Massachusetts were determined to organize themselves into autonomous congregations – congregations that would be in fellowship with, but not subject to, each other. Each congregation, therefore, would choose its own pastor and its own teacher, elect its own officers, stake out its own land, and, through the vote of free men, lay down its own laws. In general conformity to the policies of the Massachusetts Bay Company, the various villages had a great deal of local autonomy in the political and social realm. The members of each town bound themselves to each other in a common covenant with God, agreeing to serve Him, to receive His Word as their law, to follow His leading through the pastors and teachers He provided, and to rear their children and govern their civil life by the light He gave them.[9]

Membership in the church was at first limited to "visible saints," that is, to those who could profess to a saving knowledge of Christ, and whose

---

8   See William W. Sweet, *The Story of Religion in America* (New York: Harper & Brothers, 1950), chapters II and IV.

9   The close connection between many pastors, however, soon led to a form of synodical government over church life that in many ways approximated that of the Presbyterian system. See Wertenbaker, *op. cit.*, 72ff; also E.A. Gausted, *The Great Awakening in New England* (New York: Harper & Brothers, 1957), 4ff, and Perry Miller, *Jonathan Edwards* (New York: Meridian, 1959), 9-12. G.H. Sabine discusses the various political aspirations of the Puritan groups in his *A History of Political Theory* (New York: Henry Holt, 1958), 444ff, 477ff.

lives, in the judgment of the congregation, did not contradict this profession. In addition, only "visible saints" could vote in the civil affairs of the town. The children of the "saints" were entitled to baptism and were expected to make their own profession as they reached maturer years. The great religious crisis of Puritan New England occurred when a significant number of these children were unable to make a sincere profession of a saving knowledge of Christ and were honest enough to admit it.[10] The theology and ecclesiology of New England Puritanism were not prepared for such a situation. The problem was acute, inasmuch as those children of professing Christians wished for, but had not yet attained, faith in Christ, and yet nevertheless wanted their own children to receive the full benefit of inclusion within the Covenanted People of God through the rite of baptism. But such a request, if granted would seriously compromise the then existing doctrine and practice. The Church, in effect, was being asked to accept as members the children of persons who had not known God, who had not satisfied the pastor and the elders as to their conversion, and who professed no confident expectation of doing so.

After a lengthy discussion, the Massachusetts General Court asked the churches of Massachusetts to meet in Synod in Boston to discuss the matter. In 1662 they did so, and the majority of the delegates decided in favor of a proposal made earlier by the Connecticut churches, to the effect that the unregenerate children of professing Christians, who were not scandalous in life and who wished their own children to be baptized, could be made members of the Covenant with God – albeit inferior members: they could not partake of communion and could not vote in the church or the town, but their children could receive baptism. This was the famous "Half-Way Covenant," and it marked the beginning of the end of the original idea of a "godly" church. The requirements for membership grew increasingly slacker, and respectability, rather than discipleship, became the decisive prerequisite for church membership.[11] Churches were split in controversy over this accommodation to increasing worldliness, but the trend was established. (For our study of Edwards this situation is particularly important, as it was partly for his repudiation of this accommodation, and his insistence that membership in the church should be given only

---

10 Wertenbaker, *op. cit.*, 64-77, 155, 312-313. Also Sweet, *op. cit.*, 58-59, and Miller, *op. cit.*, 134.
11 Gaustad, *op. cit.*, chapter I.

to those who could profess a knowledge of Christ, that he was ejected from his parish in 1750.)[12]

If, in the view of many, religion in New England had begun a steady decline, learning, certainly, had not. The educational attainments of the leaders of the Puritan movement were impressive indeed. From the very beginning, Puritans numbered among their members some of the most eminent scholars in England. Most, though not all, were Cambridge scholars; many had been fellows and teachers at that university. Thomas Cartwright had been Lady Margaret Professor as well as University Preacher, thus embodying in himself the ideal combination of qualities prized by the whole movement. Walter Travers' *Book of Church Discipline* was so formidable an attack on prelacy and so effective a statement on the reforming ideals of Puritanism that "the rulers of the church, led by Whitgift and Bancroft, were kept busy for years in refuting it and in circumventing its author and his disciples."[13] Not only were many of the Puritan scholars as accomplished as any in England, but their pupils and their pupils' pupils became equally noted for their learning. Among these were the leaders of the New England migrations. From 1629 to 1647 more than 130 graduates of Cambridge migrated to the Puritan colonies.[14] William Ames had fled to Europe, but Thomas Hooker, Thomas Shepard, John Wilson, John Rogers, and many other men of repute as scholars, pastors, and preachers came to the New World.

One of the first programs inspired by these scholar-pastors of wilderness congregations was the successful agitation for the founding of a university, a project that the General Court of Massachusetts authorized as early as 1636. After a bad start, Harvard College was firmly established by 1640. From the very beginning the curriculum was as exacting as those of Cambridge and Oxford, and before the turn of the century, Harvard was to justify its existence by providing the overwhelming majority of churches in Massachusetts and Connecticut with their pastors, as well as many towns with their physicians, lawyers, and civil leaders.[15] Even more ministers had gone to take parishes in

---

12 Miller, *op. cit.*, 208ff. Miller erects upon the plain facts of the case his astonishing theory concerning Edwards' ingrained "secretiveness." This theory impairs Miller's judgment at many points in his interpretation of Edwards.

13 Haller, *op. cit.*, 11.

14 Sweet, *op. cit.*, 54.

15 Ibid.

England after receiving their Harvard degree.[16] The Puritans considered education a prime necessity for the preservation of the people's religion, as well as a God-given good in its own right, and the New England Puritans were resolved to do all in their power to ensure that their children and descendants would have the same caliber of religious and political leadership as they themselves had been given. Therefore, the graduates of Harvard were sent back into the parishes and villages, and many of them became teachers in local schools, preparing selected youngsters in Greek and Latin so that they too could go to college and study "grammar, logic, rhetoric, arithmetic, geometry and astronomy, metaphysics, ethics, natural philosophy, Greek, Hebrew and ancient history."[17]

One final point should be noted with respect to the learning of New England Puritanism: it was progressive, and quite open to the latest advances in European scholarship, especially in the field of natural science. Clinton Rossiter remarks of Harvard that "there is evidence that Copernicus had conquered the young Turks of the faculty as early as 1659."[18] The works of Newton, Locke, Boyle and other leaders of the then "modern" thought were eagerly received, very often years before they achieved such general recognition in Europe. Let us hear Wertenbaker:

> If one had visited the home of a Massachusetts minister in the seventeenth-century to inspect the titles of the ... volumes which lined the shelves ... in his study, one would have found among them the works of the greatest humanists and scientists of the age. Here is Francis Bacon's *Natural History* and his *De Augmentatione Scientiarum*; this much-thumbed volume is Newton's *Principia Mathematica Naturalis Philosophiae*; the one next to it his *Optics* and his *Astronomy*; here are Boyle's *Philosophical Essays, Natural Philosophy, Experiments, Physico-Mechanical Touching the Air, Of Forms and Qualities*, and other works; here Hugenius' *Discovery of the Celestial Worlds*; there Kepler's *On the Loadstone*; there Hevelius' *Machinae Coelestis* and his *Cometographis*.[19]

---

16 Wertenbaker, *op. cit.*, 137ff.
17 Ibid., 142.
18 Clinton Rossiter, *The First American Revolution* (New York: Harcourt, Brace and Company, 1956), 11.
19 Wertenbaker, *op. cit.*, 260.

Not only did the New England clergy read the latest works of European scholarship, but they were, many of them, amateur scientists and historians of better than average capacity. Newton employed the observations of two of these pastors in his *Principia*, and the writings of others appeared in the *Transactions* of the Royal Society – to this institution eleven pre-Revolution New Englanders belonged.[20]

We cannot but admire these intellectual achievements of Puritan New England, gained, as they were, in the course of a bold religious and social experiment in a new world, by a people far from home, engaged in continuous wars with the Indians who surrounded their struggling colonies. That they were able to survive at all is a marvel; that they not only survived but prevailed deserves our admiration. The stability of the political institutions they erected enabled them eventually to cut themselves off from the nation from which they had come, and the fact that they brought their English civilization with them does not detract from their achievement in applying it so well in the wilderness of North America. For our study, the success with which the Puritan congregations applied their church polity to the formation of village government in the wilderness is especially interesting. When we remember the frequency of the European wars in which the New England colonists were forced to fight England's battles – from 1689 to 1697, from 1702 to 1713, from 1745 to 1748, and from 1754 to 1763 (in addition to the unremitting guerilla fighting that raged on the Indian frontier), we will be able to appreciate somewhat the conditions under which these people lived. Having come over to forge a Holy Commonwealth, they soon found themselves in desperate defense of their social existence. The cost of this defense was variously felt, and not least in the military obligations laid on every man.

They not only survived, but they prospered. Contrary to a grand (but recent) American myth, the early colonists lived under the systematic governmental control of their economy, control by the English as well as by the local Colonial governments.[21]

Prohibited by England from almost all manufacturing, the New Englanders (most of whom were small farmers in a soil very unsuited for farming) yet turned the ingenuity for which they became famed to other areas, specifically to fishing, shipbuilding, and the distillation of

---

20 Ibid., 261f. Rossiter, *op. cit.*, 211-212.
21 Rossiter, *op. cit.*, 31. No Puritan would have accepted Rossiter's conclusion here, however.

rum. It was the success of these enterprises that brought prosperity to the colonies.

> Hundreds of ships and thousands of men were kept busy carrying cod to the Catholics of southern Europe (who welcomed it) and 'refuse fish' to the slaves of the West Indies (who did not). Rum ... was manufactured in prodigious quantities. In 1774 more than sixty distilleries in Massachusetts alone produced 2,700,000 gallons from West Indian molasses and thereby contributed decisively to the success of the slave trade... As for ship-building ... one-third of the seven thousand-odd ships engaged in English commerce were built in American yards, most of them in the small yards of the New England coast. ... Ship wharf, distillery, and countinghouse were the foundation of New England prosperity.[22]

And this, in a land in which eighty percent of the population lived on and derived its livelihood from small-time farming! The unlooked - for prosperity posed a special problem for the leaders of the Puritan movement in New England, and it was the firm conviction of some of them that the increasing wealth of the population was being used by Satan for their utter corruption.

Equally alarming was the fact that the small villages began losing more and more of their sons and daughters, as these moved west to stake out their own land. Hundreds of acres of land just over each horizon lured more and more people from the homes of their fathers. The Christian fellowship of many of these towns was thus weakened and was not as easily duplicated in the new towns being formed. The new towns could not erect the same unified structure of church and civil government that was the foundation of the old order, and the character of New England thus underwent a gradual but decisive transformation. The increasing secularization of a church that no longer expected its members to have a living knowledge of God, the slackening of public morality, and especially the gain-seeking business mentality that increasingly justified its increasingly shadier practices in the pursuit of wealth – these combined with other factors (such as a large influx of non-Christian immigrants and slaves and criminals forced upon New England by the Crown) to contribute to a visible decline in the religious and social life founded by the original Puritan congregations. New England was experiencing its own – its very own – Fall. The keeping of the Sabbath in holy pursuits such as Bible study, exhortation, and prayer became in

---

22 Ibid., 41.

many homes the barely remembered custom of an older generation. The multiplication of public taverns, the rising rate of drunkenness (the Puritans did not object to drink, but they hated drunkenness), the increasing profanity, the palpable failure of family discipline, and public misfortunes such as Indian wars, plagues, and restrictive legislation by the home government, combined to threaten the New England Puritans with what they were convinced was God's wrath outpoured in judgment on their individual and corporate existence for their individual and corporate sins.

> 'That God hath a controversy with His New England people is undeniable, the Lord having written His displeasure in dismal characters against us,' warned the Synod of 1697. 'Would the Lord have whetted His glittering sword?...Would He have sent such a moral contagion like a besom of destruction in the midst of us?...Or would He have kindled such devouring fires and made such fearful desolations in the earth, if He had not been angry?'[23]

The Synod making this judgment on the circumstances of the times had been called to meet in Boston for the very purpose of deciphering the evils that had come upon the colonies, and, hopefully, to guide the people in turning to God for mercy and forgiveness. Their report was submitted to the General Court, which caused it to be published with the title, *Necessity of Reformation*. But neither reports nor sermons, general courts nor private prayers, served to stem the tide of decay, and many New Englanders saw with horror the "return to Egypt" that they and their people had made in the "Promised Land." And in 1721 (Jonathan Edwards then being 18 years old) Increase Mather wrote in despair:

> I am now in my eighty-third year, and having been for sixty-five years a preacher in the Gospel, I cannot but be in the disposition of those ancient men who had seen the foundation of the first house, and wept with a loud voice to see what a change the temple had upon it. The children of New England are, or once were, the children of godly men. What did our fathers come into this wilderness for? Not to gain estates as men do now, but for religion, and that they might leave their children in a hopeful way of being truly religious. Oh, degenerate New England, what art though come to at this day? How are those

---

23 Wertenbaker, *op. cit.*, 171.

sins become common in thee that once were not so much as heard in this land![24]

This cry of despair from Mather is based on a profoundly theological interpretation as to the meaning of the existence of the Puritan colonies in the New World. We must turn, then, to a study of the faith that had caused these people to come to the wilderness of North America; we must see just what was the belief of those who had "seen the foundation of the first house." Let us examine now the theology of Puritanism, and especially those aspects of it most relevant to our study of Jonathan Edwards.

The Faith of the Fathers

The Puritans found themselves in basic agreement with the fundamental doctrine of the Church of England, as that doctrine was (and is) expressed in the official formularies, especially in the 39 *Articles of Religion* formally issued in Latin in 1563 and reissued with an English translation in 1571. These *Articles* are thoroughly Protestant and were written in explicit contradiction to the official Roman Catholic doctrine of the previous centuries, most especially in the decisions of the *Council of Trent*. Their publication, and the *Book of Common Prayer*, in which the Anglican exposition of Reformed theology is enshrined, constitutes the official repudiation by the Church of England of the crucial Roman Catholic doctrines of Religious Authority, of the Sacrifice of the Mass, of Grace, of Sin, of Free Will, of Works, and of Justification, against which European Protestantism had fought. The Anglican *Articles* came from the hands of Cranmer and Ridley, who had consulted with many other English and continental scholars and bishops. Revised and reduced in number they were made officially binding on the Church in 1571. G.F. Thomas writes:

> As regards the early Puritans, it must be remembered that there was a well-understood agreement between them and their opponents, i.e. the defenders of the Established Church order, on matters of doctrine. The questions in controversy were questions, not of doctrine, but of order and discipline and ceremonies. Dimock adds that the only exception to this was the observance of the Lord's Day, which was the first doctrinal disagreement.[25]

---

24 Quoted in A.S. Wood, *op. cit.*, 54. See also *The Select Works of Jonathan Edwards* (London: Banner of Truth), 23-25.

25 G.F. Thomas, *The Principles of Theology* (London: Church Book Room Press,

That so many hundreds of Puritan ministers, ardent disciples of Calvin and of other Reformed theologians, could remain within the doctrinal framework of the Established Church is proof enough of the essential Reformation principles therein contained.

> Before this time there was a general consent among our divines; for, as Bishop Carleton observes, though disputes arose between the Bishops and the Puritans with respect to Church Government, they perfectly agreed in doctrine.[26]

Furthermore, the fundamental position of doctrinal authority adopted by the reformed Church of England allowed and, in fact, required them to wage their fight for scriptural discipline and government of the church from within, as members: the Puritans campaigned for 'thorough reformation' in absolute loyalty to the Church's stated doctrine and stated doctrinal authority, in all good conscience and with no sacrifice of integrity.

To be specific, "Article VI: Of the Sufficiency of the Holy Scriptures for Salvation" of the Church of England's basic doctrinal statement, *The 39 Articles*, reads:

> Holy Scripture containeth all things necessary to salvation: so that whatsoever is not read therein, nor may be proved thereby, is not to be required of any man, that it should be believed as an article of the Faith, or be thought requisite or necessary to salvation ...[27]

Each ordained priest is asked by the bishop during the service of ordination whether he believes "that the Holy Scriptures contain sufficiently all doctrine required of necessity for eternal salvation through faith in Jesus Christ," and he is further asked whether he is "determined out of the said Scriptures to instruct the people ... and to teach nothing (as required of necessity to eternal salvation) but that which you shall be persuaded may be concluded and proved by the Scripture."[28]

In struggling for a purification of the church along biblical lines, Puritans were, in principle, faithful to their ordination vows.

With others of the specifically anti-Roman doctrines in the *Articles*, the Puritans also found themselves in fundamental agreement: the doctrines of Original Sin (Article IX) and the denial of Free Will

---

1956), xlix. With reference to Dimock, *Vox Liturgiae Anglicanae*, xx.

26   Ibid. With reference to MacBride, *Lectures on the Articles*, 30f.

27   *The Book of Common Prayer*, "Article VI."

28   Ibid., "The Ordering of Priests."

(Article X), the doctrines of Justification and Works (Articles XI, XII, XIII, and XIV), the repudiation of Roman Mariology as well as pietistic perfectionism (Article XV), and especially the absolute rejection of the official Roman doctrine of the Sacrifice of the Mass (Article XXXI).[29] In Article XXII the Roman Doctrine "Concerning Purgatory, Pardons, Worshipping, and Adoration, as well of Images as of Reliques, and also of Saints," is declared as "repugnant to the Word of God." *The Articles* concerning Holy Communion are basically Calvinistic as opposed to Lutheran expressions, but with both forms of Protestantism, they agree in repudiating the Roman doctrine of Transubstantiation (Articles XXV, XXVI, XXVIII, XXIX). The crucial Article XVII, on "Predestination and Election," while lacking the express emphases of Calvin's double predestination that the Puritans later came to insist on, yet grounds its teaching thoroughly in the free will of the gracious God.

---

29   The revival of explicitly Roman Catholic doctrine and practice within the Anglican Churches, which was begun by the Oxford Tractarians and continued by their spiritual descendants, has made it extremely difficult even for scholars to understand the historical meaning and intent not only of the Anglican Reformation, but of the stated doctrines and teachings that still inhere in the respective *Books of Common Prayer* of the various Churches of the Anglican Communion. Strong parties exist in all these Churches, using the Prayer Book and yet importing into their worship, doctrine, and life, the very Roman Catholicism that the Anglican Reformers repudiated with their life's blood. Puritanism cannot be understood if the de-mythologizing interpretation of Anglicanism practiced by so many Anglo-Catholic scholars is accepted as true. A thorough rejection of such Catholic interpretation of the essential and explicit Protestantism of Reformation Anglicanism is provided by the Roman Catholic scholar Francis Clark, S.J., in his *Eucharistic Sacrifice and the Reformation* (London: Darton, Longman, & Todd, 1960). See especially pages 23-55, 72, 115, 127ff., 131ff. Clark proves what the fifty-five volume Parker Society edition of the works of the Anglican Reformers put out in Cambridge in the last century should have demonstrated to any careful scholar – that is, the Anglican Church that emerged from the Reformation was a Protestant Church akin to that of the Lutheran and Reformed Churches of the continent. Until the change of opinion effected by partisan Catholic interpreters of Anglicanism, scholars always classified Anglicanism as Protestant, and even as Reformed, as distinguished from Lutheran. John H. Leith's introduction to the Anglican documents contained in his *Creeds of the Churches* (Garden City: Doubleday & Co., 1963), 266, is an example of the widespread misinterpretation of historical and theological fact through listening to the Catholic reinterpretation of the Protestant Reformation of the Church of England.

It was not with the reformation doctrine of the Church of England that the Puritans were at first dissatisfied, but with that church's order and discipline of ceremonies.[30] They objected strenuously to the rule of bishops over the flock of Christ – as did, indeed, many of their Anglican contemporaries. They lamented the pastoral neglect of the parishioners by so many of the clergy, the depravity and neglect into which the preaching of the Gospel had fallen, and the real lack of discipline in essential spiritual matters. Some of the defenders of the Establishment found the Puritan complaints often to be extremely petty, for example, the horror of Puritans at the giving of the Sign of the Cross at Baptism. From the Puritan point of view, however, liturgical actions that had been embedded in heretical doctrines for a thousand years had best be avoided by a Reformed church. The trappings of pomp and wealth surrounding the bishops and higher clergy were but other signs indicating to Puritan minds that these offices and men were still separated from and exalted above the Body of Christ in a most unbiblical manner.

The matter of Puritan complaint became more serious when the bishops began to contradict the doctrine of the Prayer Book and of Scripture by endorsing the semi-Pelagian theology of later Arminianism.[31] Through the rigorous opposition and persecutions of Archbishop Laud, his relentless rooting out of all opponents of his views from positions of teaching authority, and his replacing them with anti-Calvinists and explicit Arminians, a serious change took place, resulting in the hardening of Puritans against this increasing Arminianism. From then on they would call the English church "romish," "papistical," "corrupted," and would give to its leaders and policy all the epithets the Anglican Reformers had formerly reserved for Rome.

There were also more positive divergences of thought emphasized by the Puritans, and we should note the force of some of these for our understanding of Jonathan Edwards.

First, while the Anglican Reformers had been eager students at the feet of first Luther, and then Calvin, the strongest influences came to them through others of the continental Protestants, with whom they had much personal contact.[32] Cranmer had met a number of Lutheran

---

30 Wertenbaker, *op. cit.*, 22ff.

31 *The Works of Jonathan Edwards* (New Haven: Yale University Press, 1957), vol. 1, 82. This edition of Edwards' writings will henceforth be referred to as *Works* (Yale).

32 See Clark's illuminating discussion of the relationship between the Angli-

theologians while visiting Europe in 1531, and had kept up a correspondence with them. Other Anglicans had been forced to flee from
England, especially during the reign of Mary, and had found shelter
with Calvin and other Europeans, but most especially with Bullinger,
who exceeded himself in his hospitality to them.[33] In 1548 some notable
Protestant theologians from the continent had come to England, chief
among whom were Peter Martyr, Francis Dryander, John a Lasco, Paul
Fagius, Bernardino Ochino, and Martin Bucer. (It is important to note
that most of these were expressly invited to England by Cranmer.[34])
The influence of these men on the shaping of the Anglican *Articles*
and *Prayer Book*, as well as upon the theological climate in general,
was very profound.[35] The cumulative effect of these relationships with
foreign Protestant divines confirmed the architects of the Anglican
Reformation in their general Calvinism. The Puritans, however, sat at
the feet of Calvin himself, theologically, and they never relinquished
their demand for a thorough realignment of every doctrine so as to
be in detailed agreement with *their* Calvinism. That is to say, their
Calvinism was of a slightly different sort than that of the Anglican
Establishment, and the difference became increasingly manifest.

This brings us to a second major emphasis and development of Puritan
theology: the "Covenant" or "Federal Theology."[36] In the words of Karl
Barth:

> The federal Theology was an advance on mediaeval scholas-
> ticism, and the Protestant scholasticism which preceded and
> surrounded it, in that … it tried to understand the work and

---

   can and Continental Reformers, *op. cit.*, 116ff. See also John T. McNeill's *The
   History and Character of Calvinism* (New York: Oxford University Press, 1954),
   309ff., and the voluminous correspondence between Anglican and Continental
   Reformers in the *Zurich Letters* published in two volumes by the Parker Society
   (Cambridge: The University Press, M.DCCC.XLV).

33 McNeill, *op. cit.*, 310ff.

34 Clark, *op. cit.*, 117ff.

35 Ibid. See also J.R.H. Moorman, *A History of the Church in England* (New York:
   Morehouse-Gorham, 1954), 183ff.

36 See Karl Barth's critique of the Covenant Theology in his *Church Dogmatics*
   (Edinburgh: T. & T. Clark, 1956), 55-66. This is the authorized translation into
   English of his *Die Kirchliche Dogmatic* (Zollikon-Zurich: Evangelisch Verlag
   A.G., 1932). For selections from the sources consult Heppe/Bizer, *Die Dog-
   matik der Evangelisch – reformierten Kirche* (Neukirchen: Neukirchen Verlag,
   1958). See also Perry Miller's *Errand Into the Wilderness* (New York: Harper &
   Row, 1964), 55ff.

Word of God attested in Holy Scripture dynamically and not statically, as an event and not as a system of objective and self-contained truths ... This theology is concerned with the bold review of a history of God and man which unfolds itself from creation to the day of judgment. In relation to the two partners it is concerned with the history of the covenant (a history which is naturally initiated and controlled and guided to its proper end by God) – or what in the nineteenth century came to be called the history of redemption. We find something of the living dynamic of this history in the famous chapters which Calvin himself (*Institutes*, II, 9-11) had tried to apprehend the relationship between the Old and New Testament under the concept of the old covenant.[37]

Professor Barth also shows the role of Zwingli in the development of this way of theological thinking, as well as that of Bullinger.[38] (It will be remembered that these men had immense influence on the Anglican Reformers, that Bullinger himself had sheltered many of them during the Marian persecution, that their continual correspondence with him augmented his role in English theological development, and that every clergyman in the Archbishop of Canterbury's jurisdiction was in 1586 required to procure and study his *Five Decades of Sermons*.)[39]

Apparently, the first significant exposition of this form of theological thinking in England came through the writings, lectures, and sermons of William Perkins. The most noted of his many pupils was William Ames (Amesius), who was a close friend of many of the New England divines, and who, through his crucial works, *Medulla Sacrae Theologiae* and *De Conscientia*, had a decisive influence on the growth of the Federal Theology in England and America. Ames was the father of New England Congregationalism in that his views on theology as well as on the structure and government of the church were accepted as authoritative by those Puritans who migrated to America. Suppressed by his bishop, he fled to Leyden and then took a post at the University of Franeker, and, through his translation of Bradshaw's *The English Puritans*, spread the fame of that group throughout Europe.[40]

It was a student of Ames, however, who gave to this theology its classic expression. John Cocceius, in his *Summa doctrinae de foedere et testa-*

---

37   Barth, *op. cit.* 54ff.

38   Ibid., 56ff. See also James Orr's *The Progress of Dogma* (London: Hodder & Stougton, 1901), 302ff.

39   McNeill, *op. cit.*, 310ff.

40   Cf. Wertenbaker, *op. cit.*, 23ff.

mento Dei, published in 1648, conferred on the idea of Covenant a basic place in seventeenth-century theology. He saw man's relationship with God in terms of an original "Covenant of Works," by the terms of which man was expected to live a life of utter obedience to God, and by the breaking of which he lost his rights to blessedness and was then dealt with by God under the "Covenant of Grace." This whole governmental way of thinking of man's relationship to God was congenial to the thought of the seventeenth-century, and the works of such "Federal" thinkers as Hermann Witsius, and especially of Johannes Wollebius,[41] became well-known texts in the theological curricula of the Reformed Churches.

Richard Sibbes and John Preston were others of the Puritans who stressed the importance of the Covenant theology. Preston had been converted through the preaching of John Cotton (who was himself converted under the ministry of Sibbes), and as Master of Emmanuel College, Cambridge, exercised a major influence in that famous "School of the Saints." His *The New Covenant* was published in 1629.[42] Preston is noteworthy for his emphasis on the power of human reason and the capacity for good in man. This became an emphasis of fatal proportions in later New England Puritanism, especially in Thomas Hooker and Thomas Shepard.[43]

In 1647, a year before the publication of Cocceius' influential work on this subject, the *Westminster Confession* had formally incorporated this covenant emphasis into the basic dogmatic formulation of Puritanism. Part of it reads:

II. The first covenant made with man was a covenant of works, wherein life was promised to Adam, and in him to his posterity, upon condition of perfect and personal obedience.

III. Man, by his fall, having made himself incapable of life by that covenant, the Lord was pleased to make a second, commonly called the covenant of grace: whereby he freely offereth unto sinners life and salvation by Jesus Christ, requiring of them

---

41 A New English translation is provided by John W. Beardslee, III, (ed.) in *Reformed Dogmatics* (New York: Oxford University Press, 1956), 29ff. See also James Orr's discussion in his *Progress of Dogma*, 302ff.

42 William Haller discusses Preston's influence throughout his work *op. cit.* Note Perry Miller's *Errand into the Wilderness*, 58ff.

43 Miller, *Errand into the Wilderness*, 62ff, 80ff. See also *Works* (Yale), vol. 2, 53-57.

faith in him, that they may be saved; and promising to give unto all those that are ordained unto eternal life his Holy Spirit, to make them willing and able to believe.

IV. This covenant was differently administered in the time of the law, and in the time of the gospel. ... They are not, therefore, two covenants of grace differing in substance, but one and the same under various dispensations.[44]

The exponents of this way of thinking laid heavy stress on the history of God's dealings with mankind, especially in His dealings with the elect. Doctrines were studied in their relation to this history of revelation, and the present covenant relationship with believers was firmly established on the basis of the history of God's covenant dealings with His people in past ages. The importance of this for our comprehension of New England theology is made plain by the fact that in 1648 the Massachusetts churches, through their delegates, formally adopted the *Westminster Confession* as their doctrinal basis, and they adopted as well a congregational polity such as William Ames had described. Here we can see the importance of what we have already alluded to, that is, the intimate alliance of doctrine with life and with church government in the thinking of the Puritans, and most especially in the church life of the New England Congregationalists.

This view of the covenant relationship with God was expressed in three forms. First, they understood themselves, with the elect, to be bound to God through His Covenant of Grace. Second, they considered each individual congregation to be bound to God in a covenant that was an individual expression of this great, overarching Covenant of Grace through Jesus Christ. Third, the New England Puritans understood their whole migration from prelacy and persecution in England to be the progress of the elect people of God who were being set up by Him in a new, a Promised Land, where they would be a beacon to inspire the rest of Protestantism.[45] The whole of the people of the exodus from England, then, was under a social-political covenant with God, and He had promised to keep them in the truth, in this Promised Land. For their part, they were commanded to remain grateful and faithful.[46]

---

44 *The Westminster Confession of Faith*: see chapters VII and XIX in Philip Schaff's *Creeds of Christendom* (New York: Harper and Brothers, 1877), vol. III. For a Puritan commentary on the doctrine of the covenant see Thomas Watson's *A Body of Divinity* (London: The Banner of Truth Trust, 1960), 89ff., 107ff.

45 Gaustad, *op. cit.*, 7ff; Wertenbaker, *op. cit.*, 58ff, 74ff.

46 See Alan Simpson's discussion (and over-simplification) in his *Puritanism in*

"For their part" – this was the point at which the whole movement of this theology in New England stumbled and fell. It was by the increasing emphasis on *man's* part in this covenant relationship, the strenuous expositions of the works required by the original covenant of works, the repeated insistence that the reasonableness of God, and His works with men, demanded of men attitudes and responses that He would surely (by grace, of course) answer – it was by throwing their weight on the duties of man and of the (almost obliged) covenant faithfulness of God to answer the covenant faithfulness of men that this theology fell into Arminianism,[47] which they had always regarded as Pelagianism in disguise!

It happened before they knew it, and when, in 1734, Jonathan Edwards plainly named the current theology "Arminian," he incurred the undying enmity of some of the most influential of the New England clergy.[48] The matter had really been settled, however, by the doctrinal presuppositions underlying the "Half-Way Covenant" of 1662, for in granting a form of church membership to persons who admitted they did not know God, and in including them and their children in the realm of the promised, covenanted benefits of God, the Puritan churches had already turned away from their original doctrine of election by God's sovereign grace. Formally, they had always insisted on grace and on divine sovereignty and had always held that man can do nothing to earn salvation. In practical effect, however, they had ceased to rely on this doctrine. They had really accepted another in its place, a doctrine that stressed the degree to which God Himself was bound to – perhaps not *reward*, but at least – *answer* with graciousness those who had done "their part."[49]

We will mention Edwards' relationship to this covenant theology in a later section. It is sufficient for our purposes at this point to realize that it was one of the means through which theology in New England was transformed from Puritan Calvinism to a form of Arminianism

---

Old and New England (Chicago: The University of Chicago Press, 1955), 19-38.

47　See footnote 43.

48　*The Works of President Edwards in Four Volumes*, a reprint of the Worcester Edition (New York: Leavitt & Allen, 1858). We shall refer to this edition henceforth as *Works in Four Volumes*.

49　See Shepherd's preface to Bulkeley's sermons in *The Gospel-Covenant; or the Covenant of Grace Opened*, as well as Perry Miller's introduction to this work: Miller, *The American Puritans*, 143ff. Note also Bulkeley's remarks, 150-152. Cf. Gaustad's discussion in his first chapter, *op.cit.*

that was utterly at variance with their original intention and with their original trust in God's mercy alone for every aspect of their salvation. Further, the understanding gained through this covenant insight led the Puritans to rejoice over the "reasonableness" of God who had contrived such a scheme of redemption. This reasonableness was so exalted, and the agreement of man's reason with God's so emphasized, that even Preston was led to say that "faith teacheth nothing contrary to sense and reason."[50] Such an attitude was safe only so long as God's revelation itself remained the judge of human "sense and reason": otherwise it became an open invitation to rationalism. The invitation was accepted almost immediately by many Puritan thinkers, although some of the consequences were not recognized until Edwards named names a century after Preston's death.

In addition to its strict Genevan Calvinism, and the acceptance of the covenant theology, there was yet another important emphasis of Puritan theology, which deeply affected New England theology, and that was the doctrine of the Church as it manifested itself in the profound theological attention given to the guidance of souls under conviction, conversion, and sanctification. The most outstanding and learned of the renowned Puritan authors of ponderous Latin tomes of theology were at the same time widely known among the English populace for their down-to-earth books on "practical godliness." To understand Jonathan Edwards and his theological works, we need to be aware of this part of the tradition into which he was born. It is difficult perhaps for our time to appreciate this emphasis of Puritan theology. We must mention a few instances.

William Perkins was, just before his death in 1602, "by far the most important Puritan writer" of his time.[51] His influence on theologians of the movement was immense, but he was also renowned in humble Christian homes for his *Golden Chaine*, a "descriptive psychology of sin and regeneration."[52] In Haller's description:

> In lucid and eminently readable prose he set forth the process by which, as anyone might observe, God converts the sinful soul into a state of grace, the technique by which man comes to be born again. In the *Golden Chaine* he even supplied a graphic chart or diagram of all the steps by which man mounts to heaven and in a parallel column those by which he may descend to hell

---

50   Quoted in Miller's *Errand Into the Wilderness*, 13.
51   Haller, *op. cit.*, 91.
52   Ibid., 92.

> ... Composed and first published in Latin, they were soon put out by his pupils in English translations. ... His influence was particularly felt by other preachers. From him, probably, more than from any other, the members of the brotherhood, i.e. the Puritan preachers, learned to transpose the abstract doctrine into a rule of practice, into a method of spiritual self-help which they could set forth in sermon, tract, and treatise for common men to apply to their own lives. In a few years, a whole literature appeared on the bookstalls for the purpose of teaching the people how to dissect and physic their soils.[53]

Perkins' *Combate Betweene Christ and the Devill* was another detailed treatment of the struggle of man's soul after godliness and was intended as a guide for troubled consciences.

The influential William Gouge's *The Whole Armor of God*, John Preston's *The New Covenant* and *The Breast-plate of Faith and Love*, as well as Richard Sibbes' *The Bruised Reed and Smoking Flax* were but some of the many works of practical theology that indicate the overwhelming importance given this subject by leading Puritan theologians. The significance of this aspect of the theological tradition for Jonathan Edwards becomes more apparent when we find him recounting the effects on his parishioners' consciences of the newly imported Arminianism, his decision to preach extensively on "Justification by Faith Alone," the blessing this doctrine of justification proved to his people, and the place it had in the dramatic "outpouring of the Spirit" in 1734.[54] New England Puritans felt their very existence as God's people, as well as the salvation of each individual soul in their congregations, depended upon "right doctrine" in their preaching and pastoral care. The revival of a neo-Calvinism at the time of the Great Awakening of 1740 is to be explained, in part at least, by the conviction of many of the pastors that God was honoring a right, a doctrinally correct, preaching of His Word at this time. Their relationship to their English Puritan heritage is nowhere more apparent than in this application of doctrine to personal Christian experience, and in the testing of such doctrine by the help it afforded souls in their daily life with God.

Finally, we must note a fourth major emphasis of Puritan theology, that is, the attention given to the doctrine of the Person and Work of the

---

53 Ibid.
54 *Works in Four Volumes*, vol. 3, 232ff.

Holy Spirit. It was here that the Puritans made perhaps their greatest positive contribution to Protestant theology.

> It appears ... that a large influence in directing the Puritans' attention to the doctrine of the Holy Spirit was the preaching of Richard Sibbes, whose *Bruised Reed* played a part in converting Baxter, and whose writings were published, both before and after his death in 1635, every year from 1633 to 1641 inclusive.[55]

This is not to claim that there were not other Puritan theologians equally interested in the doctrine of the Spirit, but the work of Sibbes was persuasive, and he may be considered one of the leading exponents of this doctrine in early Puritanism. Naturally, the doctrines of Calvin were completely accepted by these men, and the Trinitarian economy as described in the *Institutes*[56] was upheld in the midst of heated controversy with Unitarians. But the Puritans devoted more attention to the doctrinal explication of the Person and Work of the Spirit than had been done before their time.

The variations of the *Westminster Confession* from the *Thirty- Nine Articles* present an immediate shift of emphasis towards a stated reliance on the Holy Spirit and constitute the best presentation of this emphasis for our study of Edwards and the theological tradition that he inherited. So also does *The Savoy Declaration* of 1658, the Confession of the "Independents" or Congregational Puritans, as they distinguished themselves from the Presbyterians. Largely the work of John Owen, *The Savoy Declaration* makes apparent at once the intense interest of this branch of Puritanism in the Holy Spirit.[57] Especially in the twentieth chapter of this *Declaration* is this emphasis on the Holy Spirit most vividly portrayed. Although John Owen's *Pneumatologia* is perhaps the greatest and one of the best known Puritan studies of the Holy Spirit and His work in convicting, converting, and sanctifying

---

55 Geoffrey F. Nuttall, *The Holy Spirit in Puritan Faith and Experience* (Oxford: B. Blackwell, 1947), 14. *Works* (Yale), 69-70.

56 See Nuttall's discussion of the Puritan controversy with the Quakers (the evidence he himself here adduces should have warned him against concluding that Quakerism was the logical outworking of Puritan theology), *op. cit.*, 150ff.

57 See Schaff, *op. cit.*, for these documents. See also Erik Routley, *Creeds and Confessions* (London: Duckworth, 1962), 117-127. Not only the *Confession* but also the Catechisms of Puritanism must be studied if this theology is to be understood. See volume III of Schaff, *op. cit.*, and T.F. Torrance's *The School of Faith* (New York: Harper & Brothers, 1959), 181-234.

men, the Puritan literature as a whole is filled with lesser books, treatises, and sermons on the subject.[58]

It is important for us to note two factors in this Puritan emphasis on the Holy Spirit: the Trinitarian foundation of their doctrine (and thus the relationship of the Spirit to the Word), and the criteria for testing the Spirit and His work.

The Puritan movement as a whole, in the midst of many controversies over the subject, held tenaciously to the traditional Western Trinitarian doctrine, and thus to the assertion of the closest relationship between the Son and the Spirit of God. Especially in their writings on the Scripture and its authority is this correspondence of Word and Spirit apparent. As the Spirit had inspired the biblical witnesses to write the Scriptures, so must He also illumine the hearts of Christian readers if they are to understand the written words as the very words of God.[59] When Quakers and "enthusiasts" arose who wished to claim a knowledge and reception of the Spirit apart from, and not necessarily subject to nor defined by, the written Word, the main stream of Puritanism recoiled. Let us hear Richard Sibbes:

> God, joining with the soul and spirit of a man whom he intends to convert, besides that inbred light that is in the soul, causeth him to see a divine majesty shining forth in the Scriptures, so that there must be an infused establishing by the Spirit to settle the heart of this first principle ... that the Scriptures are the word of God ...
>
> The breath of the Spirit in us is suitable to the Spirit's breathing in the Scriptures; the same Spirit doth not breathe contrary motions ...
>
> The word is nothing without the Spirit; it is animated and quickened by the Spirit.
>
> Oh! The Spirit is the life and soul of the word.[60]

---

58 Haller, *op. cit.*, 23ff.

59 In this respect they carefully followed John Calvin; cf. his *Institutes of the Christian Religion*, John T. McNeill, ed. (Philadelphia: The Westminster Press, MCMLX), Book I, 6-9; Book III; Book IV, 4. Cf. chapters I and VIII of the *Westminster Confession*.

60 Quoted in Nuttall, *op. cit.*, 23-24, from *Works of Richard Sibbes* (Edinburgh: Names Nichol, 1862-3).

John Owen remarked, "… he that would utterly separate the Spirit from the Word had as good burn his Bible."[61] Richard Hollinworth said:

> God's people are led by the Spirit, when they are led by the word inspired by the Spirit, and they are taught by God, when taught by His Book: no Spirit of Christ doth abstract any man's faith from the Word of God. … We are not warranted to expect or trust to Enthusiasms, or praeter-scriptural, much less contra-scriptural Revelations.[62]

The Puritans as a whole were emphatic in asserting that it is God's own Holy Spirit with whom we have to do in the gospel of His Son. The Spirit given men by the Son is the Spirit of the Father, the Holy Spirit of the Triune God.

Their orthodox Western Trinitarianism was coupled with their acceptance of the authority of the apostolic and prophetic description of the work of the Spirit. The Scripture had for them the weight it had for the Genevan Reformer. The criteria of the Spirit's work, therefore, are to be found in the writings of the apostolic and prophetic witnesses, in the Canon of Scripture. This position was basic to the whole of Puritan theology. It was as exegetes of Scripture that many of the Puritan preachers and theologians had begun their ministry, in posts created for them and for their biblical instruction, and their whole campaign against the "popery" and "prelacy" of the Establishment had been on the basis of their reading of Scripture and the pattern of church government they claimed to find in the apostolic and prophetic writings.[63]

We are not surprised, therefore, to find Baxter saying:

> We must not try the Scriptures by our most spiritual apprehensions, but our apprehensions by the Scriptures: that is, we must prefer the Spirit's illuminating of us to understand them, or before any present inspirations, the former being the more perfect. … This trying the spirit by the Scriptures, is not a setting of the Scriptures above the Spirit itself; but is only a trying of the Spirit by the Spirit; that is, the Spirit's operations in ourselves and his revelation to any pretenders now, by the Spirit's operations in the apostles, and by their revelations recorded

---

61 Ibid., 31, from John Owen's *Pneumatologia*, *Works of John Owen* (Edinburgh: Johnstone & Hunter, 1851-2), II, 4.

62 Ibid.

63 Haller, *op. cit.*, chapter III.

for our use. For they and not we are called the foundations of the church.[64]

The Scriptures were for the Puritans the key to the discernment of the work of the Spirit. When troubled by "strong Illusions," we are, says Sibbes, to "Bring them therefore to some rules of discerning. Bring all your joy, and peace, and confidence *to the word*. They go both together. As a pair of indentures, one answers another."[65]

Far more important than mere reason, greater than the convictions of conscience, stronger than the assurances of the Church, the witness of the Bible to the work of the Spirit is in the theology of Puritanism, the only sure guide in discerning the works of God from the actions of the devil and of the flesh. The Scriptures were given by God for this very purpose. Christian "experience," therefore, was *Christian* when it conformed to the biblical description of the work of God's Spirit in the persons and lives of His elect. However it shocked the timid and offended the rationalists, however it outraged the enthusiasts by the restrictions is imposed, the biblical description of the work of the Spirit of God was the only one the Puritans accepted as authoritative because it was the only one given by God to men.

The writings of Jonathan Edwards in this field must be read in the light of what his fathers had done before him. Likewise, we cannot appreciate the problems of his situation without some awareness of the degree to which eighteenth-century New England Puritanism had deviated from its seventeenth-century theological foundations. Later in our study, we shall find Edwards accusing his contemporaries of refusing to test the Spirit by the Word of God and by the whole of the biblical witness to the Spirit's work. Some of his contemporaries, on the other hand, objected to him on grounds of "reason," "conscience," and other criteria drawn from their "enlightened" age. Whether they were right or wrong in so doing is not for us to say at this point: but it *is* necessary that we notice the original Puritan criteria for evaluating the work of the Spirit, and the original insistence that the Spirit who is shed abroad in the hearts of believers is the Spirit of Christ, and thus the Holy Spirit of the Triune God, who is described authoritatively and sufficiently in the Scriptures, and nowhere else.

---

64 Quoted by Nuttall, *op. cit.*, 32.
65 Ibid., 43.

Let us summarize what we have said concerning those aspects of Puritan theology most needed for an appreciation of the thought of Edwards and of the theological tradition into which he was born:

Puritan theology was, essentially, the theology of the Anglican Reformation as that theology was formulated on the basis of the Reformers' positive doctrinal constructions in deliberate opposition to what they considered the heresies both of Rome and of Radical Anabaptism. But those who came to be called Puritans had emphases of their own, and it is these which set them apart as a particular "school" of Anglican theology.

First, they were rather more strict Calvinists than the Calvinists who became the leaders of the Established Church. In doctrine as well as in the realm of church order, government, and discipline, the pattern of Geneva was the one they considered most true to the explicit biblical witness, and they therefore strove to "purify" the Church of England so as to conform to that pattern.

Second, Puritan theology came to be dominated by the idea of the Covenant. Of this Covenant Theology, Karl Barth has written that "in the second half of the seventeenth-century it was the ruling orthodoxy of the Reformed Church."[66] This reading of biblical revelation through the dynamic historical perspective of the covenant theology was so influential in New England Puritanism that not only their doctrine but also their whole migration from England, as well as the actual formation of each new congregation, was seen in the light of this covenant relationship with the God who had called them out on this mission to the Promised Land. Furthermore, the increasing emphasis on their covenant obligations led to an emphasis on *human* "works" that opened the gates wide to Arminianism and Pelagianism in the eighteenth-century.

A third major emphasis of Puritan theology was its intense preoccupation with soul-care. The most influential Puritan theologians were also widely known for their practical works for humble Christians, works in which the path to heaven was carefully described, as well as the typical assaults of Satan, and the ways by which he should be avoided in the believer's pilgrimage to the New Jerusalem. Puritan theologians and pastors were expected to give such guidance to the souls under their care, and they were trained accordingly.

---

66 Barth, *op. cit.*, 55.

Finally, a fourth major emphasis of Puritan theology was the attention it gave to the doctrine of the Holy Spirit and His work. From the very beginning the Puritans had concentrated on giving full credit to this aspect of dogmatic theology, and they did so on the basis of an orthodox Trinitarian doctrine of God, which, based on the testimony of Scripture, revealed, they claimed, the closest possible connection and relationship between the Word and the Spirit of the Living God. They insisted also that the written Word of God is the only criterion given us for evaluating the working of the Spirit, as well in the Church as in the world.

We have dealt with these aspects of Puritan theology at this point because no accurate proper grasp of Jonathan Edwards is possible apart from an appreciation of them, and certainly no fair evaluation of his doctrine of regeneration can be had without an awareness of the close attention his "fathers in the faith" had given to the Person and the work of the Holy Spirit. Edwards is considered by many to be the greatest theologian of whom Christ's Church in America can boast, but we must not romanticize him. He stood in a great tradition, and he made great use of it. We will see later in our study that his experience was perhaps richer in the area of our interest than was that of some of the men whose works he read, but while we acknowledge the greatness of his theological achievement, we must not underestimate the magnitude of his debt to the tradition in which he was born.

"Tares Amongst the Wheat"

We have examined aspects of New England Puritanism's history and theology that help to illuminate the life and thought of Jonathan Edwards. We must now glance briefly at significant elements of the intellectual history of the eighteenth-century as these conspired to transform the religious culture established by the Puritans in New England. When Jonathan Edwards began his ministry in 1722, the future of religion in New England appeared dark indeed: defections from its ranks displayed its inner weakness, and the open attacks by "ungodliness," and the inner poison of "heresy" were causing the "orthodox" immense grief and trembling. To the orthodox, the power of Satan seemed unbounded. This could only mean that God's wrath was being poured out upon them for their base ingratitude and their open sin.

Because of the astonishingly high intellectual caliber of Puritan leadership (lay as well as clerical) and the close ties with the intellectual life of the Old World, the restless currents of eighteenth-century thought flowed across the Atlantic to burst upon the shores of the New World with unabated power. Every intellectual attack sustained by orthodox Christianity in the British Isles was felt also by the churches of the Puritans in North America. In later chapters, we shall note that Jonathan Edwards set himself, from his early years, to engage and dispute those ideologies that tore at the heart of the Christian faith and that all his works must be seen in the light of his lifelong engagement with the major forces of Anglo-Saxon intellectual life. Here, however, we will merely mention several of the most important of these intellectual currents for our correct knowledge of his theology, so that the audience to whom most of his published works were directed may be held in mind as, in succeeding pages, we examine the details of his thought.

We cannot, of course, do justice to the whole "Age of Reason" in these few pages, but we must name some of the names that ruled the thought of the time, and characterize the manner in which their works influenced adversely the religion of Edwards' land.

Reason

The title "Reason" points more to a spirit than to a creed, more to a temper of mind than to a specific platform. Yet the reality to which it points is the whole attitude of thought as this had developed in the seventeenth-century. Men of that age had embarked on a course that would, they thought, emancipate mankind from the barren sterility of scholastic theology, from the vicious brutality of priestcraft and the ignorance of superstition engendered by centuries of fable, lies, and childish deceits.

> It was in the seventeenth-century that modern European thought seems first to have assumed, once more, that its appointed task was *La Recherche de la Verite*, the discovery and declaration, according to its lights, of the True Nature of Things ... It was then, too, that the concepts of "truth," "reality," "explanation," and the rest were being formed, which have moulded all subsequent thinking.[67]

It was at this time that the *kind* of "truth" sought was substantially different from that which had satisfied European man for well over a thousand years. The Scholastic-Aristotelian discussions of the *Why?* of things were shelved; what people now wanted was to know *How?*

---

67 Basil Willey, *The Seventeenth-century Background* (London: Penguin Books, 1962), 9.

What they now sought to know was the measurement – not the metaphysical status – of created things. Added to the exciting discoveries of Galileo was the pious apology of Bacon to the effect that, since God worked throughout His creation by secondary causes only, it was no disrespect, but indeed the most proper honoring of Him, to study the laws of His manner of working.

The interest shifted from Metaphysics to Physics, from Being to Becoming. The "Reality" that more and more came to be the object of thinkers' seeking was of a type easily measurable by means of human science – a significant departure, needless to say, from the type of "Reality" sought by the scholastics. For various reasons and in different ways, European scholars bent their gaze to the wonderful world of measurable Things. The exhilarating successes of mechanical studies elevated a *method* of Natural Science into a *principle* of a new, often unacknowledged, metaphysics, and the unbounded confidence in man's reason to discover things-as-they-really-are by means of disciplined, unfettered investigation expressed itself in every area of intellectual life. Speaking of this period, a Roman Catholic historian remarks:

> The Western mind has turned away from the contemplation of the absolute and eternal to the knowledge of the particular and the contingent. It has made man the measure of all things and has sought to emancipate human life from its whole intellectual and social order being subordinated to spiritual principles; every activity has declared its independence, and we see politics, economics, science, and art organizing themselves as autonomous kingdoms which owe no allegiance to any higher power.[68]

The brilliant achievements of Descartes and those who followed him impressed upon the mind of the age the conviction that what is true can be described with rational clarity by means of mathematics. What disciplined reason finds to be mathematically true of the object of its study, is true. The terrifying unveiling of the untrustworthiness of human sense perception through the work of Galileo and others only increased the gratification felt at the thought that, though senses deceive, reason and mathematical investigation do not. The hypotheses that Kepler gave to the new astronomy were crowned in 1687 with brilliant success through the synthesis of all natural principles in

---

68   Quoted by Willey, *op. cit.*, 16.

the *Principia* of Sir Isaac Newton. Reason had triumphed indeed! The inner secret of Creation itself had been discovered.[69]

The philosophical concerns of this "Age of Enlightenment" are likened by Wilhelm Windelband to those of the Greek Sophistic movement of the 5th century B.C. He writes:

> ... the tendency as a whole and the objects of thought, the points of view and the results of the philosophizing, show an instructive similarity and kinship in these two periods so widely separated in time and so different in the civilizations which formed their background. There prevails in both the same turning away from metaphysical subtleties with doubt and disgust, the same preference for an empirical genetic consideration of the human psychical life, the same inquiry as to the possibility and the limits of scientific knowledge, and the same passionate interest in the discussion of the problems of life and society.

> But the basis for the Enlightenment of the eighteenth-century was given in the general features of a secular view of life, as they had been worked out during the Renaissance by the fresh movements in art, religion, politics, and natural research.[70]

The philosophical foundation of the Enlightenment in England was laid by John Locke in his popular *Essay Concerning Human Understanding*. Here the Cartesian worldview was assimilated to an empirical psychological procedure that promised quick success in every area of philosophical and ethical concern. The study of the inner capacities of the mind of man that Locke inaugurated captured the imagination of many thinkers, and the setting aside of metaphysical problems seemed eminently justified in the light of that age's firm conviction that man's "proper study" is Man, and that this study could profitably be carried out by man's own employment of his greatest gift, his reason.

Nature and Nature's Religion

Another determinative concept of the thought of this age was that of Nature and its Religion. The triumphs of sixteenth and seventeenth-century science were so impressive, the success with which its view of the world as a Great Machine so effectively dramatized, and the infiltration of this new worldview into all areas of eighteenth-century thought so

---

69 See Emanuel Hirsch, *Geschichte der neueren evangelischen Theologie* (Gutersloh: Gerd Mohn, 1960), vol. i., 113-218, for broad treatment of this theme.

70 Wilhelm, Windelband, *A History of Philosopy*, English translation by James H. Tufts (New York: Harper & Brothers, 1958), vol. II, 437f.

extensive, that even a cursory study of this period must acknowledge the magnitude of the intellectual revolution that occurred. Professor Willey says of this new way of thought:

> The laws of nature are the laws of reason; they are always and everywhere the same, and like the axioms of mathematics they have only to be presented in order to be acknowledged as just and right by all men. The historic role of "Nature" at this time was to introduce … peace, concord, toleration, and progress in the affairs of men; and in poetry and art, perspicuity, order, unity and proportion.[71]

Shocked by the spectacle of the vicious religious wars of the sixteenth and seventeenth centuries, eighteenth-century people turned with gratitude to the order and peace, the security and the surety of the study of Nature and all its ways. Though men had been able to wrest even the Bible to their own deluded ends, yet God had given a record of Truth that lay open to all honest inquirers, and whose "truths," these men hoped, could not be gainsaid. The Great Machine loomed in majestic splendor over the petty creedal squabbles of priests and fanatics, and Reason, by thinking God's thoughts after Him, in accord with the pattern revealed by the Celestial Mechanik, would discern those truths of physics and ethics that would enable men to live at peace with themselves and with God.

> Nature and Nature's laws lay hid in night:
> God said, Let Newton be! and all was light.[72]

These words of Alexander Pope express one of the major convictions of the age. They force us also to remember that the leaders of the English Enlightenment considered themselves to be truly on the side of God and the angels and that although the new way of thought was anti-metaphysical, it did not at first consider itself anti-religious.[73]

For this reason, many Christians found comfort in the "truths" of Nature being discovered in this exciting time. Others used these "truths" to buttress traditional Christian teaching. The Anglican Bishop Tillotson, for example, wrote, "All the duties of the Christian religion … which respect God, are no other but what natural light prompts

---

71 Basil Willey, *The Eighteenth-Century Background* (London: Penguin Books, 1962).
72 Ibid., 13.
73 Ibid., 11.

men to, excepting the two sacraments, and praying to God in the name and by the mediation of Christ."[74]

It is not easy to understand how a well-trained New England pastor steeped in the Puritan tradition could find himself attracted to the writings of the Anglican Bishop. Yet such was the case. In the early years of Jonathan Edwards' ministry in Northampton, the writings of Tillotson and other like-minded authors of the new age were eagerly studied in the colleges and pastorates of New England. One wonders how these words of Tillotson that we have just quoted were harmonized with the first chapter of the *Westminster Confession*, which reads, (concerning the "Holy Scripture"):

> Although the light of nature, and the works of creation and providence, do so far manifest the goodness, wisdom, and power of God, as to leave men inexcusable, yet they are not sufficient to give that knowledge of God, and of his will, which is necessary unto salvation; therefore it pleased the Lord ... to reveal himself, and to declare his will unto his Church: and afterwards ... to commit the same wholly into writing; which maketh the Holy Scripture to be most necessary ... [75]

The full implications of the developing naturalism became more and more clear as the theological inhibitions of its spokesmen became less and less bound to the doctrinal exposition of traditional Protestantism. The church then found itself attacked from without as well as from within; which attack was the more lethal is difficult to say.

Freed from the shackles of ignorance, priestcraft, and superstition, these "Freethinkers" allowed their unfettered minds to roam at will over the glorious wealth of material available for man's search for Truth. The cults of Reason and of Nature early found devotees among the ranks of New England Puritanism. A few decades after the foundation of Harvard University, complaints were raised as to the doctrinal orthodoxy of teachers and students. From 1688 to 1692 the liberal tutors John Leverett and Thomas Brattle ran the college. In 1707 there were so many supporters of the liberal faction that Leverett was elected president of the institution.[76] His colleague, Brattle, had, some years before, been instrumental in the founding of the Brattle Street Church in Boston. The significance of this particular church lay in the fact

---

74 Ibid.
75 John H. Leith, ed., *Creeds of the Churches* (Garden City: Doubleday & Co., Inc., 1963), 193.
76 Wertenbaker, *op. cit.*, 152f.

that the terms of its organization 1) repudiated the traditional pattern of requiring some profession of Christian belief from new members, 2) endorsed the provisos of the Half-Way Covenant, 3) altered the standard form of Puritan worship, and 4) allowed non-communicant churchgoers to vote in church matters. No more drastic departure from the religiously disciplined congregations of earlier decades could have been imagined, and loud was the cry that went up from the conservatives who deplored this abject surrender to the secularism of the "modern" age, the age of "Reason" and "Tolerance." The ripple became a flood as the ideas of the Enlightenment crossed the Atlantic and seeped into the parishes and schools of the New World, the New Jerusalem.

There were other forces at work in the New England of the late seventeenth and early eighteenth centuries, forces of direct, open opposition to traditional Christian doctrine and to the pattern of life the descendants of the Puritans had sought to erect upon their view of God's revelation. We must now turn to a brief examination of some of the more explicit "heresies" that engaged the attention of pastors, theologians, and laymen of the New England colonies during this period.

Heresy

There were three "heresies" that assumed special importance during this time: Arminianism, Quakerism, and Socinianism. Let us look at each of these in turn, remembering that they in no way exhaust the intellectual movements of this period, but only that for the purposes of our study of Edwards' theology they deserve special attention.

Arminianism

Arminianism, of course, was the dirtiest word extant in the lexicon of orthodox Calvinism. Since the famous Synod of Dort had met in 1619 to consider the Five Points of the Remonstrants and had decisively repudiated these objections to the prevailing doctrines of Calvinism, persons who objected at any point to any of the orthodox answers to the Remonstrants' objections were immediately branded with the epithet, "Arminian." Jonathan Edwards considered this brand of theology to be the most dangerous single intellectual threat to the life and doctrine of the parishes of his time, and it is necessary for us to appreciate the points at which it disagreed with the doctrines of Calvinism that he espoused.

So fearful were the New England Puritans of this "heresy," and so active were they in their opposition to it, that in 1726 the influential pastor Cotton Mather claimed that there was not one such heretic in Puritan New England (the scattering of Anglicans, Roman Catholics, and others in the colonies could not, of course, be considered a part of "Puritan" New England). A bare eight years later, however, Jonathan Edwards was speaking and preaching in such a manner as if the New England churches were in danger of being overcome by *native* manifestations of this heresy.[77] That such an implication was horrifying for the orthodox to contemplate may be gathered from an earlier, classic expression of Puritan opinion concerning Arminianism. Stanley Gower, a member of the Westminster Assembly and a Puritan divine of high repute, had this to say:

> There are two rotten pillars on which the fabric of late Arminianism (an egg of the old Pelagianism, which we had well hoped had long since chilled, but is sit upon and brooded by the wanton wits of our degenerate and apostate spirits) doth principally stand.
>
> The one is That God *loveth all alike*, Cain as well as Abel, Judas as the rest of the apostles.
>
> The other is, That *God giveth* (nay is bound, 'ex debito,' so to do) *both Christ, the great gift of his eternal love, for all alike to work out their redemption, and* 'vires credendi,' *power to believe in Christ to all alike to whom he gives the gospel;* whereby that redemption may effectually be applied for their salvation, if they please to make right use of that which is so put into their power.
>
> The former destroys the *free* and *special* grace of God, by making it *universal*; the latter gives cause to man of glorifying in himself rather than in God, God concurring no farther to the salvation of a believer than a reprobate. Christ died for both alike; God giving power of accepting Christ to both alike, men themselves determining the whole matter by their free-will; Christ making both savable, themselves make them to be saved.[78]

In 1633, fourteen years previous to the publication of Gower's definition of Arminianism, William Laud had been made Archbishop

---

77 *Works in Four Volumes*, 3, 233f.

78 Quoted by John Owen in his *The Death of Death in the Death of Christ* (reprinted in London: The Banner of Truth Trust, 1959), 35.

of Canterbury. His deliberate policy was to dismiss from ecclesiastical office those Anglicans of Puritan sympathy, replacing them with anti-Puritans and open Arminians. Consequently, while the fundamental doctrinal statements and their expressions in the words of Anglican worship remained unchanged, a larger and larger proportion of Church of England pastors and theologians came to preach the open Pelagianism that characterized later Arminianism. In 1710, an Anglican polemicist, Daniel Whitby, published an attack on the Calvinistic "Five Points." Ramsey says of the ensuing controversy:

> In 1710 Whitby became engaged in refuting the Calvinism of John Edwards, who had been forced in 1670 from St. John's College at Cambridge because of his views. Anthony Colling in his *Discourse on Free-Thinking* was able to list on the Calvinist side, no one among the Anglicans worth naming except John Edwards. Collins and Whitby both observe that most Anglicans were Arminians. An Anglican of the eighteenth-century was surprised to learn that until about the time of Archbishop Laud the clergy were universally Calvinist, and that in those days the anti-Calvinists were the despised 'Anabaptists.' Arminianism permeated the eighteenth-century, and in mild form the whole of the Church of England in this century, becoming in a sense not heresy but orthodoxy.[79]

The book of Whitby's against the Calvinistic theology was among those given to the Yale library, and perhaps one of the ones responsible for "corrupting" the minds of the Rector and two tutors in the "Great Apostasy" of 1722, when these men and several other Congregationalists repudiated Congregationalism and declared for Anglican orders.

To a people that regarded Arminianism as but another form of Pelagianism, the successful appeal of Church of England Arminians to the minds of Puritan pastors and teachers was a horrible thing to contemplate, yet this is exactly what began to happen around the turn of the eighteenth-century. Such crucial teachings as those of God's sovereign control of history, His electing grace, the desperate nature and extent of sin, and man's absolute dependence on God for every aspect of his salvation – all of these were seen by the Calvinists to be compromised and thus negated by both the spirit and the letter of Arminian theology. The erection of a Church of England Chapel in Boston in 1723 (the congregation had organized in the 1680s) was clear evidence (to them) of Satan's power in sowing tares amongst the wheat. (The fact

---

79   In his introduction to *Works* (Yale), vol. 1, 82.

that this first Anglican Chapel later became the first Unitarian Church in the area did nothing to convince later Calvinists that their fathers had misread the signs.)

Even before the introduction of Arminian doctrine from England, however, the establishment of the Half-Way Covenant, and the consequent emphasis on man's part in "owning the covenant," had already committed large sections of New England Puritanism to a *practical* agreement with the essence of doctrinal Arminianism: i.e., to a decreased reliance upon God for their salvation and an increased reliance upon their own works of preparation, obedience, etc.

> The Puritan fathers had held that conversion was solely the work of God, but with the second and third generations, as the number of conversions decreased, gradually the idea began to emerge that there were certain 'means' which might be used in putting the soul in a position to receive the regenerating influence of the Spirit of God. Such 'means' were owning the covenant, attending divine worship, leading a moral life, reading the Scriptures and prayer. Thus there came to be more and more reliance upon the use of 'means' and less and less upon the miraculous power of God ... [80]

But other "heresies" were brewing for New England.

Quakerism

The arrival of Quaker missionaries in Boston, in the year 1656, inaugurated yet another assault on the Puritan establishment. In the eyes of conservative Puritans, the Quakers posed a major and two-dimensional threat to the New England colonies. Socially and politically, as well as theologically, the Quakers assaulted the very foundations.

Socially and politically the Quakers were a direct threat to New England society because, by their denial of the Puritans' right to govern the colonies according to Puritan religion, they challenged the basis of the colonial government and discipline. The Puritans had set up their society on the basis of their conviction that God had called them out of Old England for this very purpose, and that He had commanded them to establish a commonwealth governed by His will as revealed in His written Word. The government of each town and congregation was based on the adults' comprehension of the Bible's guidance in these matters. The Quakers, however, rejected the right of the Puritans to establish set up such a community, and in their rejection they appealed

---

80 Sweet, *op. cit.*, 65.

to "the Spirit within" themselves, over and against the Puritan appeal to the injunctions of the written Word. From the Puritan point of view, to relinquish their responsibility to govern the body politic on biblical lines (as they understood them) would constitute a total repudiation of their calling, and of their covenant responsibility to the God who had appointed them to organize a holy commonwealth. This would amount to national apostasy and would be followed by God's dreadful vengeance on them, their children, and their children's children as well. Were they to allow individual Quakers, appealing to "the Spirit within," to cause them to throw over the authority of the Bible and the responsibilities of their offices, they would bring about the destruction of their society and the loss of their own souls. They thus tried to keep the Quakers out. When they were unable to prevent them from infiltrating their towns and proselytizing their people, they reluctantly resorted to threats, then punishments, then imprisonment, and, finally, execution. The Quakers thrived on these repressions, however, and eventually, under pressure from England as well as from troubled consciences within their own ranks, the Puritans gave up the struggle and allowed the "error" to settle among them. By 1674 the Quakers were meeting regularly in Boston.[81]

The theological threat of Quakerism was twofold: by giving to human opinions concerning the Spirit's immediate revelations the same authority they gave to Scripture, the latter was effectively supplanted by the former, as God's Word was replaced by men's words; and, by divorcing the Spirit from the Son of God whose Spirit He is, God's Triune nature was misunderstood and thus misrepresented. Repudiating, in effect, the decisive and exclusive authority of the Bible in religious matters, by their claim to immediate revelations from God's Spirit, they separated the Word from the Spirit in a manner repugnant to Puritan conscience and potentially disastrous to Puritan religion. We fail utterly to appreciate the situation if we do not understand the Puritan reaction to Quakerism to be analogous to Luther's reaction to the subjectivism of the Anabaptists in their similar separation of the Word of God from His Spirit, and their giving the greater practical authority to their view of the illuminations of the latter over the written witness of the former.[82]

---

81 See Wertenbaker's fine discussion in *op. cit.*, 208ff. For Puritan interpretation read Thomas Hooker's words in *The American Puritans*, 153ff.

82 Nuttall, *op. cit.*, 20-47. See Martin Luther's discussion of this basic doctrine of Classical Protestantism in the English translation of his *Galatians*, 360ff. This

By allowing the Quakers to settle in their midst, the conservatives knew themselves to be violating the express injunctions of the *Westminster Larger Catechism* (QQ. 107-110) as well as their practical obligation to protect themselves and theirs from the influence of such error.[83] Such an open opposition to their Trinitarian dogma and to the Bible as the basis of their religious and social authority was regarded by many at the time as a grievous wound from the Enemy, a wound permitted by God who in His wrath punished His people for their disobedience and ingratitude.

Socinianism

Perhaps the most shocking – because most obviously basic – heresy to strike at Puritan theology was that revival of a form of Arianism to which Faustus Socinus (d. 1604) gave his name: "Socinianism." Explicitly denying that God is Triune, this movement struck at the very heart of orthodox Christian doctrine – the doctrine of God. The Puritans in New England fought side by side with their brothers in England, and with Anglicans as well, in opposing this emasculation of the Christian message. The fact that this "error" came to be established, however, and the fact that books promulgating it could be published, proved to the saddened Puritans that the Church of Christ had entered into a new, a dark, and a fearsome day.

Samuel Clarke in England launched his attack against traditional Trinitarian dogma in his *Scripture Doctrine of the Trinity*, published in 1712, in which the dogmas of God and the traditional creeds were thoroughly denied. Daniel Waterland replied in 1719 with his *A Vindication of Christ's Divinity*. Even before this, however, and certainly long after it, the presses were flooded with heated polemical works, and the doctrine of the Triune God was torn apart, patched up, defiled, and yet defended in a manner undreamed of within the confines of European Christianity since the close of the 5th century.

---

emphasis on the fidelity of the Spirit's teaching to the written prophetic and apostolic testimony to the Son of God was basic to the Reformation repudiation both of Roman Catholicism on the one hand, and of radical Anabaptism and Spiritualism on the other. See *Luther's Works*, American Edition (Philadelphia: Fortress Press, 1958), vol. 40, 45-223. Also vols. 26 and 27. See his *Commentary on St. Paul's Epistle to the Galatians* (Westwood: Fleming H. Revell Company, reprint from the first publication of 1535).

83   Torrance, *op. cit.*, 207ff.

Anti-Trinitarianism had, of course, found fervent support at the time of the Reformation. Much of Calvin's exploration of the Christian doctrine of God must be seen in terms of his vigorous arguments with Michael Servetus, Giorge Blandrata, Valentine Gentile, Gianpaulo Alciati, and Matthaeus Gribaldi.[84] The *positive* doctrinal and ethical constructions of the Socinians, however, made an immediate appeal to English rationalism, humanism, and Deism. English anti-Trinitarianism thus assumed the assertive stance associated with early Unitarianism.

(We shall see in a later chapter that Edwards considered Arminianism to be based upon principles basically and essentially anti-Trinitarian. He opposed both, and in the same manner, by portraying the person and the work of Christ Jesus. More explicitly, Edwards found the doctrine of Christ's sacrificial death for man's sin to be the crux of the polemical issues of the eighteenth-century.)

More important for comprehending the explicit form of this "heresy" that American Puritanism faced was Thomas Chubb's defense of Arianism published in 1715.[85] Chubb's works enjoyed huge success in New as well as Old England, although surreptitiously in America at first. Not until after the Revolution did an explicit anti-Trinitarian campaign get started in America, but the conservatives in general, and Jonathan Edwards in particular discerned the necessary direction of the principles expressed in the earlier English literature, named them, and began the fight long before the Revolution began.[86]

Summary

We have discussed the "spirits" that informed men's "reason" in the seventeenth and eighteenth-century world of Anglo-Saxon thought, and, under three main headings, we have noted the opposition to Puritan theology that was implicit and explicit in these new winds of doctrine.

The cult of Reason, the cult of Nature, the religion derived from both – these combined with a number of specifically Christian "heresies" to

---

84   See *Institutes* I.13.2; II.14.3, 6, 8. The edition of the *Institutes* that we have cited has excellent notes and bibliographical suggestions that illuminate Calvin's exposition.

85   *The Supremacy of the Father Asserted: or, Eight Arguments from Scripture to Prove that the Son of God is a Being Inferior and Subordinate to the Father, and that the Father Alone is the Supreme God.*

86   *Works* (Yale) 1, 62ff; 129ff; 203ff.

shake the foundations upon which the Puritans had based their beliefs, and by which they conducted their lives.

The powerful currents of eighteenth-century thought seemed all to share an allegiance to the exaltation of man at the expense of God. Puritan New England was not exempt from this threat by its distance from the Old World. Let us quote again from Professor Willey's *The Seventeenth-century Background*:

> The 'inner light' of the Quakers ranks with the 'Reason' of the Platonists, the 'clear and distinct ideas' of Descartes, or the 'common notions' of Lord Herbert of Cherbury, by which the century was testing the legacy of antiquity and declaring its spiritual independence.[87]

Before Jonathan Edwards came on the scene, the whole character of the Puritan Experiment in North America had been altered, the structure in many ways had deviated seriously from the foundation the founding fathers had laid, and, in the minds of many, the cause was so far lost that the accumulation of natural catastrophes, the increasing severity of the Indian campaigns, the vastly increased criminality, and the lowered standards of public morality were but natural symptoms of the fact that the whole land was groaning and suffering under the outpoured wrath of God. This was an interpretation frequently heard from the pulpits and in the presses of New England in the decades before the Great Awakening of 1740.[88] We must take into consideration the seriousness with which they held this interpretation if we are to appreciate the tremendous repercussions of the Great Awakening, the role of Jonathan Edwards in it, and the confidence he had in God's vindication of his theology of the Holy Spirit and His work in regeneration.

The Great Revival

The third and fourth decades of the eighteenth-century witnessed an astonishing "revival" of religion in New England.[89] Many people were convinced that God had at last turned back in mercy towards His people in the Puritan colonies, forgiving their individual and corpo-

---

87   Willey, *The Seventeenth-Century Background*, 72.
88   Wertenbaker, *op. cit.*, 159ff. A.S. Wood, *op. cit.*, 53ff.
89   E.A. Gaustad's *The Great Awakening in New England* (New York: Harper & Brothers, 1957) is a superb description of this remarkable religious movement. His balanced judgments, his documentation, and his bibliographical information are excellent.

rate apostasies and filling scores of villages with the power of His Holy Spirit. Many thousands of formerly nominal church members became ardent Christians filled with love for God and with zeal for His cause. Thousands of others were brought from unbelief to a living fellowship with God. In spite of the many excesses that marred the course of this revival, literally thousands of people were convinced that God was answering His peoples' prayers for an outpouring of His Spirit. The whole character of New England society was affected. Never before had these settlements witnessed a religious movement of such power. It fell to Jonathan Edwards to be a leading spokesman for the churches during this time; to guide many people in understanding what was occurring; and to help them sift the wheat from the chaff, to see what was the work of God and what was the work of the devil. We must turn now to a survey of these religious events, in order to follow the development of Jonathan Edwards' life and thought.

Early Revivals

The first definite signs that the religious situation of the Puritan colonies might be improving were to be found in Northampton, Massachusetts, under the ministry of Jonathan Edwards' grandfather, Solomon Stoddard. Stoddard was the leading ecclesiastic in the colonies, and during his ministry in Northampton, five revivals of religious life occurred. In the years 1679, 1683, 1696, 1712, and 1718 this pastor "reaped" what he termed five "harvests." During these "harvests" the lives and characters of many of his parishioners were significantly altered, and many professed to have been brought to conversion and to a saving relationship with God in Christ. There was a final, smaller revival in 1729, just before Stoddard's death, and just after Edwards had come to Northampton to be his grandfather's assistant; in this revival, about twenty people professed conversion.[90]

In 1705, an impressive revival occurred in Taunton, after the minister, Samuel Danforth, had begun studying and praying regularly with some of his people. It is important for our purposes to note that this revival, that affected over three hundred persons in this small town, was, on the human level, first inspired by a reading of a description of the flourishing religious societies in England. Similarly, news of this revival in Taunton spurred other New England congregations to hope

---

90   *Works in Four Volumes*, vol. 3, 232ff. contains Jonathan Edwards' famous *A Faithful Narrative of Surprising Conversions* to which we shall often refer. This piece is indispensable for our knowledge of the happenings at Northampton.

for such a visitation of God's Spirit. In 1720 many more souls were brought to a profession of conversion through the ministry of Theodore Freylinghuysen, a Dutch Reformed minister in New Jersey. Six years later, other Presbyterian churches in that area were experiencing general "awakenings" and individual conversions. In 1730 and 1732, a most impressive revival occurred among the Presbyterians under the ministries of Gilbert and his brothers John and William Tennent. Just prior to this, in Windham, Connecticut, eighty persons had professed conversion, all within a space of six months, and in a town of only about two hundred families. The work was so extensive in this village that the minister wrote, "the town was never so full of love, joy, thanksgiving and praise."[91] The pastors in these situations testified over and over again to the love, to the joy, and to the peace that filled the hearts and minds of persons involved in these revivals. They testified as well to the radically altered character and behavior of the persons converted – character and behavior that evidenced, among other things, deep love to God and love of His revelation through the Scriptures.

There were other instances of revival in New England in the period just prior to the Great Awakening of 1740, but the most outstanding of all was that which took place (again in Northampton) under the ministry of Jonathan Edwards.[92] This revival began in 1733, and the effect and the extent of it were so profound, the influence upon other New England towns so extensive, that the leading minister in Boston, Benjamin Coleman, wrote Edwards for an account. Edwards replied in May of 1735, and Coleman was so moved by this narrative and so convinced as to its accuracy from conversations with other persons who knew of the situation, that he published Edwards' letter and sent it to some of the leading non-conformist theologians in England. Edwards was asked to expand his original report for regular publication. He did so, and this revised edition was published in London in October of 1737 by Isaac Watts and John Guyse. The publication created an immediate sensation. "It went through three editions and twenty printings by 1739," says Perry Miller, "and a hundred years later was still a handbook of revivalism in Illinois and Wales."[93] The objectivity of the account Edwards had written, the scriptural background of the evaluations it contained, the pastoral experience evidenced, and the openness of the author's mind to the obvious variety of the Spir-

---

91   Wood, *op. cit.*, 57. See Edwards' account in his *Narrative*, footnote 91 above.
92   Wood, *op. cit.* 56ff.
93   Miller, *Jonathan Edwards*, 136f.

it's workings all combined to raise the thirty-four-year-old pastor to a position of leadership that he himself did not feel competent to assume.

In the account, entitled *A Faithful Narrative of Surprising Conversions*, Edwards told of his pastoral labors as these were directed to awakening his people to a proper sense of God and of His will. He described how he had persuaded them to form into groups for prayer and study; of his sustained preaching on the themes of God's electing grace and His justification of sinners through faith in Christ Jesus; of his guidance of the persons "affected"; and of the course of the revival that occurred.[94] Edwards emphasized that this revival was just like the earlier ones Northampton had experienced, and for this reason, the people were convinced that they were once again being visited by the Spirit of God. The unusual feature of this occasion, however, lay in the rather remarkable power and extent of the movement among the people. Otherwise, it was similar to the other revivals then occurring in New England, particularly in the Connecticut Valley, in the early 1730s. In Edwards' own words:

> This work of God, as it was carried on, and the number of true saints multiplied, soon made a glorious alteration in the town; so that in the spring and summer following, anno 1735, the town seemed to be full of the presence of God: it never was so full of love, nor so full of joy; and yet so full of distress as it was then. There were remarkable tokens of God's presence in almost every house. It was a time of joy in families on account of salvation's being brought into them ... The work that has now been wrought on souls, is evidently the same that was wrought in my venerable predecessor's days; as I have had abundant opportunity to know, having been in the ministry here two years with him, and so conversed with a considerable number that my grandfather thought to be savingly converted under his ministry before. And I know of no one of them that in the least doubts of its being the same spirit, and the same work ... And God's people that were formerly converted, have now partook of the same shower of divine blessing, in the renewing, strengthening, edifying influences of the Spirit of God that others have in his converting influences; and the work here has also been plainly the same with that which has been wrought in those of other places that have been mentioned, as partaking of the same blessing. I have particularly conversed with persons about their experiences, that belong to all parts of the country, and in various parts of Connecticut, where a religious concern has

---

94 *Works in Four Volumes*, 3, 233ff.

lately appeared; and have been informed of the experiences of
many others by their own pastors.[95]

Edwards listed more than twenty-five towns where revival had occurred,
usually giving the name of the pastor as well so that those who wished
could write and secure first-hand information for themselves.

The most notable progress of the revival occurred in 1734 and 1735.
Its power abated after that, proving to Edwards and to many others
who shared his interpretation of these events that, with all the human
elements involved, the whole thing was primarily a case of God giving
and then withdrawing the mighty operations of His Holy Spirit.[96]
Many, many persons remained permanently altered in mind and heart
and life. Edwards says:

> But as to those that have been thought to be converted among
> us, in this time, they generally seem to be persons that have
> had an abiding change wrought on them: I have had partic-
> ular acquaintance with many of them since, and they gener-
> ally appear to be persons that have a new sense of things, new
> apprehensions and views of God, of the divine attributes, and
> Jesus Christ and the great things of the gospel: they have a new
> sense of the truth of them, and they affect them in a different
> manner ... [97]

As late as 1737, persons were still experiencing the powerful works of
the Spirit, but the dramatic visitations that had come upon hundreds
of people within a few months had ceased. About forty towns in all
were thus affected in this revival, and the reports of conversions and of
growth in Christ electrified many other congregations in New and Old
England. The thanksgivings aroused in the hearts of those who had
longed for such a blessing from God, and among those who had been
unexpectedly blessed, were intense. To those who knew the history
of the Puritan movement, it appeared to be a divine justification of
the faith of their fathers, and of the classical Protestant theology that
had shaped those pastors who preached the message that had been so
dramatically blessed.[98]

---

95   Ibid., 235.
96   Ibid., 270-1.
97   Ibid., 271.
98   This point is important. The clergy who preached not the "new" doctrines but
     the "old" ones were the ones whose parishes were experiencing revival. These
     men demanded that the "liberals" and the "rationalists" show similar fruits in
     the lives of *their* congregations. Once again, the Puritan concern for *doctrine*

But this revival was soon to be overshadowed by a bigger one – the greatest New England had ever known.

The Great Awakening of 1740

In September of 1740 the Reverend George Whitefield, a clergyman of the Church of England, came to Newport, Rhode Island, and preached his first sermon of what was to be a remarkable "crusade." Word of the astonishing power of this young man had crossed the Atlantic before him. News of his preaching success in Delaware, New York, Pennsylvania, and the Jerseys had reached New England and had produced tremendous excitement concerning his visit. Whitefield proceeded to Boston, where the buildings were unable to contain the multitudes who came to hear him preach, forcing him to preach in the open air, to crowds that grew from five, to eight, to fifteen thousand hearers.[99]

> Although Whitefield only spent a month in and around Boston, the results of his visit were phenomenal. Gilbert Tennent continued the work for four further months and all the signs of genuine revival were displayed. Pastors confessed that more people resorted to them in spiritual need within that short period than they had previously known throughout their entire ministry. William Cooper, Coleman's assistant, met about six hundred and John Webb ... received over a thousand. 'There repaired to us boys and girls, young men and women, Indians and negroes, heads of families and aged persons,' reported Thomas Prince ..."some in great distress for fear of being unconverted; others lest they had all along been building on a righteousness of their own, and more still in the gall of bitterness and bond of iniquity; some fearing lest the Holy Spirit should withdraw Himself; others in great anxiety lest He should leave them forever.' Other equally remarkable results ensued. No less than thirty religious societies were formed in the city. Churches were overcrowded. Ministers preached in private houses almost every evening. 'Our lectures flourish,' wrote Coleman to Isaac Watts, 'our Sabbaths are joyous, our churches increase, our ministers have new life and spirit in their work.' It was said that the very face of Boston was strangely altered. Even the street loafers no longer made themselves objectionable and the taverns were well-nigh deserted.[100]

---

evidenced its immediate relevance for *life*.
99 Wood, *op. cit.*, 63ff. See Whitefield's own account in *George Whitefield's Journals* (London: The Banner of Truth Trust, 1960), 451ff.
100 Wood, *op. cit.*, 64f.

Whitefield then went to Northampton, staying with Edwards and his family, preaching four sermons from Edwards' pulpit and instigating a new revival that lasted for two years.[101] In his *Journals* Whitefield recorded:

> ... we crossed the ferry to Northampton, where no less than three hundred souls were saved about five years ago ... Mr. Edwards is a solid, excellent Christian, but, at present, weak in body. I think I have not seen his fellow in all New England. When I came into his pulpit, I found my heart drawn out to talk of scarce anything besides the consolations and privileges of saints, and the plentiful effusion of the Spirit upon believers ... Felt great satisfaction in being at the house of Mr. Edwards. A sweeter couple I have not seen ... Mrs. Edwards is adorned with a meek and quiet spirit; she talks solidly of the things of God, and seemed to be such a helpmeet for her husband, that she caused me to renew those prayers, which, for some months, I have put up to God, that He would be pleased to send me a daughter of Abraham to be my wife.[102]

The work commenced by Whitefield grew rapidly. Hosts of ministers pressed upon their people the need to open their hearts and lives to the rich blessings the Spirit of God was pouring out upon them. Whole communities – more than one hundred and fifty of them – were drastically reformed. Contemporary accounts are full of the evidence concerning the changed lives of many hundreds of people, and of evidence concerning the conversion of hundreds, and even thousands, more. Ministers, who had been brought up on the lamentations of their fathers concerning the degeneracy of the Puritan cause, now saw for themselves – and to a far greater degree – the divine blessings their fathers had known. To many of these people, it appeared as if the second coming of Christ was being heralded by these momentous events.

A host of problems quickly arose. Whitefield, through youth and inexperience, rashly advised his hearers to forsake "spiritually dead" ministers. Each person, then, was to consider himself spiritually mature enough to perform such a judgment on ministers' souls. Many people began at once to do just this. Further, Whitefield's practice of touring from town to town was a new feature to the New England churches, and many people, who felt themselves "converted" and "called," began to do the same. Uneducated, ill-qualified, and incompetent "itiner-

---

101 Sweet, *op. cit.*, 132f. See *George Whitefield's Journals*, 475ff.
102 Ibid.

ants" began to tour the land, gathering crowds, preaching whatever came into their heads, and playing havoc with the parish structure of the New England churches. The regular pastors came more and more under the fire of these self-appointed evangelists, and many newly "awakened" persons, spiritually immature themselves, were led to despise the experienced pastors who could have been of real help to them at that time and to follow instead the itinerants. What Jonathan Edwards was to regard as the very worst feature of this situation, the practice of judging and condemning the spiritual state of others, came to be common coin. But this was not all.

The dramatic *effects* that now attended not only the preaching of White-field and Edwards but of the sermons of many others as well, began to be sought as ends in themselves. Just as in England and in Wales and in Scotland, so also in North America at this time, the powerful preaching of the gospel was accompanied by faintings, cryings out, and other bodily effects among some of the hearers. The journals of the Wesleys and of others testify to these effects. The majority of the New England pastors were sufficiently satisfied with the biblical witness not to give too much credence to these phenomena, nor to rule out the possibility of their being caused by the very powerful outworkings of the Spirit of God. But the frequency of such bodily effects in some of the parishes most renowned for revival of religion gave these inci-dental physical effects a place in the popular mind out of all proportion to their real worth, as the majority of ministers understood this matter. More and more, then, the people of New England began to be less and less restrained in this regard. Many people actually began to ape the shouting, the fainting, the shaking, and the shrieking that occurred in other towns. The result was chaos in many parishes.[103]

A number of churches were plunged into the controversy over this issue. Persons who considered the various manifestations of revival to be all of the Spirit of God came to be called the "New Lights." Those who opposed them – the "Old Lights" – saw only the hand of Satan involved. Individualism ran riot. Many people cast themselves off from their churches and from the guidance of their ministers. They put themselves unreservedly into the hands of self-appointed "evan-gelists" and "exhorters," men with no training or experience in the guidance of souls. The excesses of the movement caused many people formerly neutral in judgment to decide that there could be nothing

---

103 Miller, *Jonathan Edwards*, 171-176; Cf. *Works in Four Volumes*, 3, 292ff. for Edwards' own careful evaluation.

good in it at all. Thus, a full twenty-five years before the outbreak of the American Revolution, the spirit of individualism, of "democratic" self-expression, of man's exaltation of himself (a mark of the whole eighteenth-century) found ample expression within Puritan culture during this religious revival.

On the other hand, a powerful antidote to this whole spirit of individualism and subjectivism also showed itself in the dynamic renewal of Puritan theology that accompanied the revival. Many ministers in New England churches rejoiced in the return to classical Calvinistic doctrines. Strong exponents of traditional Puritan church life came to the fore, although Jonathan Edwards was unquestionably the most outstanding of all. His influence was widespread, reaching across the Atlantic to the British Isles and to Europe. He trained a group of personal disciples who carried on and developed (not without modifications) the theological movement of which he was the acknowledged leader. Joseph Bellamy and Samuel Hopkins, Jonathan Edwards, Jr. and Timothy Dwight – these were among the figures that rose to leadership, becoming the spokesmen of what came to be called the "New England Theology." Their religious leadership evidenced power and influence well into the nineteenth century.[104]

The educational effects of the Awakening were perhaps the most far-reaching and profound. Princeton, the University of Pennsylvania, Queen's College, Dartmouth, Brown University, Liberty Hall (later Washington and Lee University) and Hampton-Sidney were direct products of the religious revival. In addition to these colleges, many private schools arose, and these prepared hosts of leaders for later roles of major importance in the new nation.[105]

Another well-known effect of the Great Awakening was the impetus given to the evangelization of the Indians. Edwards wrote an account of David Brainerd's life and work, and had this published with Brainerd's own diary. This book, says Sweet, "proved a tremendous stimulus in promoting the cause of missions."[106] This enterprise elicited a significant help from the churches in England.

---

104 For a brief sketch, see J.L. Neve's *A History of Christian Thought* (Philadelphia: The Muhlenberg Press, 1946), 276ff. His presentation of Edwards' own theology is very inaccurate, however. See Sweet, *op. cit.*, 134ff.
105 Sweet, *op. cit.*, 140ff.
106 Ibid., 162.

The Great Awakening, in fact, had an incalculable influence upon American society, and not the least of its effects was the increased humanitarianism it inspired. The historian William Sweet remarks:

> One of the immediate byproducts of the great colonial awakenings was the rise of a new social consciousness and a broad humanitarianism, which manifested itself in a greater concern for the poor and the alleviation of distress and suffering. The central emphasis in the revivalistic theology of Samuel Hopkins [Edwards' brilliant disciple] was *disinterested benevolence* [the central theme of Edwards' *The Nature of True Virtue*] or complete unselfishness in the interests of others. The theology gained a great vogue throughout New England congregationalism ... Samuel Hopkins may be called the father of the antislavery movement in America.[107]

Hopkins was among the first to see the evil of the slave trade, and he crusaded, from door to door, to bring it to an end. Curiously, the practice (on both sides) of making slaves of captives during the Indian wars had early accustomed New England to such a situation. These colonies became the center of that terrible trade, and not till 1769 (eleven years after Edwards' death) did Hopkins begin the campaign that eventually enlisted the support of most of the Congregational ministers and resulted in the emancipation acts passed during and just after the Revolution (too late, however, to release the economy of the Southern states from dependence on the ghastly institution).

With such a variety of effects, therefore, it is no wonder that the Great Awakening gave rise to a wide range of interpretations. Perry Miller has written, "I am ready to say that the Great Awakening was the point at which the wilderness took over the task of defining the objectives of the Puritan errand,"[108] and again,

> What was at work throughout the Western world is fairly obvious: the upper or the educated classes were tired of the religious squabbling of the seventeenth-century, and turned to the more pleasing and not at all contentious generalities of eighteenth-century rationalism; the spiritual hungers of the lower classes or of ... 'ordinary' folk were not satisfied by Newtonian demonstrations that design in the universe proved the existence of God. Their aspirations finally found vent in the revivals ... the era of Pietism or Evangelicalism ... [109]

---

107 Ibid., 171.
108 Perry Miller, *Errand into the Wilderness*, 153.
109 Ibid., 156.

Sweet, in his history of Christianity in America, finds the major "causes" of the Awakening to be "the presence among the people" of New England of a "tremendous amount of latent fear" due to the continued Indian wars, plus "the doctrine of human responsibility in conversion" that came to be stressed in the degenerated covenant theology of the later seventeenth and early eighteenth centuries.[110]

Ola Winslow, in her biography of Edwards, considers the "shallow sensationalism" of George Whitefield to be the major human cause. Her lurid (and very inaccurate) description of Whitefield, his adventures and critics, is perhaps designed to protect Edwards from the fundamental criticisms leveled at the English preacher and at the entire Awakening by a small but quite articulate group of New England clergy.[111]

These clergymen published a manifesto against the whole revival. This was answered, a few months later, by a document which, while deploring the excesses and faults accompanying, yet saw the Awakening as the work of God's outpouring of His Spirit upon New England. One hundred and eleven of the Massachusetts clergy signed this document[112] – a large majority of those involved in the controversy in that state.

The dispute raged for many years and has not yet ended. Nor can it be. In the final analysis, one's interpretation of the Great Awakening depends in part, at least, upon one's convictions as to the manner of the working of God's Spirit among men: which is to say, it depends on one's decision concerning the doctrine that this present study seeks to explore.

Before examining Jonathan Edwards' doctrine of the regenerating work of God's Spirit in men, we must sketch, briefly, his life, and note those aspects of his studies, his experiences, and his theology that qualified him to write on this subject.

---

110 Sweet, *op. cit.*, 127f.

111 Ola Winslow, *Jonathan Edwards*, (New York: Collier Books, 1961). This biography of Edwards is marred throughout by the author's open hostility to Puritan doctrine and life. A reliable biography of Edwards is very much needed.

112 See Gaustad's careful evaluation of the contemporary evidence in his fifth chapter, *op. cit.*

2

The Man

Early Life

Jonathan Edwards was born on the 5th of October, 1703, in East Windsor, Connecticut, then a town on the Indian frontier.[113] His father was the Reverend Timothy Edwards, a Harvard graduate and minister of East Windsor for over five decades. Jonathan's mother was the former Esther Stoddard, a daughter of the famous Solomon Stoddard, and a woman of eminent character and piety who lived until 1771, thus surviving her only son by thirteen years. Jonathan was the fifth child and, with his ten sisters, received his early schooling from his father, who taught him Greek, Latin, classical literature and other subjects that were prerequisites for entrance into the universities of New England.

Jonathan early proved to be an exceptional student and an acute observer of nature. At the age of twelve he wrote his famous essay, "Of Insects," and a year later his equally remarkable analyses "Of Colors" and the "Rain-Bow," as well as a treatise on the immateriality of the soul. His works on colors and the rainbow show an acquaintance with Newton's *Opticks*, or at least with the results of that epochal study.[114]

---

113 Winslow, *op. cit.*, Iain H. Murray, in *The Select Works of Jonathan Edwards* (London: The Banner of Truth Trust), has given a brief biographical sketch in vol. 1, 13-59. The best biography of Jonathan Edwards is that of Sereno Dwight in his *The Works of President Edwards* (New York: S. Converse, 1829-1830), vol. 1. (Since the writing of this book, several other fine biographies have appeared. See the Bibliography. Ed.)

114 See the selections in Vergilius Ferm's *Puritan Sage* (New York: Library Publishers, 1953), 1-93.

They evince also that intense interest in the physical sciences that remained with him to the end of his life.[115]

From his earliest days he was deeply concerned with the things of God; when he was about thirty-two years old he wrote:

> I had a variety of concerns and exercises about my soul from my childhood; but had two more remarkable seasons of awakening, before I met with that change by which I was brought to those new dispositions, and that new sense of things, that I have since had. The first time was when I was a boy, some years before I went to college, at a time of remarkable awakening in my father's congregation. I was then very much affected for many months, and concerned about the things of religion, and my soul's salvation; and was abundant in duties. I used to pray five times a day in secret, and to spend much time in religious talk with other boys; and used to meet with them to pray together. I experienced I know not what kind of delight in religion. My mind was much engaged in it, and had much self-righteous pleasure; and it was my delight to abound in religious duties. I with some of my school-mates joined together, and built a booth in a swamp in a very retired spot, for a place of prayer. And besides I had particular secret places of my own in the woods, where I used to retire by myself; and was from time to time much affected. My affections seemed to be lively and easily moved, and I seemed to be in my element when engaged in religious duties. And I am ready to think, many are deceived with such affections, and such a kind of delight as I then had in religion, and mistake it for grace.[116]

A few years afterward he entered Yale College. At this time, even though engaged in preparation for the ministry, he had lost what he had formerly thought was "peace with God," and was often in a state of extreme distress about it. He continues:

> ... I entirely lost all those affections and delights and left off secret prayer, at least as to any constant performance of it; and returned like a dog to his vomit, and went on in the ways of sin. Indeed I was at times very uneasy, especially towards the latter part of my time at college; when it pleased God to seize me with a pleurisy, in which He brought me nigh to the grave, and shook me over the pit of hell. And yet, it was not long after my recovery, before I fell again into my old ways of sin. But God

---

115 We have already noticed the intense interest of the Puritans in the natural sciences, above, p. 14

116 *Works in Four Volumes*, 1, 14f.

would not suffer me to go on with any quietness; I had great and violent inward struggles, till, after many conflicts with wicked inclinations, repeated resolutions, and bonds that I laid myself under by a kind of vows to God, I was brought wholly to break off all former wicked ways, and all ways of known outward sin; and to apply myself to seek salvation, and practice many religious duties; but without that kind of affection and delight which I had formerly experienced. My concern now wrought more by inward struggles and conflicts, and self-reflections ... but yet it never seemed to be proper to express that concern by the name of terror.[117]

He then tells of his early abhorrence of "the doctrine of God's sovereignty, in choosing whom He would to eternal life, and rejecting whom He pleased; leaving them eternally to perish, and be everlastingly tormented in hell. It used to appear like a horrible doctrine to me."[118] We are justified in regarding this as perhaps one of his deepest problems: his hatred of God's so acting towards so many men. Accepting this traditional interpretation of the doctrine of God's sovereignty and predestination, he could not honestly love God's action – as he knew he should love all of God's doings. That is to say, his will was not in agreement with God's will: he not only did not accept it, he considered it horrible.

But later there occurred "a wonderful alteration in [his] mind, with respect to the doctrine of God's sovereignty." He became satisfied of God's justice in this regard and was brought to consider God's sovereignty as "exceeding pleasant, bright, and sweet. Absolute sovereignty is what I love to ascribe to God. But my first conviction was not so."[119]

The persuasion of God's goodness in all that He does seems to have marked a turning point in Edwards' life. He continues:

The first instance that I remember of that sort of inward, sweet delight in God and divine things that I have lived much in since, was on reading those words, I Tim 1:17, 'Now unto the King eternal, the only wise God, be honor and glory forever and ever, Amen.' As I read the words, there came into my soul, and was as it were diffused through it, a sense of the glory of the Divine Being; a new sense, quite different from any thing I ever experienced before. Never any words of Scripture seemed to me as these words did. I thought with myself, how excellent a Being

---

117 Ibid.
118 Ibid.
119 Ibid., 15.

that was, and happy I should be, if I might enjoy that God, and be rapt up to him in heaven … I kept saying and as it were singing over these words of Scripture to myself; and went to pray to God that I might enjoy him, and prayed in a manner quite different from what I used to do; with a new sort of affection. …

From about that time, I began to have a new kind of apprehensions and ideas of Christ and the work of redemption, and the glorious way of salvation by Him. An inward, sweet sense of these things, at times, came into my heart; and my soul was led away in pleasant views and contemplations of them. And my mind was greatly engaged to spend my time in reading and meditating on Christ, on the beauty and excellence of His person, and the lovely way of salvation by free grace in Him. … Not long after I first began to experience these things, I gave an account to my father of some things that had passed in my mind. I was pretty much affected by the discourse we had together; and when the discourse was ended, I walked abroad alone, in a solitary place in my father's pasture, for contemplation. And as I was walking there, and looking up on the sky and clouds, there came into my mind so sweet a sense of the glorious *majesty* and *grace* of God, that I know not how to express. I seemed to see them both in a sweet conjunction; majesty and meekness joined together; it was a sweet and gentle and holy majesty; and also a majestic meekness; an awful sweetness; a high, and great, and holy gentleness.[120]

From this time on, he says, this "sense of divine things gradually increased, and became more and more lively, and had more of that inward sweetness."[121] Prayer now became the breath and the joy of his life. The whole world seemed filled with the beauty of God's goodness, and wherever he found himself he "was almost constantly in ejaculatory prayer."[122] His delight in God continued to increase. A year and a half after this new relationship with God began, he went to New York to be pastor of a small Presbyterian church. He was then in his nineteenth year.

His father's guidance and ministry, and the events that occurred in his parish during Edwards' youth appear to have profoundly impacted his character and religion. The earliest extant writing from his pen is a

---

120 Ibid., 16.
121 Ibid.
122 Ibid., 17.

letter he wrote to an absent sister in May 1716 (Jonathan was twelve years old). He writes: "Through the wonderful goodness and mercy of God, there has been in this place a very remarkable outpouring of the Spirit of God. It still continues, but I think I have reason to think it is in some measure diminished, yet I hope not much … I think above thirty persons come commonly on Mondays to converse with father about the condition of their souls."[123]

This was one of several periods of awakening under his father's ministry, and the importance of it for our study of Edwards' theology cannot be overlooked. Jonathan Edwards was reared in the home of a pastor who guided his people in their pilgrimage with Christ, and who thus exemplified the traditional Puritan concept of the pastor's role.[124] Furthermore, he was brought up in a town that considered itself to have been blessed with outpourings of God's Spirit. We see also that in his earliest – as in his latest – writings, Edwards considered such an "awakening" the work of divine "outpouring," in "goodness and mercy," a matter quite clearly of God's sovereign initiative.

Education

Edwards entered Yale College in September of 1716, just one month before his thirteenth birthday. He graduated three years later but remained at the college two more years in order to prepare for the ministry. Because of the importance of his studies during this for the development and later shape of his theology time has not yet been appreciated to the degree that it should, nor its relationship with his theology properly understood, we must make some remarks concerning his education at Yale.[125]

---

123 Select Works, vol. 1, 14.

124 Haller, *op. cit.*, 24-66; see Edwards' sermon, "The True Excellency of a Gospel Minister," in *Works in Four Volumes*, 3, 580ff. He says, in part, "Ministers are set in the church of God to be the instruments of this comfort and refreshment to the souls of men and to be the instruments of leading souls to the God of all consolation … they are sent as Christ was, and as coworkers with Him, to preach good tidings to the meek, to bind up the broken-hearted, to proclaim liberty to the captives … and to comfort all that mourn; they are to lead those that 'labor, and are heavy laden' to their true rest, and to speak a word in season to him that is weary; they are set to be ministers of the consolation and joy of the saints." See also the following sermon, "Christ the Example of Gospel Ministers," *op. cit.*, 593ff.

125 The finest study that we have seen is Samuel S. Miller's *The Younger Jonathan Edwards* (unpublished book presented to the University of Chicago, 1955).

Basic to the Yale curriculum were the linguistic studies whereby the Hebrew, Greek, and Latin texts were analyzed and exegeted. In addition to the Bible itself, basic theological works of Calvinism were thoroughly mastered by the young students in a program that included not only careful reading but much memorization and seemingly infinite debating. Each day an "analysis" of the Bible reading given in chapel was presented to increase the students' skill in Scripture, logic, and rhetoric. Through Latin manuals of logic, the students were trained not only in *method* but also in the *content* of traditional scholastic philosophy. Logic was regarded as crucial to their education. The policy of Yale, as Samuel Miller has shown, was to expose the men to various leading logicians of the past and present. To this end they studied not only John Locke (as recent research on Edwards has emphasized), but also (and more important for our purposes) the logics of Aristotle, Suarez, Francis Bacon, Ramus, the Port Royal Logic, and that of the Dutch Calvinists Adrian Heereboord and Franciscus Bergersdicius. The works of these last two were favorite texts in the New England of Edwards' time.[126] The theological training of Yale (and Harvard also), therefore, was based upon prior preparation in the classical languages, scholastic metaphysics (both directly and indirectly through the theological works of seventeenth-century Calvinists), and the usual studies of natural science, mathematics, history, geography, etc., popular in the universities of the time.

The importance of the metaphysical and logical studies cannot be underestimated. Before the students came to their theological training (properly so called), they were grounded in the metaphysics that seventeenth-century Calvinism had taken from the scholastics, especially the Thomistic metaphysics of Suarez. Even the biblical studies with which they began their education (as they studied the Hebrew and Greek Scriptures) were accompanied by texts that incorporated this metaphysical framework. For example, their Old Testament studies were assisted by the text of the Basel theologian, Johannes Wollebius, in his *Compendium theologiae christianae*, 1626. This work had been prepared for the help of Wollebius' students of the Old Testament and

---

Miller's studies call in question most of what has been written of Edwards' education and intellectual makeup by twentieth century writers. Our present study is heavily indebted to Miller's findings. [Not even Marsden's massive biography discusses in much detail the connection between what Edwards studied at Yale and his later thought. Ed.]

126 Ibid., 75ff.

aimed at presenting the framework of Christian theology to assist the students' awareness of the significance of their Old Testament studies. Wollebius was a student of Amandus Polanus, an Aristotelian by way of Ramus, and thus through these men, the Yale students were receiving metaphysical presuppositions concerning the nature of "being" and of "reality" that were profoundly in opposition to the prevailing tendencies of eighteenth-century thought.[127]

These students heard other voices, as well. The theology and the metaphysical presuppositions of William Ames, also enjoyed widespread popularity in New England Puritanism, and his opposition to the metaphysics of Protestant Scholasticism was also an ingredient of the Yale education.

When the students at Yale came to the study of John Locke (regarded primarily as a logician), therefore, they did so from a background in metaphysics and logic much wider and deeper than is sometimes appreciated. Edwards' reading of Locke took place in this context. Furthermore, decisions as to Edwards' "philosophy" must now be reexamined in the light of Samuel Miller's detailed analyses of Edwards' thought, and the metaphysical and logical studies that were influential throughout Edwards' whole life.[128]

Having said this, we must now mention Edwards' words to a friend in the last years of his life, as he told of discovering Locke's *Essay Concerning Human Understanding* in his second year of college. He said he had more pleasure studying this book "than the most greedy miser finds, when gathering up handfuls of silver and gold, from some newly discovered treasure."[129] Let us see what he could have meant by this.

The unitary view of man's nature as propounded by Locke (Chapter XXI, Book II of the *Essay*) met with immediate approval from Edwards. He agreed with Locke's rejection of the medieval faculty-psychology

---

127 Ibid., 82ff. A new English translation of Wollebius' influential *Compendium* has been published in *Reformed Dogmatics* (New York: Oxford University Press, 1965), edited by John W. Beardslee, III.

128 Samuel Miller's study proves that some interpretations of Edwards' intellectual heritage are grave oversimplifications, and thus distortions. The role of John Locke has been seriously overemphasized, and other, more substantive factors in his early study and training have been almost ignored. See Harold Simpson's discriminating discussion of this point in his *Jonathan Edwards: Theologian of the Heart* (Grand Rapids: William B. Eerdmans, 1974), 23ff.

129 *Works* (Yale), 1, 47.

that divided up man's nature into "faculties" such as reason, appetites, and will, ascribing particular capacities and functions to each. With Locke, he asserted that man is a unitary being, that it is not a separate "faculty" of will but the man himself who wills, the man himself who reasons, and the man himself who has appetites. With Locke, he also thought that the traditional problem of "freedom" or "bondage" of the will could be more easily settled once the old tripartite psychology upon which the arguments were often based was discarded.[130]

Edwards went even farther than did Locke in this matter, however, and later disagreed with the latter's apparent falling back into that type of psychology he had at first criticized. Edwards, in fact, came to have a more unitary dcotrine of human nature than did Locke and was sensitive to any kind of distinction in analysis that would tend to compromise this view of the basic integration and co-inherence of man's capacities, desires, appetites, and reflections.[131]

In a notebook he began in college entitled *Notes on the Mind*, Edwards shows not only his direct dependence on Locke for his view of the relationship of "ideas" (item no. 6) but, almost immediately afterwards, his radical adaptation and alteration of this view (items no. 10, 11, 72 in Townsend's edition).[132] When we remember that Edwards' *Notes* were written sometime between his fourteenth and seventeenth years, we can only marvel at his brilliance, not only in understanding and so readily applying Locke's radical views, but also in criticizing and adapting them. His critical discernment in his study of Locke shows itself again in his repudiation of the latter's theory of "uneasiness" and its relationship to the decisions of man's "will."[133]

Locke's view of perception, and the role of man's senses in this process profoundly influenced Edwards' thought. For the rest of his life, this concept of the process of perception was evidenced by its role in his sermons and writings.[134] We must not overestimate this, however, as Perry Miller in his study of Edwards has done. The Puritans had

---

130 See Locke's discussion in his *Essay Concerning Human Understanding* (New York: Dover, 1959), Book II, chapter XXI. Cf. Paul Ramsey's treatment of Edwards' relationship to Locke in his editor's introduction to *Works* (Yale), 1, 47-65.

131 For Edwards' criticisms of Locke, see *Works* (Yale), 1, 138ff.

132 H.G. Townsend, editor, *The Philosophy of Jonathan Edwards from his Private Notebooks* (Eugene: The University Press, 1955), 28-29, 30-31, 72ff.

133 Ibid., 67.

134 Cf. his discussion in Ibid., 113-126.

long spoken of a "sense" and "relish" of divine things, which God gave through the revelation of His Son. Edwards undoubtedly contributed to a deeper explication of the nature of man's new "sense" of God and of divine things, and he did so with the help of John Locke's own discussion. The rich examination of perception Locke propounded was not in its essence original with him, however, nor was Edwards' use of it in theology a brand new thing. In a later chapter we shall have occasion to discuss Edwards' comprehension of this point in relation to both, and here the language of John Locke will appear in a framework clearly recognizable in its relationship to the Reformation doctrine of faith, not as mere *notitia historica* but as *fiducia*, with all that the latter entails.

Paul Ramsey has also criticized Miller for overestimating the role of Locke in Edwards' teaching on man's perception of God:

> These three consecutive references drawn from the *Treatise Concerning Religious Affections* demonstrate, I judge, how wrong it is to reduce JE's system to that of John Locke ... not giving equal weight to his Augustinian doctrine of illumination. Insofar as Locke had great influence, it was not to make JE some sort of religious naturalist or sensation empiricist, but to provide him with a different philosophical manner of stating the truth contained in these earlier theological points of view.[135]

It would be more accurate to call Edwards' view of illumination "Puritan" rather than "Augustinian," but that it is "traditional" is certainly Edwards' real contribution, as we shall see later – and it is a contribution John Locke helped him to make – is the rich development and explication of this traditional view of the nature of man's perception of God through the work of the Holy Spirit in giving faith in Christ.

There is another aspect of Edwards' debt to Locke that we should notice, as it seems to show him becoming a more consistent Lockean even while disagreeing with his mentor, because of his more consistent explication of Locke's own principles. Let us hear Perry Miller's judgment:

> Modern criticism has been fascinated with the 'Notes' mainly because Edwards made the brilliant stroke of extending to primary quantities the critique which Locke applied to the secondary. As the history of philosophy is written, at least in this country, Edwards' lonely performance appears ... astounding.

---

135 In his editor's introduction to *Works* (Yale), 1, 43, n. 5

Undoubtedly this feat is testimony to Edwards' genius for abstract speculation, or at least to his knack for improving upon his sources. According to the mechanics of sensation as Locke conceived them, the color, sound, or taste habitually attributed to objects actually exists only in the senses of the spectator, and therefore such qualities which he called secondary, had to be 'mental.' But the qualities which, by his reasoning, were inseparable from the nature of body itself – solidity, bulk, extension, number, figure, mobility – by any honest consideration must be granted the status of objective reality; these characteristics impress upon the senses a motion which 'must be thence continued by our nerves, or animal spirits, by some parts of our bodies, to the brains or the seat of sensation, there to produce in our minds the particular ideas we have of them.'[136]

Edwards accepted this analysis of the secondary qualities and agreed that the mind can be aware of physical objects only through *ideas* presented to it through the senses – ideas clothed in those secondary qualities of color and taste and sound. The basic physical objects themselves, however, those hard bodies of "solid, separable, moveable parts" whose best name is "solidity" – whose existence Locke did not doubt – these Edwards questioned.[137]

Edwards asked why we may not consider the "idea" of "solidity" as "mental" as the "idea" of "color." On the basis of Locke's principles of human perception, Edwards' questioning of "solidity" was as valid as Locke's questioning of "color" and "sound." Basically, said Edwards, what the eighteenth-century accepted as the material stuff of the universe was, according to Lockean principles, as much a matter of mental reconstruction, on the basis of the impressions of the senses, as was the existence of the secondary qualities of the objects perceived. That is to say, both primary, as well as secondary, qualities were but "mental existences." In point of fact, our senses prove only that there are "resistances" to be encountered in the so-called material world. In his own words:

> Therefore, there is nothing out of the mind but resistance. And as resistance is nothing else but the actual exertion of God's power, so the power can be nothing else but the constant law or method of that actual exertion. ...The world is therefore an

---

136 Perry Miller, *Jonathan Edwards*, 60.
137 Cf. Locke's' section "Of Solidity," Book II, chapter iv, *op. cit.* Compare Edwards' remarks in Townsend, *op. cit.*, 36f.

ideal one; and the law of creating, and the succession of these ideas, is constant and regular.[138]

We hasten to add that for the world to exist "mentally" did not, in Edwards' thinking, mean that it was any less "real" than in the thought of the most pedestrian materialist. It was as real as could be. Only, it was "mentally" real. It was the effect of the constant (and free) action of God who had decided to act in such a manner and to make and maintain such a world. It existed because God had decreed that it should; He formed it in His mind; He conceived it, and it came to pass. He decreed that we, too, should, in our own and of course inferior and limited way, perceive it also. We must make no mistake: the world *is* real, says Edwards, because, of course, God's acting is real. Our study of "natural" science is valid, then, because "to find out the reasons of things in natural philosophy [Edwards' term for what we call 'science'] is only to find out the proportion of God's acting. And the case is the same, as to such proportions, whether we suppose the world only mental, in our sense, or no."[139]

Later scholars have been so impressed by this philosophical achievement of the young Edwards that they have labored to prove that he learned it from Bishop Berkeley. There is no evidence for this assertion. Edwards, in his notebooks, always acknowledged his sources, and, furthermore, these show the progression of his thought in this matter. We get a glimpse of the intellectual stature of this young Puritan when we realize the depth of his philosophical thought in his teens and early twenties, the years in which he was writing his *Notes on the Mind* and *Notes on Science*.

The latter series of notes has connections with his earlier studies, which issued in his precocious works "Of Insects" and "Of the Rainbow," and reveals a fine acquaintance with Isaac Newton's *Principia*. Edwards studied the *Principia* while still an undergraduate; and although the work was being bitterly contested in England and Europe, he accepted it immediately for what it was, namely, the most up-to-date natural science of the age. He began a notebook in which he discussed such topics as "Of Being," "Of Atoms and of Perfectly Solid Bodies," proving his propositions with diagrams and close reasoning.[140] He also listed

---

138 In Townsend, *op. cit.*, 36f; see also 40–47.

139 Ibid., 39. yet Edwards' "Idealism" is different than that of Berkeley's. Cf. Perry Miller, *Jonathan Edwards*, 61f.

140 See Ferm, *op. cit.*, 48–92, for the text of this work by the young Edwards. Edwards felt free to read Newton as critically as he had read Locke. Ramsey notes

many "Things to be Considered, or Written Fully About," among which are the following:

1. To observe, that Incurvation, Refraction, and Reflexion, from concave surfaces of drops of water, etc., is from Gravity ...

5. To observe, that the cause that an object appears not double, being seen with two eyes, is, that all the parts upon the retina, that exactly correspond, end upon the same spot of the surface in the brain, which received the images ...

9. To show, that the different refrangibility of rays must of necessity be owing, either to their different velocity, or different magnitude ...

11. To show, from (Sir) Isaac Newton's principles of light and colours, why the sky is blue; why the Sun is not perfectly white, as it would be, if there were no atmosphere, but somewhat inclining to a yellow, even at noonday; why the Sun is yellow, when rising and setting, and sometimes, in smoky weather, of a blood-red; why the Clouds, and the Atmosphere, near the horizon, appear red and yellow, before sun-rising, and after sun-setting; why Distant Mountains are blue, etc.[141]

He included plans to study thunder, the weight of the ascending and descending blood in man's veins, the various properties of light in varying weather, the colors attaching to sunlight as it passes through the leaves of a tree, and the small six-pointed particles of a frozen fog he had observed one morning. His powers of exact observation were immense.[142]

He wrote out a "Second Series" of "Things to be Considered," and a few quotations will give us some appreciation of the range of Edwards' thought:

1. To prove the Universe, or Starry World, one vast Spheroid ...

2. To demonstrate that all the matter, which is without the Spheroid, is so disposed, as that there should be an equal attraction on all sides, and so probably an equal quantity of matter. ...

---

concerning Edwards' view of causation in the human will and in the created order, "So far was Edwards from having succumbed to the Newtonian world view and the binding operation of secondary causes. ..." *Works* (Yale), 112.

141 Ferm, *op. cit.*, 62f.

142 Ibid., 65.

4. To know the shape of the Spheroid of the Universe, by observation of the Milky Way; and to know whereabouts our System is in it; 1st with respect to the plane of the greatest circles, from observations of the ratio of the brightness of the opposite sides compounded with several other ratios. 2nd. with respect to the latitude, or the axis of the Spheroid, by observing how much the Milky Way differs from a great circle …

5. To show that the Starry World cannot be infinite, because it is a Spheroid …

7. To write concerning the distance of the Sun, by observation of the enlightened part of the Moon, when exactly in quadrature …

9. To show how Infinite Wisdom must be exercised, in order that Gravity and Motion may be perfectly harmonious; and that, although the jumble of the Epicureans be allowed … it be, in fact, impossible …[143]

This last point about Infinite Wisdom governing Gravity and Motion is important. Contrary to the fears some men had of "atheistical" tendencies in Newton's science, Edwards found in it a thrilling confirmation of the unbelievable wisdom of God, in holding the whole of His Creation in His thought, and governing it as He did. He considered this science to be also an incredible demonstration of the *power* required to hold together each atom on earth as well as in the myriads of stars in the Milky Way. He adds, "To show how God, who does this, must be necessarily *Omniscient*, and know every the least thing, that must happen through Eternity."[144]

To Edwards, the study of Newton offered thrilling testimony to the magnitude of God's creation and the wonder of His maintaining it. The absolute consistency of God's acting, with the marvelous harmony of His providential control of all the parts of the creation, stirred Edwards to the depth of his heart.

In these intellectual pursuits Edwards reveals himself a true child of his age. We have mentioned the interest of the Puritans in the latest learning of the day – especially the newest developments in natural science. Even in the wilderness of New England, they had pursued this interest and had participated actively, through correspondence

---

143 Ibid., 64f.
144 Ibid.

and periodical journals, in the scientific investigations then being conducted in England and Europe. The grand rationalism of the age contributed to an equally confident rationalism among Christian scholars, and Jonathan Edwards shared with many of them the conviction that investigations into the nature of God's creation would, by God's providence, add to the store of man's knowledge concerning the whole of created reality and thus give Christians deeper insight into the manner of God's working within it.

Now, it is extremely important to note that Edwards did not succumb to the eighteenth-century conviction that God worked in the world by secondary causes. In opposition to one of the basic beliefs of the age, Edwards insisted on the actual present action of the Creator at each moment in each part of His creation, working, sustaining, guiding towards His intended result in history. What many regarded as "laws" of Nature, Edwards regarded as *patterns of God's past and present acting* – inasmuch as men could discern and interpret that acting. Let us hear him refute Hobbes, Deism, and all forms of mechanistic determination in one short paragraph, written probably before his twentieth year: "Hence we see what's that we call the laws of nature in bodies, to wit, *the stated methods of God's acting with respect to bodies and the stated conditions of the alteration of the manner of His acting.*" The conclusion to be drawn from this is obvious:

"Hence we learn that there is no such thing as mechanism if that word is taken to be that whereby bodies act each upon the other purely and properly by themselves."[145] God did not at one point in time create the world and then leave it to run by its built-in-powers and principles. On the contrary, asserted Edwards, God created the world *ex nihilo* and creates it anew each moment – *ex nihilo*; it exists each moment by the power of His acting and the constancy of His will and plan for it. The Great Machine of eighteenth-century thought was spoiled by this New

---

145 Ferm, *op. cit.*, 60. This should show the falsity of Perry Miller's assertion that "Luther, Calvin, and the founders of New England frequently utilized the physics of their day, which was still scholastic, for illustration of confirmation of their doctrines, but they never dreamed of resting the case for Protestantism upon the laws of nature. Edwards saw at a glance that no theology would any longer survive unless it could be integrated with the *Principia*" (Perry Miller, *Jonathan Edwards*, 74). The very opposite is true: for Edwards, *no* findings of "natural reason" ever could or ever would provide the content of God's revelation as that is attested in the Scriptures, and by Christian doctrine. See his *The Insufficiency of Reason as a Substitute for Revelation* in Ferm, *op. cit.*, 93-109.

England theologian of the glories that the Enlightenment had lavished upon it: the Machine was Great, but it was not independently so – God upheld it every second. He was present to all parts of it at all times. The supreme achievement of the new science, then, lay in its disclosure of the magnitude and power of the immediate working of the Creator within His creation.

We have spent so much time on our discussion of Edwards' studies of John Locke and Isaac Newton, not because he read nothing else in college, but because his use of these seminal figures shows us both the power of his own intellect as well as the range of his acquaintance with the latest thought of the age. On the other hand, his college studies also included the standard subjects required at this time, and he seems to have had some advantage in hearing of the more modern European studies through one of Yale's tutors, Samuel Johnson. [146]Edwards studied the usual curriculum, which was patterned after that current in England and included the traditional "grammar, logic, rhetoric, arithmetic, geometry and astronomy, metaphysics, ethics, natural philosophy, Greek, Hebrew and ancient history."[147] Under Samuel Johnson's tutelage the students concentrated on logic (especially that of Ramus) and languages, in the first year of college; ontological studies and Ramus and Burgersdicius received prominent attention in the second year; physics and mathematics followed and, in the fourth year, "pneumatology and a system of ethics" were studied along with standard works in divinity.[148] Johnson's list of what he considered the best works in Pneumatology survives:

> On *Pneumatology* read LE CLERC'S Pneumatologia, LOCKE'S Human Understanding passim, WOLLATTSON'S Religion of Nature, CLARKE'S Letters to DODWELL and LEIBNITZ, MALABRANCH, DESCARTES Metaphysics, NORRIS' Ideal World, Bp. BERKELEY'S New Theory of Vision, Principles of Human Knowledge, Dialogues et Tract. De Motu ... SHAFTESBURY'S Philosophical Rhapsody; WATTS' Philosophical Essays.[149]

---

146 This Johnson, an extremely dissatisfied Puritan, occasioned so many complaints from his students that he finally resigned to take a parish. Shortly afterwards, through reading the works of some Anglican theologians, as well as a good deal of polite literature, he threw up Puritanism entirely, traveled to England and was ordained in the Established Church.

147 Wertenbaker, *op. cit.*, 142.

148 Samuel Miller, *op. cit.*, 187ff.

149 H.W. Schneider, ed., *Samuel Johnson: His Career and Writings* (New York: Co-

This list indicates that the older scholastic training of Puritanism was combined with the newer studies from England and Europe and that Johnson's students were exposed to, and in fact trained in, the leading intellectual currents of the era. John Locke was only one of the important forces in the thought of Johnson, Edwards, and other New Englanders, and he was studied, in Yale at least, in a context of deliberate eclecticism, whereby various philosophies were evaluated in terms of other viable options and the successful defense each might be able to make against the more important criticisms of the other systems.[150] This was not without its disadvantages for the students. The horror at Johnson's defection to Anglicanism tainted also the studies that had driven him "back to Egypt," and the atmosphere after 1722 was thus considerably less open to the newer learning.

Edwards, however, had left the school in 1722, and had already begun to prepare for his Master's examination. Furthermore, his whole career was to prove that, whatever he gained from the wide range of modern learning under Samuel Johnson (which was considerable, as we shall see), his own approach to Scripture and theology was not troubled by the form of Anglicanism embraced by his mentor. In fact, we shall claim later that Edwards is a classic example of a Christian theologian who, while engaged in intense dialogue with the leading intellectual leaders of his time and culture, and fully cognizant of the best thought of the time, yet retained in substance and in form the biblical theology whose content he offered to the culture of his time.

It is important that we should not omit the range of studies and of literary interest in Puritan New England. All the classical subjects admired by the English Puritans – valued for their own sake, be it known – were prized also by the Puritans of New England. Professional theological training in Harvard and Yale began *after* the Bachelor's program was completed. This latter included (as it did in Cambridge) studies in the traditional Seven Arts. (The "narrow bigotry" of American Puritanism is the creation of bigoted nineteenth century American "liberalism" and "humanitarianism.")

The literary education of Jonathan Edwards was considerably enhanced by the famous Dummer Library of several hundred works, presented to Yale in 1714. From this collection, he and the other students were

---

lumbia University Press, 1929), Vol. II, 368.

150 See Samuel Miller's whole chapter, "The Eclecticism of Yale College," *op. cit.*, 64ff.

able to sample the very latest English thought, including that of the Deists, Arminians, and Naturalists of the time. He was able to read the *Republic of Letters* and widely-prized *Philosophical Transactions of the Royal Society*, which put him abreast of the cutting-edge literary and scientific works of Enlightenment England. Fortunately, his own *Catalogue* of books (read or to be read) has survived, and we can see from this the contact he had with the thought of the period. Not only his thorough acquaintance with the major works of Puritan theology, practical theology, and ethics, but also his cognizance of moral and literary theory and especially his wide and deep familiarity with the best histories available – secular and ecclesiastical, Catholic and Protestant – appear through this list of his reading.[151]

Even a sketchy acquaintance with the intellectual currents of the Anglo-Saxon world will significantly illuminate the theological writings of Edwards, and we shall show in other pages that his polemical theological works were conceived and written in deliberate consciousness of, and dialogue with, the formative movements of English thought.

It is to be expected that the texts for advanced theological training at Yale (as well as at Harvard) were those of the leading European and English Calvinists. The treatises of William Ames, John Owen, Richard Sibbes, John Goodwin, William Perkins, John Preston, Thomas Shepard, John Flavel, Philip Doddridge, Theolophilus Gale, as well as New England writers such as Thomas Hooker, the Mather brothers, and Solomon Stoddard, and the Europeans Wollebius, Turretin, von Mastricht – these were the volumes studied by the young men who trained for the ministry of urban and rural New England. We should remember that many of these works were read by the students before they left their homes to go to college, and in this Edwards was no exception. It is easy to discern the special liking Edwards had for Owen, Flavel, Sibbes, and Stoddard, but he prized Petrus von Mastricht's *Theoretico-practica Theologia* above all, and wrote to his close friend Joseph Bellamy that as a "universal scheme of divinity" it was "better than Turrentine or any other book in the world, excepting the Bible, in my opinion."[152]

The publications of theological opponents were also carefully read. The titles in Samuel Johnson's lists show how the various aspects of theological debate were considered – and in their best expression – and to

---

151 See Samuel Miller's chapter, "The Background of Reading," *op. cit.*, 227ff.
152 Douglas J. Elwood, *The Philosophical Theology of Jonathan Edwards* (New York: Columbia University Press, 1961), 121.

the end of his life Edwards procured from his friends in Boston and the British Isles the most up-to-date and influential of the theologians who opposed the doctrines he himself held and defended. Much of his power and effectiveness must be traced to his thorough mastery of those views against which he wrote.[153]

153 See Ramsey's remarks in *Works* (Yale), vol. 1, 65f.

3

The Role

The Pastor

Edwards graduated from Yale in September of 1720 but remained for two more years preparing for the ministry. In August of 1722, he completed his studies and accepted a call to a small Presbyterian church in New York. (It is interesting to note that Edwards, a Congregationalist of the Independent tradition of Puritanism, began his ministry as pastor of a Presbyterian church and ended it as president of a Presbyterian college.) He served there for eight months and then, for various reasons, decided to leave. The decision was not easy for him to make, apparently, and he deeply missed the very close friends he had made in that congregation. He wrote of his parting:

> I came away from New York in the month of April, 1723, and had a most bitter parting with Madam Smith and her son. My heart seemed to sink within me at leaving the family and city, where I had enjoyed so many sweet and pleasant days. ...as I sailed away, I kept sight of the city as long as I could. However, that night, after this sorrowful parting, I was greatly comforted in God … It was sweet to me to think of meeting dear Christians in Heaven, where we should never part more.[154]

Edwards spent the summer in study, and in September returned to New Haven to receive his Master of Arts degree. At this time he was elected to be a tutor at Yale. He then studied until taking up the post of Senior Tutor the following June. This office entailed not only teaching, but also the actual administration of the College, and it was a heavy burden for his twenty-one-year-old shoulders to bear. Apparently,

---

154 *Works in Four Volumes*, 1, 19.

however, he gave full satisfaction as, with the help of one other tutor, he taught the sixty students then attending.

He occupied this office for two years. Then, in November of 1726, he was invited by the Reverend Solomon Stoddard and the church at Northampton to come to assist his aging grandfather. In February of 1727, he was ordained in Northampton and began his apprenticeship with that most renowned of the New England pastors of the day. He took the regular Thursday lectures, preached regularly, and shared with his grandfather the pastoral administration of the large inland parish. He participated also in the meetings of the Hampshire Association, a "presbytery" of neighboring ministers organized by Stoddard in defiance of both Congregational tradition and the wishes of the conservatives in Boston.

In July, Edwards married Sarah Pierrepont of New Haven, a young woman of remarkable beauty and piety, who made him an outstanding wife and who drew from George Whitefield the praise we have already recorded. They were to have eleven children, and it was because of Sarah's government of the household and management of their affairs that her husband was able to devote himself to his work to the degree that he did. He did not enjoy good health, and it is difficult for us to credit him with the volume of work he produced. It was by the most stringent discipline of time, diet, and habit that he was able to do so much. From his private diary and from the remarks of his family and friends we know a bit about his private habits.[155] He prayed often and regularly; he fasted often, and regularly; he rose at four in the summer, and by five in the winter, and he averaged from twelve to thirteen hours of study each day. He was very strict with his diet, having earlier determined which foods, and in which quantities, best enabled him to remain alert and fit for work. He exercised regularly by riding, walking, and chopping wood. On such rides or walks, he would take pen and paper, and make notes on the predetermined subjects of his meditations. He had early accustomed himself to record in writing his reading and reflections, and he would rewrite the results in his notebooks. This, in fact, is commonly acclaimed as one of the keys to the productiveness of his thinking. He began to keep a notebook of "Miscellanies" while still in college, and in this he would make notes, compose serious essays, record valuable findings from the books he had read, and store up the fruits of his intensive studies. This work grew to nine volumes of one-thousand-three-hundred and sixty entries, all carefully indexed.

---

155 See *Works in Four Volumes*, 1, 24ff.

We have mentioned already his "Notes on the Mind" and "Notes on Natural Science." Added to the monumental "Miscellanies" and these earlier works is another project, his "Notes on Scripture,"[156] which began as comments on an interleaved Bible and developed into three extra volumes. These show not only his own massive biblical learning but also his acquaintance with the major works currently valued in Calvinistic circles abroad.[157] From these notes, he illumined his weekly sermons and lectures, as well as every one of his publications.

In February of 1729, Solomon Stoddard died, leaving the twenty-five-year-old Edwards in charge of the largest and most prominent of the inland Massachusetts congregations. His pastoral responsibilities were now very heavy. After a keen analysis of his own character and capacities, he decided he was incompetent to turn the customary chat of the visiting parson into channels profitable for his parishioners. He then adopted the policy of calling his people, singly as well as in small groups, to his study, where he would talk with them about their souls, pray with them, and guide them into a deeper knowledge of their religion.[158] He always visited those in need or those who requested that he come. He was frequently requested to preach to small groups in private homes. This latter exercise was a notable activity of many of the pastors during the Awakening.

In July 1731, he was invited to Boston to give the important "public lecture" during Commencement Week at Harvard. This was the most prestigious speaking honor New England offered at that time, and Edwards' efforts were so well received that his lecture was published the following month with an enthusiastic preface by two of the leading neo-Calvinist ministers in Boston.[159]

---

156 See Vol. IX of Dwight's edition, *The Works of President Edwards*. Excerpts from these "Notes" are included in *Selections from the Unpublished Writings of Jonathan Edwards*, edited by Alexander B. Grosart (Edinburgh: Ballantyne & Co., 1865). This contains also the very important *Treatise on Grace*, which is also reproduced in a less reliable condition in Ferm, *op. cit.*

157 Edwards valued especially Matthew Poole's five volume *Synopsis Criticorum*, highly esteemed by Puritan commentators, as well as Theophilus Gale's four volume *The Court of the Gentiles*.

158 [This modifies considerably the impression that he spent thirteen hours in study each day; rather, he spent that amount of time in his study, often in pastoral conversations with his congregation. Ed.]

159 See Perry Miller's dramatic and delightful description of this event in his *Jonathan Edwards*, 3-34. His interpretation of the theological meaning of Edwards' lecture is wholly misleading, however; see Edwards' own words in *Works in*

This lecture, entitled, "God Glorified in Man's Dependence," is unparalleled as a summary of Edwards' thought, touching, as it does, upon all the major doctrinal emphases, the explication of which was to occupy the rest of his life. [160]

In 1733 his preaching began to have an increasing effect upon his people in Northampton, and by the following year the famous revival there was at its height. The revival subsided by 1737, leaving many of the citizens deeply affected and many converted. For our study of Edwards, it is important that we recognize the pastoral role he exercised during this time: not only did he converse with and guide the more than three hundred members of his own parish who were affected by the "outpouring of the Spirit," but he also compared notes with many, many other persons in other parts of New England where similar events occurred. He corresponded with many of the pastors whose names he listed in his *Narrative of Surprising Conversions*. He also visited others of them and was, in turn, visited not only by ministers but by lay members of the churches of other towns. The publication of his *Narrative*, as we have seen, catapulted him into a position of leadership in the revival movement, and from that time his extensive correspondence with foreign divines began. Edwards had in the early years of his ministry, therefore, the benefit of considerable experience in guiding souls under the convictions, and conversions, as well as the delusions and misapprehensions that were to characterize the momentous spiritual events of his time. His later writings on this subject, therefore, were the result, not merely of the theological deposit of a past era, but also of a significant amount of personal experience with several hundred people.

In 1739 he preached thirty sermons that were to form the outline of a projected *History of Redemption*;[161] this was to be a great, many-volumed work in which the doctrines of Christianity were to be introduced in a vast historical perspective, in the order in which God had revealed them to His Church.[162]

Four Volumes, 4, 169-178. (This is also included in the Banner of Truth edition of *Select Works*, II, 33-48.)

160 [For a very brief discussion and its impact upon Edwards' career, see Marsden, *Jonathan Edwards*, 140-142. Ed.]

161 *Works in Four Volumes*, 1, 295-516. This work has been conveniently reprinted in a separate volume by The Sovereign Grace Book Club (Evansville, 1959). We shall refer to this edition in our study.

162 See Edwards' own description of this project in *Works in Four Volumes*, 1, 48f.

In 1740 George Whitefield began his momentous preaching tour of New England, and Jonathan Edwards joined in the movement to the extent of accepting invitations to preach in various parishes, consulting with many in his own and other churches as to the state of their souls, corresponding heavily with ministers and laymen throughout New England and, as we have mentioned, with ministers in Scotland. He made several extended tours, traveling in the western part of Massachusetts, and down into Connecticut as well, preaching in one pulpit after another. In July of 1741, he preached the famous sermon, "Sinners in the Hands of an Angry God," to a spiritually deadened congregation – which immediately came to life. In September of the same year, he preached in Yale, and his sermon was published under the title, "Distinguishing Marks of a Work of the Spirit of God" (a crucial document among those that deal with evaluating the work of the Spirit).[163]

In 1742 and 1743 he delivered the sermons that became the basis for his definitive study of the work of God's Spirit in Christians, *A Treatise Concerning Religious Affections*. Published in Boston in 1746, in Edinburgh in 1772, reprinted abridgments many times, and translated into Dutch in 1779 and Welsh in 1883, this work became Edwards' most widely read book.[164]

The revival had considerably subsided by 1744. In this year a controversy broke out in Northampton which, coupled with Edwards' sudden announcement that he no longer agreed with the Half-Way Covenant policy his grandfather had inaugurated in Northampton, and that he now considered it essential for persons to make some brief form of confession of Christian knowledge and personal experience before becoming members of the church and receiving communion, combined with other factors to contribute to that sad controversy between Edwards and his people that resulted in his dismissal in 1750. He found himself, then, at the age of forty-six, with a family of eleven children, cast out from a ministry that had been more spectacularly blessed than any in New England history, from among a people to

---

163 *Works in Four Volumes*, 1, 519-562.

164 See John Smith's excellent editor's introduction to the Yale edition in *Works* (Yale), 2, 1-83. *Religious Affections* had been preceded in 1740 by another study of great importance, his *Some Thoughts on the Revival of Religion in New England*. This was Edwards' most extensive evaluation of the whole revival, with studies of the good and bad elements in it, and detailed suggestions as to how Christians should conduct themselves in that time of God's dramatic activity. See *Works in Four Volumes*, 3, 274-425.

whom he had been bound in love and prayer and service for twenty-three years. His own health at this time was (and had been for some years) very poor. He was unfit for anything but that ministry to which he had given his life; but, because of a fierce campaign of vilification (conducted primarily by close relations whom he had offended by his lifelong campaign against Arminian theology), he was not at first called to another church. Later, he received calls from Connecticut, Virginia, and Scotland. He accepted, however, a call from a mission station in Western Massachusetts, which had been established both to convert and educate the Indians in that region, as well as to provide an administrative center for their pacification.

He brought his family to Stockbridge in 1751 and entered upon the last stage of his pastoral ministry. Iain Murray provides an interesting summary of Edwards' duties at this hazardous outpost:

> Stockbridge was an isolated frontier village, on the western borders of New England, next to the province of New York ... An Indian mission had existed there since 1735, and two schools had been established for Indian children. This was to be the scene of nearly all that remained of Edwards' life. His weekly duties for the greater part of the next six years consisted of preaching two sermons a week to the white congregation, one, by an interpreter, to the Housatonnucks, and one to the Mohawks – as long as they remained at Stockbridge; besides this he was responsible for the catechizing of the children, both white and Indian, and for the general supervision of the schools. ...Two obstacles, however, impeded the usefulness of his labours in these spheres. After his arrival at Stockbridge he soon found himself opposed by the avarice and intrigue of a group of traders [the leader of which was a member of the family whose Arminian leanings provoked them to engineer Edwards' expulsion from Northampton], who had been making money at the expense of the Indians. They had succeeded in embezzling for their own purposes funds that had been sent to Stockbridge for the benefit of the Indian children, and by the sale of rum and spirits they had greatly hindered the moral improvement of the Indians.[165]

Edwards' only resources against such disastrous mismanagement of a potentially explosive Indian situation were his faithful ministry to the Christian Indians there and his heavy correspondence with the mission officials in Boston and London. In 1754 the bloody French and Indian

---

165 *Select Works*, 1, 46f.

War broke out. Edwards and his family remained, however, and it was during these years that he completed those works whose publication established his reputation, to this day, as America's greatest theologian: *A Careful and Strict Inquiry into the Modern Prevailing Notions of that Freedom of the Will, Which is Supposed to be Essential to Moral Agency, Virtue and Vice, Reward and Punishment, Praise and Blame* (1754); *The Great Christian Doctrine of Original Sin Defended* (1758); and two posthumously published treatises, *The Nature of True Virtue*, and *Concerning the End for Which God Created the World*. While these books were the product of a lifetime of note-taking and deep study, it is not easy to conceive how Edwards produced them in these years of struggle, Indian unrest, and his own continual sickness.

In September of 1757, Edwards was invited by the Board of Trustees of the College of New Jersey (later Princeton) to become the President of that institution, as successor to his able son-in-law, Aaron Burr, whose early death had just distressed the College and Edwards' family. After being advised by a council of neighboring ministers to accept (Edwards wept at their decision but accepted it as the will of God; one is reminded of Farel's charge to John Calvin in 1536), he went ahead to take up his duties, leaving his family to follow. A smallpox epidemic broke out in New Jersey; Edwards was inoculated, apparently successfully, but his body was so broken in health that complications developed, the proper medicines could not be administered to him, and he died after six weeks of illness in March of 1758.

We will end this sketch of his life with a quotation taken from the biography which precedes his *Works in Four Volumes*:

> After he was sensible that he could not survive that sickness, he called his daughter to him, who attended him in his sickness, and addressed her in a few words, which were immediately taken down in writing ... 'Dear Lucy, it seems to me to be the will of God that I must shortly leave you; therefore, give my kindest love to my dear wife, and tell her, that the uncommon union which has so long subsisted between us, has been of such a nature, as I trust is spiritual, and therefore will continue forever; and I hope she will be supported under so great a trial, and submit cheerfully to the will of God. And as to my children, you are now like to be left fatherless, which I hope will be an inducement to you all to seek a father who will never fail you ...'

> He said but very little in his sickness; but was an admirable instance of patience and resignation to the last. Just at the close of his life, as some persons who stood by, expecting he would

breathe his last in a few minutes, were lamenting his death, not only as a great frown to the college, but as having a dark aspect on the interest of religion in general; to their surprise, not imagining that he heard, or ever would speak another word, he said, 'Trust in God, and ye need not fear.' These were his last words.[166]

The Theologian

Jonathan Edwards was a Puritan theologian. That means that he was a theologian of Scripture, standing in the Calvinist (or Reformed) tradition and shaped by the particular influences and characteristics of the Puritan movement and its American development. It cannot be taken for granted that the implications of this will be immediately apparent to our generation, since a long period of time and a good amount of misinterpretation stand between us and Edwards, between our age and New England Puritanism. We shall look for a moment at the salient features of his theology, so that in our later study of his doctrine of regeneration his real meaning may be appreciated. To do this, we will first note Edwards' relationship to those aspects of Puritan theology that we have already singled out for attention; next, we will examine Edwards' theology in relationship to some of the major intellectual movements of his time; finally, we will indicate those aspects of his theology that render him unique.

Edwards and Puritan Theology

In our study of "The Faith of the Fathers," we noted four major emphases of Puritan theology that distinguished that theology from the teachings of other churches, and that were important in the life of the New England colonies. Edwards was an heir of the Puritan movement, and of the distinctive theological interests it displayed: of its Calvinism, its federal theology, its practical application in the doctrine of the Church and in soul-care, and its intense concern with the person and work of the Holy Spirit. Let us look at each of these in turn.

In his defense of "Calvinistic" doctrine against the Arminian doctrine of the freedom of man's will to choose for good or evil, Edwards declares:

> ... I should not take it at all amiss, to be called a Calvinist, for distinction's sake: though I utterly disclaim a dependence on Calvin, or believing the doctrines which I hold, because he

---

166 *Works in Four Volumes*, 1, 51.

believed and taught them; and cannot justly be charged with believing everything just as he taught.[167]

Edwards does not quote Calvin often in his writings. Yet he was regarded then and considered himself to be, a defender of the doctrine traditionally associated with "Calvinism"; and, if the "Five Points" of the Synod of Dort are any test, he was a "Calvinist" of the purest type. He firmly believed that the Scripture proved all men to be totally sunk in sin, and unable of their own power to save themselves; he believed also that God elects certain of His creatures to salvation and life, and that this electing is based on no merit to be found in the men chosen, but is rather a decision of sovereign and unconditioned mercy on the part of God. He believed, further, that the sacrifice of Christ for the sin and crime of the world was the major means through which God works our salvation. With the majority of Protestants, he believed that the application of the redemptive effects of Christ's sacrifice was not made to all individuals born into the world, but was limited to those whom God chose for eternal life. He agreed with the Synod of Dort in believing that the calling, the revelation, and the conversion God effected through His Son, by which He delivered people from bondage to sin and death, were works of sovereign, saving, and irresistibly working grace. He also agreed with Dort in believing that God would not betray those to whom He gave His Spirit, and that, though they might fall again into sin, they would not fall away; God would effect their perseverance unto everlasting life.[168]

By the standards Calvinists usually applied to themselves, therefore, Edwards was a Calvinist theologian.

We noted previously that the theology of Puritanism was characterized also by its interest in the "covenant theology" of Calvinistic orthodoxy. At this point, Edwards presents us with a problem. On the one hand, he accepts and employs the traditional terms, and some of the concepts, of this type of theology. He speaks of a "covenant of works" that God made with Adam and a "covenant of grace" that God made when man's sin had destroyed his former relationship with his Lord.[169] On the other hand, he repudiates aspects of this theology that were integral to the use others had made of it. His sermons on "Justification Through Faith Alone" and "Sinners in the Hands of an Angry God" utterly deny that men, by availing themselves of certain "means of grace," could

---

167 *Works* (Yale), 1, 131.
168 *Works in Four Volumes*, 4, 101f; 176ff; 2, 301-510; 527ff; 547-597; 3, 509-537.
169 Ibid., 4, 130; 2, 457; 1, 113; *Works* (Yale), 2, 222.

thus "fulfill their part" of a bargain and thus bind God to fulfill His.[170] Against the terms of the "Half-Way Covenant," Edwards asserted that God is bound to grant salvation only to whom He has predestined to faith. He is bound, therefore, to extend the blessings of the covenant only to those persons (and, *if He so pleases*, their children) whom He has bound to Himself by the gift of His Spirit and consequent faith in His Son. In giving persons his Spirit, and faith in His Son, God is certainly "rewarding" virtue (to use the covenant theology terminology): but this virtue is not their own, it is Christ's. It is His, Who Himself merited all favor for men and Who, in His indwelling of the elect, ascribes to them the virtue that is properly His own. The foundation of men's acceptance with God under the new covenant, then, is not built upon their obedience to His commands: "We suppose the foundation of this to be Christ's worthiness and righteousness" while the other interpretation "supposes it to be men's own virtue."[171] Men cannot, therefore, lay claim to His benefits, for themselves or for their children, by nominal membership in His church; nor does one's being born into the fold of the New Israel automatically assure one of salvation. Through faith in Christ, and through faith in Him alone, men are brought to life with God. There are *no* "means" by which man can render God favorable to him. With Luther, Edwards insisted that the *only* sure "preparation" for grace is the eternal predestination of God; it is God's mercy in electing and saving: "The best and infallible preparation for grace and the sole means of obtaining grace is the eternal election and predestination of God." Luther's following thesis is equally clear: "On the part of man, however, nothing precedes grace except ill will and even rebellion against grace."[172] Faith itself is the gift of God the Spirit, working through the proclamation of the gospel of the Son. "We are dependent on God's power through every step of our redemption. We are dependent on the power of God to convert us and give faith in Jesus Christ, and the new nature."[173]

It was his allegiance to this cardinal biblical doctrine – that *God* is the author of man's election, forgiveness, and salvation –that led Edwards to repudiate the teaching of those theologians who assigned to man

---

170 *Works in Four Volumes*, 128ff.

171 Ibid., 129.

172 Martin Luther, "Disputation Against Scholastic Theology," *Luther's Works*, vol. 34, 11, theses 29 and 30.

173 *Works in Four Volumes*, 4, 172. See here Edwards' careful questioning of the term "condition" when used of faith in relation to justification.

a share in any part of the divine work, preparatory or otherwise. It was this that led him first to question and then to repudiate the policy his grandfather Stoddard had inaugurated in Northampton of inviting "unbelievers" to partake of the Lord's Supper, with the common expectation that, by their taking the first step, God might be moved to save them. This conviction also protected him from following those theologians, such as Cocceius, who ascribed to natural man's conscience and reason a capacity to discern the original covenant God made with mankind.[174] For the same reason, it is a complete misunderstanding of Edwards' theology to call it "mystical," if that term is understood in its usual sense. *No* capacity in man, no *act* or program or contemplation of any sort could ever enable a man to attain to a knowledge of and fellowship with God.

Edwards did, however, make a very positive use of the covenant way of thinking. As we have seen, he planned a substantial work of theology entitled "A History of the Work of Redemption," which was to be "a body of divinity in an entire new method, being thrown into the form of a history," "a method which appears to me to be the most beautiful and entertaining," and in which he intended to elaborate all of the major Christian doctrines, as the Scripture revealed them in historical perspective.[175] This may have been inspired by his reading of Petrus von Mastricht's *Theoretico-practica Theologia*. Edwards never completed his project, but from the sermons that were to form its basis, we gain some appreciation of his positive relationship to the covenant way of thinking.[176]

We have said enough, however, to show that Edwards both learned from and freely criticized the theological tradition in which he was nurtured.

We noted that a third major emphasis of Puritan theology as a whole was its attention to the practical application of the doctrine of the church, especially in the guidance of persons under conviction and conversion, and in their life in Christ. A Puritan minister was expected to be a man whom God had called to be a preacher, a teacher, and

---

174 See Edwards' extensive remarks in his *Inquiry Concerning Qualifications for Communion*, as well as his reply to the Reverend Solomon Williams, in *Works in Four Volumes*, 1, 85-292; see especially 117ff, 150ff, 250ff. For Cocceius cf. Heppe/Bizer, *op. cit.*, 229ff. Again note Edwards' treatment in *Works* (Yale), 2, 222.

175 *Works in Four Volumes*, 1, 48f.

176 *The History of Redemption*, 74ff, 102ff, and 182, especially.

a guide to his people. The most important Puritan theologians were noted for their works that sought to guide the faithful in the life of the Spirit. Thomas Brooks' *Heaven on Earth* and William Bridge's *A Lifting Up for the Downcast* show just how Puritan theology was applied to daily Christian living.[177] They show us also what was expected of Jonathan Edwards, and we are thus not surprised to find that his *Treatise on Religious Affections*, his *Charity and its Fruits* (a more than three hundred and fifty page commentary on I Corinthians 13), his *Justification Through Faith Alone* and his *History of Redemption* were all originally and primarily sermons delivered to his congregation. We have already quoted from his observations concerning God's work in his own conversion and growth,[178] and it is important for us to appreciate the obligation he was under to guide others in the life of God, and to know for himself the snares of the "wilderness" that were likely to entrap his people. His "Farewell Sermon" to his congregation reveals, as perhaps nothing else can, the awful responsibility he felt in this regard.[179] All of his writings against Arminianism and all of his publications dealing with the discernment of God's Spirit in the midst of the revival in New England are evidence of his attempts to fulfill this responsibility laid upon him as a Puritan preacher.

The final aspect of Puritan theology to which we have called attention is its emphasis upon the work and the person of the Holy Spirit. This, of course, is the central concern of our study, so we shall not anticipate our later findings here, except on these important points: Edwards was true to the whole Puritan tradition in proclaiming the Spirit as the Holy Spirit of the Triune God, the Spirit of the Father, the Spirit of the Son. We will comment later on his use of some of Luther's writings against the "enthusiasts" in this regard.[180] Edwards was also consistent with the central tradition of Puritan theology in insisting that the *only* criterion

---

177 See Heller's fine treatment in *op. cit.*, 83ff; his historical descriptions are far more trustworthy than his theological interpretations. See the very poor treatment of Calvinism in general, and the doctrine of predestination in particular, 83-90. The Banner of Truth Trust has reissued fine paperback editions of William Bridge's *A Lifting Up for the Downcast* (London, 1961) and Thomas Brooks' *Heaven on Earth* (London, 1961).

178 See above, p. 95-100 and *Works in Four Volumes*, 1, 13ff.

179 *Works in Four Volumes*, 1, 63ff. See also 3, 364ff.

180 This point cannot be over-emphasized: with Luther (and Classical Protestantism), Edwards was convinced that Satan worked his greatest harm in God's church through persuading folks that "new" teachings were yet of God's Spirit. See *Works* (Yale), 86, 87, 144, and 145.

God has given for us to recognize the work of His Spirit is the gospel of His Son. Specifically, it is the prophetic and apostolic testimony as recorded in the Holy Scriptures. (In the fourth chapter of our study we will deal with the Trinitarian foundation of Edwards' doctrine of the Spirit, and in chapter six we will examine the biblical criteria by which Edwards said Christ's Spirit was to be distinguished from other spirits.)

In 1654 Thomas Brooks had written:

> ... The witness of the Spirit is *ever according to the Word.* There is a sweet harmony between the inward and the outward testimony, between the Spirit of God and the Word of God. The Scriptures were all indited by the Spirit, 2 Pet. 1:20; and therefore the Spirit cannot contradict himself, which he would do, if he should give any testimony contrary to the testimony of the Word. It is blasphemy to make the testimony of the Spirit contradict the testimony of the Word. The Spirit hath revealed his whole mind in the Word, and he will not give a contrary testimony to what he hath given in the Word.[181]

We shall hear Edwards saying the same thing. Further, we shall find him claiming that the *purpose* of the major outpourings of the Spirit in Christian history was to exalt and glorify the Son of God.[182]

Jonathan Edwards conducted a continuous critical, yet appreciative, dialogue with Puritan theology throughout his entire life. He was no proud destroyer of ancient landmarks, nor was he a blind slave to doctrinal precedent. His creative application of Puritan themes and his appreciative and critical reworking of them in the light of his own continual exegesis of Scripture gave to his writings and to his preaching extraordinary depth and power. He sought to be, in the very best sense, a "Reformed" theologian – that is, a theologian of that branch of Christ's church that knew it should submit itself and all its works continually to the correcting, purifying light of the written Word of God.

Edwards' Theology and Eighteenth-century Thought

The study of Edwards' relationship to the intellectual movements of his own time in New England, the British Iles, and Europe is a project that deserves a book of its own. We cannot do this here, of course, but will attempt instead merely a sketch of some of the important connections between – and divergences of – Edwards' theology and major aspects

---

181 Thomas Brooks, *Heaven on Earth* (London: The Banner of Truth Trust, 1961), 302f.
182 *Works in Four Volumes,* 3, 311f, 316, 364ff; 4, 128f.

of eighteenth-century life and thought. Though we must touch upon material already mentioned in preceding pages, and must also anticipate matters that will receive fuller development in later chapters, we feel that a summary presentation at this point might serve to place Edwards even more clearly within the context of his own age.

First, we are not surprised to find Edwards in frank opposition to the developing Deism of the era. The enthusiastic embracing of the investigations of natural science led many theologians (and scientists) suddenly into a position where the role of God in His world seemed only explainable by a form of pious Deism. Also, the enthusiastic embrace of the newly-revived Renaissance ideals of man (in all his glory and with all his majestic powers) led people also to a situation where the deistic removal of God to a safer distance seemed more consistent with their other theological presuppositions. Edwards, on the contrary, with all of his study of Newton, and all of his interest in the workings of the natural world, resolutely opposed Deism at every point. Instead, he asserted – against Newton's "secondary causes" – the direct and continual action of God, in every aspect of His creation, at every moment, maintaining its present constitution and causing to come to pass what actually did come to pass. His doctrine of God, and of Providence, set him directly against the tendency to Deism so prevalent in his time.[183]

Second, and closely allied to the first, he did not share at all the eighteenth-century's enthusiastic estimation of man's essential goodness, and of his natural moral powers. As we shall see in our later presentation of his docttrine of sin, Edwards considered man in his fallen state to be capable of much good – when compared with earthly standards – but deserving of horrible punishment for his radical selfishness and sin – when compared with God and with God's intention for men's lives. His powerful work on *Original Sin* was a total attack on the easy optimism that had infiltrated and subverted Christian theology. Such optimism, he thought, was an agent of Satan, for it blinded men to their true state, lured them away from seeking salvation in Christ, and thus misrepresented God's "design" for "our redemption."[184] In *Freedom of the Will*, Edwards refuted the revived Pelagianism and Arminianism by asserting that their exalted view of man was not only false – it was

---

183 See Ramsey's discussion in his introduction to *Works* (Yale), 1, 34ff, 67f. See also Edwards' correspondence to earlier Calvinistic orthodoxy in Heppe/Bizer, *op. cit.*, 114-116.

184 *Select Works*, 2, 46.

so false that it of necessity contradicted every Christian doctrine, and theoretically removed God from His position as Lord and Governor of the world, and as Savior and Redeemer of men.[185]

A third aspect of the thought of the age (which was grounded, of course, in the exaltation of man we have just discussed) was its prevailing subjectivism. This appeared in many forms, as well in the pretensions of religious "enthusiasts" in Europe and New England, as in the lofty detachment and superiority of the "rationalists." In either case, Edwards claimed, men set themselves apart from and above not just each other but also God. The "enthusiasts" of all sorts distinguished themselves on the basis of *their* "visions" or views or interpretations or "experiences." Edwards, as we shall see, opposed them by asserting that God's witness through the scriptural writers is more authoritative than their pretended experiential authority. The "rationalists" raised themselves above men and angels by the pretensions of the power of their own "reason." Edwards, again, opposed them on the basis of God's revelation, and of His judgment on the deceitfulness of sin and the corrupt nature of fallen man's mind. The heart of all Edwards' writings on the work of the Spirit in the Great Awakening in New England contains exegetical passages that refute and nullify all the categories of analysis and judgment by which men of the time wished to evaluate the work of God.

In fact, Edwards so strongly negated all forms of subjectivism that he has been considered a "theonomist." Many are repelled by what seems a bloodlessly narrow view of man's nature and of the beauty of human life. (Whether such a charge is valid must depend, however, on an evaluation of such of his works as *The End for Which God Created the World,* which will be treated in our fourth chapter.)[186]

A fourth aspect of eighteenth-century culture was its vigorous moralism. This expressed itself in many ways in the different Christian churches, and in New England, it also took various forms in Edwards' time. Active as he himself was in the promotion of what he considered God's work, and often as he himself urged his people to extend themselves in the same cause, he also strove to lift their thoughts to *God* and to *Heaven,* and to persuade them that the love of and glorification of *God* was their *primary* task, one that was served by, but which was

---

185 See footnote 28.
186 Elwood has distorted Edwards' true position in this regard; *op. cit.,* 15.

not to be made subservient to, their good works toward men.[187] He lamented the fact that the latter view had taken precedence over the former.

Fifth, in connection with the eschatological interest of eighteenth-century thought, Edwards appears as a child of the age. When one remembers the amount of time and thought Isaac Newton (to name only one) spent on the problem of discerning the "last things" and on understanding the apocalyptic literature which treats of these matters, as well as the stark chiliasm prevalent also in Europe, Edwards' own eschatological thought seems indeed to be the expression, in part at least, of a burning issue of his generation. The fact that momentous events in New England lent weight to this concern, and that many other persons who shared Edwards' own chiliastic convictions, and his expectation of the imminent coming of Christ, show further his intimate connection with the preoccupations of his century.[188] With respect to the fate of the damned, his view closely parallels the traditional one and is quite similar to that of other Reformed theologians.

In another area also, Edwards appears a pure child of the eighteenth century. One might label this aspect of that age "imperialistic rationalism." We have noted already his complete opposition to that feature of rationalistic thought which overlooked the blindness and the incapacity of man's sin-polluted reason, in regard to divine things, as well as in regard to the machinations of man's own deceitful heart. But when one remembers the all-embracing attempts of eighteenth-century thought to order and to enfold all knowledge and all meaning into comprehensive "systems," whether of philosophy or science, or whatever, Edwards' own grand plan to write a "Rational Account of the Main Doctrines of the Christian Religion Attempted" seems quite in keeping with the tenor of the age. As a matter of fact, his major works, *Freedom of the Will* and *Original Sin*, were but the preliminary volumes of this mammoth project, which was to encompass all Christian doctrine and to relate it to all human knowledge. This program, planned in his youth and never completed, yet provided the motive for much of his study and for hundreds of his notes.[189] His logical defenses of traditional doctrine, as well as his "rational" expose of the "irrational" presuppositions and arguments of those he opposed, while always grounded in

---

187 See his sermon "The Advantage of a Thorough Knowledge of Divine Truth" in *Works in Four Volumes*, 4, 1-15.

188 See again *The History of Redemption*, 302ff.

189 Perry Miller, *Jonathan Edwards*, 49, 127, 266, 285, and 304.

convictions that he claimed came not from rational inquiry but only from revelation, still show his correspondence with the methodology of his time in its attempt to exploit the power of thought in the service of grand themes. The ambitious confidence in the feasibility and necessity of such endeavors was shared by Calvinists and deists alike, and Jonathan Edwards was no exception.

In relation, therefore, to his Puritan heritage and to the powerful intellectual currents of the eighteenth-century, we see Edwards both as an heir and as a critic. Considering his appreciation for his theological heritage as well as for the new learning of his time, it is interesting that he felt as free as he did to criticize aspects of both that many regarded as integral to the systems from which they were drawn: e.g., the covenant theology, church polity, Newton's powerful presentation of "secondary causes" in the ordering of the material universe. Let us turn now to an examination of characteristics of his theology that make him of special interest to students of Christian thought.

Chief Characteristics of Edwards' Theology

A mid-twentieth-century evaluation of Edwards' theology, from the position of contemporary English Calvinism, reads:

> Saint, scholar, pastor and theologian, Jonathan Edwards ... was one of the greatest evangelical writers of all time. His outlook was essentially that of the Puritans, but he presented Puritan theology with a massiveness of strength and cogency which few of the Puritans themselves could equal.[190]

In calling attention to those facets of his theology which are either of special importance for understanding him, or which serve to distinguish him from other theologians, we will mention first his emphasis on the beauty of God, second, his emphasis on love – both God's and man's – third, his exegetical intent, and, fourth, his rather frequently articulated Trinitarianism.

First, Edwards' emphasis on the *beauty* of God in His love and in His holiness is so pronounced that it must be mentioned in any survey of his thought. This could be illustrated from many, many places in his writings. The following is taken from his *Religious Affections* under the section entitled, "Truly gracious affections are attended with a reasonable and spiritual conviction of the judgment, of the reality,

---

190 From the dust jacket of vol. 2, *Select Works*.

and certainty of divine things."[191] He explains that this conviction and "certainty" includes a "sense and taste of the divine, supreme, and holy excellency and beauty of those things."[192] Edwards writes:

> Men by seeing the true excellency of holiness, do see the glory of all those things, which both reason and Scripture shew to be in the divine Being; for it has been shown that the glory of them depends on this: and hereby they see the truth of all that the Scripture declares concerning God's glorious excellency and majesty, his being the fountain of all good, the only happiness of the creature, etc. And this again shows the mind the truth of what the Scripture teaches concerning the evil of sin against so glorious a God ... and this sense of spiritual beauty ... enables the soul to see the glory of those things which the gospel reveals concerning the person of Christ; and so enables it to see the exceeding beauty and dignity of his person ... And thus the Spirit of God discovers the way of salvation by Christ ... A sense of true divine beauty being given to the soul, the soul discovers the beauty of every part of the gospel scheme ... This shows the truth of what the gospel declares concerning the unspeakable glory of the heavenly state.[193]

This "beauty" of God, this "excellency" of His holiness, this "glorious excellency and majesty" that cause Him to be the "fountain of all good" is so basic to all of Edwards' thought that it may be termed one of the most decisive characteristics of his theology. (It is important to realize, however, how intimately dependent this "beauty" of God is upon his *moral* "excellency" and "holiness." One study of Edwards has misunderstood this: "The primacy of aesthetic appreciation over moral submission in Edwards' personal response to God led him in a direction away from the naked worship of sheer power which has too often characterized the Calvinist."[194] On the contrary, God was beautiful primarily because of His moral excellency – His holiness.)

---

191 *Works* (Yale), 2, 291.
192 Ibid., 301f. See his sermon "A Divine and Supernatural Light" in *Works in Four Volumes*, 4, 438ff.
193 Ibid.
194 Elwood, *op. cit.*, 31. Elwood here parrots the familiar clichés of secular humanism. "The naked worship of sheer power" had no place ever in orthodox Calvinist theology, as any honest study of Calvinistic discussion of God and His Providence would prove in a moment. Significantly, Elwood gives no reference for his sweeping statement. Cf. the English translation of Heppe/Bizer, *Reformed Dogmatics*, translated by G.T. Thomson (Ann Arbor: Baker, 1978), 105-280.

This distinguishing mark of his thought will become more apparent in our next three chapters, as we see how basic to the work of Christ is the communication to men of a true knowledge and "sense" of God's beauty and holiness.[195]

We should remember that earlier Reformed theologians had also expressed this connection of God's holiness and goodness and worth. What we are saying here is that Edwards stands out sharply from other writers in the degree to which the sense of God's beauty, His loveliness, and worthiness, and goodness dominates his thought – as indeed it dominated his conscious life.[196]

The second major emphasis of Edwards' theology, which distinguishes him from so many other theologians, is the degree to which *love* governs both his doctrine of God and of his teaching about men who are in fellowship with Christ. This, of course, is intimately connected with – in fact, it is based upon – the characteristic of God's beauty which we have just discussed, but it is so prominent in his writings and sermons that we must mention it here. In succeeding chapters, we shall see how integral Edwards' understanding of God's love is to his view of regeneration and faith; we shall see too how decisive the *works* of love prove to be in attempting to evaluate the presence of the Lord of love in the lives of His people.

These two characteristics – the beauty of God in His loveliness and holiness, and love - may be said to be the outstanding, distinguishing marks of Edwards' theology. There are two further characteristics of his theology which – while certainly not peculiar to Edwards – are yet basic to all of his theology, will thus appear in our later discussions, and so should be pointed out at this time.

The first is the *exegetical* character of his theology. As a Calvinist and Puritan, he naturally sought to teach as doctrine only what God had revealed through the Scriptures. We have noticed already his criticism of what he considered extra-biblical elements in Puritan theology. We saw also, in connection with his scientific studies, how strongly he insisted that only through God's revelation as attested in Scripture do men have any true knowledge of God, and that the Scripture was

---

195 Compare the statements of Reformed thought along these lines in Heppe/Bizer, *op. cit.*, 78ff.

196 See especially *Works in Four Volumes*, 4, 443. The whole treatise illustrates this point. Ibid., 438-450.

"the only rule"[197] by which they could seek to serve God. We should mention now (in preparation for our later treatment of the work of the Spirit) how vital it was to him that the Scriptures be understood as subservient to the electing, revealing work of God Himself, in the Persons of His word (Christ) and Spirit.

> ... no natural man *knows* the Scripture to be the word of God ... although such may *think* so, yet they do not *know* it ... *No natural man is thoroughly convinced, that the Scriptures are the word of God* ... For it is only the *word of God* in the Holy Scriptures that gives a man a right to worship the Supreme Being ...[198]

In line with this, God's Lordship over the Scriptures is maintained in the actual process of exegesis. That is, the exegete is to interpret the Bible *by* the Bible, and not by principles and beliefs of his own drawn from sources not given by God through the prophetic and apostolic testimony. *Scriptura Scriptura interpretata.* "But here again I desire that the Scripture may be allowed to be its own interpreter."[199] From Scripture alone does the Holy Spirit explain the scriptural revelation, and as a matter of fact, one of the chief works of the Holy Spirit is to give people a love of the Scripture: "He establishes them more in their truth and divinity."[200] Against the Arminians and other "modernists" of his own time Edwards asserted:

> Certainly we must allow the apostles to be judges of the importance and tendency of doctrines; at least the Holy Ghost in them. And doubtless we are safe, and in no danger of harshness and censoriousness, if we only follow him, and keep close to his express teachings, in what we believe and say ... Why are we to blame, or to be cried out of, for saying what the Bible has taught us to say, or for believing what the Holy Ghost has taught us to that end that we might believe it?[201]

The Spirit does not reveal new doctrines, but rather explains to us the meaning of the ancient truths given through the biblical witnesses.

---

197 *Works in Four Volumes*, 1, 188.
198 Ibid., 170f.
199 Ibid., 130.
200 Ibid., 541.
201 Ibid., 4, 129.

Nor do men discover new doctrines through their philosophical or scientific inquiry. They never have, and they never will.

> God was pleased to suffer men to do the utmost that they could with human wisdom, and to try the extent of their own understandings to find out the way of happiness, before the true light came to enlighten the world; before he sent the great prophet to lead men in the right way to happiness. God suffered these great philosophers to try what they could for six hundred years together; and then it proved, by the events of so long a time that all they could was in vain; the world not becoming wiser, better, or happier under their instructions, but growing more and more foolish, wicked, and miserable. He suffered their wisdom and philosophy to come to the greatest height before Christ came, that it might be seen how far reason and philosophy could go in their highest ascent, that the necessity of a divine teacher might appear before Christ came ... *And after God had showed the vanity of human learning, when set up in the room of the Gospel*, God was pleased to make it subservient to the purposes of Christ's kingdom, and as handmaid to divine revelation ...[202]

In our final chapter, we will study Edwards' method of drawing doctrine from Scripture. At this point it is necessary to emphasize – against the tendency to call him "mystical," "philosophical," etc. – that everything he published was founded on what he considered biblical teaching, that it was always supported by a extensive citations from the Scriptures, and that his polemics against other writers were occasioned by what he considered to be their denial or falsification or misunderstanding of Scripture. We cannot say of any man – Edwards included – that he fully succeeded in explicating only biblical truth. Some interpretations have completely neglected this basic characteristic of his theology – its exegetical foundation and intent – and we must be clear at the outset that this was actually one of the determining factors in all his thought.

The second characteristic of Edwards' theology which, while not peculiar to him, yet manifests itself repeatedly throughout his works, is his consistent or *explicit Trinitarianism*. When one remembers the basic Trinitarian structure of Calvin's *Institutes* (following, of course, the structure of the Apostle's Creed) one is not surprised that later Calvinists would be affected by this emphasis of the Genevan Reformer. But we must mention it as a peculiarity of Jonathan Edwards because of the consistent, explicit articulation of this theme. Again and again,

---

202 *The History of Redemption*, 154f.

we hear him discussing the work of the Son in relation to the love He bears for the Father, the work of the Sprit, for the glorification the Father desires for His Son, etc. The work of the Triune God in terms of the inter-relationship between the Father, Son, and Spirit dominates Edwards' writings and will be especially prominent in our next chapter. An awareness of this point is foundational for the comprehension of Edwards' views concerning all of God's gracious dealings with and for men, and we will see in our chapter on regeneration (Chapter Five) the place this has in his thought.

But the most important contribution to theology made by Edwards, we believe, is the depth and breadth of his view of God's regenerating work among people. While elements of his doctrine are clearly based on earlier theological writings (especially those of Calvin and the Puritans) the profundity and richness of his own treatment of this subject deserve much more attention than it has sometimes received. This theme is a key which unlocks almost the whole of Edwards' theology, involving, as it does, his doctrines of God and all His works, and his doctrines of man, his nature, situation, and destiny. From what we have already noted of Edwards' life and study, his background and interest, we see how eminently equipped he was to write on this subject and to assume a leading role in the revivals of eighteenth-century New England. Let us summarize: Edwards was qualified to write on the regenerating work of the Holy Spirit a) through his participation in the Puritan movement, which had been especially interested in this theme; b) through his own immense biblical learning; c) through his acquaintance with the major theological works of Reformed theology in Europe; d) through his deep familiarity with the most advanced secular thought of the age, including the scientific and philosophical works of Newton and Locke, which were then revolutionizing the intellectual life of Anglo-Saxon culture; e) through his participation in "revivals" in his father's parish, in Solomon Stoddard's veteran congregation, and his own active role as a pastor during the dramatic events of the third and fourth decades of eighteenth-century New England; and finally, f) through the advantage of his outstanding intellect – his was one of the finest minds in American history. What he wrote on a subject of such importance and with which he was so familiar deserves to be heard. In the sixth chapter of our study, we will see his discriminating use of all of his qualifications in sifting the good from the bad, the wheat from the chaff, in his analysis of the Spirit's regenerating work during the revivals. Edwards towered above the controversies concerning this revival by his *discriminating* studies of what was *not* the work of God's Spirit (against the enthusiasts) and of what *was* the proper work of that Divine Spirit (against the rationalists).

Let us turn, now, to the Trinitarian foundation of Edwards' view of the person of the Holy Spirit (as this relates to His regenerating work in men). The Spirit of God, he insists, is the Spirit of the Father *and of the Son*. Through the Son – through Him alone (*solus Christus*) – He is made present to men. As such, He is described by the only witnesses God appointed to witness to His coming to men in the Person of His Son – which is to say, the Spirit of God, who is the Spirit of Jesus Christ, is witnessed to by the writings of the Old and New Testament Scriptures (*sola Scriptura*).

4

The Holy Spirit of Christ

O Glorious NATURE! supremely Fair, and sovereignly Good!
All-loving and All-lovely, All-Divine!...O mighty NATURE!
Wise Substitute of Providence! Impowered CREATRESS!...

All Nature's Wonders serve to excite and perfect this Idea of
their AUTHOR. 'Tis here he suffers us to see, and even converse
with him, in a manner suitable to our Frailty; How glorious is it
to contemplate him, in this noblest of his Works apparent to us,
The SYSTEM OF THE BIGGER WORLD.

Lord Shaftesbury

Universal consent, then, should be regarded … as the first and
sovereign Theology and Philosophy, and to this end divine
providence greatly assists …

Now we derive this universal consent not only from laws, religions, philosophies, and the written remains of all kinds of
authors, but we claim that there are certain faculties innate
in us by means of which these truths are vouched for … it is
easy to establish the general truths which are necessary, and
… universal consent (which can only be arrived at by divine
providence) is the sole criterion of the truth of these necessary
things.

Lord Herbert of Cherbury

God has not given us his PROVIDENCE, but his WORD, to be
our governing rule … And, strictly speaking, this is our ONLY
rule …

This is the main thing that fallen men stood in need of divine
revelation for, to teach us how we that have sinned may come to
be again accepted of God; or, which is the same thing, how the

sinner may be justified. Something beyond the light of nature is necessary to salvation chiefly on this account. Mere natural reason afforded no means by which we could come to the knowledge of this, it depending on the sovereign good pleasure of the Being that we had offended by sin … What is the gospel, but only the glad tidings of a new way of acceptance with God unto life …?

Jonathan Edwards

Introduction

Whether explicit or implicit, whether acknowledged or unacknowledged, any discussion of the *work* of the Holy Spirit is informed by a prior knowledge of His *nature*. While He reveals His nature through His work, nevertheless our evaluation of His work depends on our knowledge of His person.

The repudiation, by much of eighteenth-century thought, of God's role in creating, sustaining, and governing the universe, as this had been traditionally understood, was based in large part on a real, though unacknowledged, rejection of the traditional interpretation of His Person. Therefore, the controversies in which Jonathan Edwards found himself, as they related to the problem of evaluating the Spirit's work in men, concerned even deeper problems concerning the very nature of God Himself. In this chapter, then, we must seek to understand Edwards' doctrine of the Holy Spirit of God in terms of eighteenth-century controversies over the Trinity, the Spirit, God's relation to the world, and the proper relationship of men to God.

In order to accomplish this, we shall first survey some of the leading themes of eighteenth-century thought in these areas; then, in the second part of the chapter, we shall present Edwards' own views. In our exposition of Edwards' doctrine, we shall see his explicit handling of issues vital not only to his own time but also to ours. For we live in an age that is also deeply informed by the presuppositions and prejudices which came to power in the eighteenth-century, and our views of nature, of God's acting in nature and in history, and of man's obligations to God, are based often on principles similar to those with which all of Edwards' theology was in conscious dialogue.

The Spirits that Whispered in Reason's Ear

For a brief moment in the history of Western thought, a matter of immense consequence was held in balance: the *source* of the authority by means of which people could discern Truth. The New Learning did not at first claim to replace God's personal revelation of Himself to humans; rather, it sought only to isolate those areas which God had given to men for the full play of their inquisitiveness and their reason. In the words of Francis Bacon (he wrote this in 1620):

> Sacred theology must be drawn from the word and oracles of God, not from the light of nature, or the dictates of Reason.

> We are obliged to believe the word of God, though our reason be shocked by it.[203]

A mere seventy-six years later, John Toland inaugurated the Deistic controversy through his book, *Christianity Not Mysterious*, in which (manifesting the widespread anti-supernaturalism that had developed since the time of Bacon) he had this to say:

> What is revealed in religion, as it is most useful and necessary, so it must and may be as easily comprehended, and found as consistent with our common Notions, so what we know of Wood or Stone, or Air, or Water, or the like ... As for God, we comprehend nothing better than His Attributes.[204]

This passage reveals the collapse of the famous "Two Books of Revelation" argument that had sought to justify God's revealing of Himself through both the Scriptures and through natural science and philosophy, for the work of the Holy Spirit through the apostolic testimony came to be of less and less importance to a generation that found it could discern so much truth by its own unaided mental resources. The anti-supernaturalistic bent of the modern thought claimed that the truths of religion were fairly plain and accessible to rational men, and were, moreover, really quite reasonable. The Bible was thus superfluous to a mentality like Toland's which could, of itself, discern the principles by which truth could be found – and could do so on the basis of a study of the "Common Notions" of mankind. The truths of religion were thus found to be just what cultured men of the time would have expected them to be.

A tremendous controversy arose in England after the publication of Toland's work. To be sure, John Locke had just the previous year expounded similar (though not identical) themes in his *The Reasonableness of Christianity*, but Locke had not drawn the negative conclu-

---

203 Quoted in Willey, *Seventeenth-century Background*, 32f.
204 Quoted in Willey, *Eighteenth-century Background*, 16.

sions which so appealed to Toland, and could thus be cited by people on both sides of the furious debate.

Two years after the appearance of Toland's book, Charles Leslie's *Short and Easie Method with the Deists* added new fuel to the fire by staunchly attacking the attackers of the traditional doctrines. Attack and counterattack thus followed one another as the orthodox became increasingly shocked at the relatively new and blatant contempt with which the Deists assaulted the old Christian doctrines. The Religion of Nature claimed to be able to dispense with the "superstition" and "ignorance" of the old Religion of Revelation. In 1730, a new note was sounded by the publication of the Deists' Bible: *Christianity as Old as Creation*. This work by Matthew Tindal joyously portrayed the basic harmony that existed between nature and the moral law, by means of the principles of Natural Religion, based on Reason. The "innovations" associated with traditional Christianity were judged to be false, and the moral principles of the universe were said to have informed the history of mankind long before the creation of church dogma.[205]

A clear exposition of what was involved in this development occurs in the works of Lord Shaftesbury:

> O Glorious NATURE! supremely Fair, and sovereignly Good! All-loving and All-lovely, All-Divine!...Whose every single Work affords an ampler Scene, and is a nobler Spectacle than all which ever Art presented! O Mighty NATURE! Wise Substitute of PROVIDENCE! impowered CREATRESS! O Thou impowering Deity, supreme Creator! Thee I invoke, and Thee alone adore. To Thee this Solitude, this place, these Rural Meditations are sacred; whilst thus inspir'd with Harmony of Thought, unconfin'd by Words, and in loose Numbers, I sing of Nature's Order in created Beings, and celebrate the Beautys which resolve in Thee, the Source and Principle of all Beauty and Perfection.
>
> All Nature's Wonders serve to excite and perfect this Idea of their AUTHOR. 'Tis here he suffers us to see, and even converse with him, in a manner suitable to our Frailty; How glorious is it to contemplate him, in this noblest of his Works apparent to us, the SYSTEM of THE BIGGER WORLD.[206]

Vigorously opposing both the atheists and the orthodox, staunchly denying that either man or nature is seriously corrupted through the

---

205 See Moorman's discussion in his *History of the Church in England* (New York: Morehouse-Gorham, 1954), 273f.
206 Quoted in Willey, *Eighteenth-century Background*, 65-66.

fall and through sin, repudiating the notion of future punishments and other supposed barbarisms such as divine wrath, Shaftesbury proclaimed the happy gospel of harmony and justice in nature and in moral law, of beauty and order in the structure of creation, and of man's capacity to exercise the essential goodness of his nature by imitating in his soul and in his life the harmony and proportion so clearly portrayed in the external and internal universe.[207]

Views such as these burst upon the rocky shores of New England with all the force with which they had shattered the structures of thought in the Mother Country. American Protestantism at first presented a more united front – not to new knowledge – but to the ideologies which contradicted basic doctrinal positions. How could a well-trained Puritan theologian reconcile those views of Shaftesbury with Chapters I, III, V, VI, VIII, IX, XIV, XIX, or XXI of the *Westminster Confession*? For instance, Chapter XXI begins with the words, "The light of nature showeth that there is a God, who hath lordship and sovereignty over all ..." Though this small bit alone might seem to furnish some support for Shaftesbury's view, such an interpretation would be utterly ground-less when taken with the words that follow:

> But the acceptable way of worshipping the true God is insti-
> tuted by himself, and so limited to his own revealed will, that
> he may not be worshipped according to the imaginations and
> desires of men or the suggestions of Satan ... or any other way
> not prescribed in the Holy Scripture.[208]

The following paragraph condemns the notion that there is any other mediator but Christ Jesus between God and men, ruling out the role which Shaftesbury would wish to assign to nature.

It was not long before the winds of new doctrine blew into New England and succeeded in raising up dust from that soil. In 1688 Harvard College was in the practical control of two liberal tutors who, while certainly not out - and - out deists, yet breathed with a spirit different from that which had inspired the writing of the *Westminster Confession*. The future pastors, teachers, doctors, and magistrates of New England were being wooed by the spirits of Reason and Nature that had captivated the minds of their teachers.

It is important that we note, also, some of the issues raised by the new ways of thought. The stark materialism of Hobbes had, in England,

---

207 Ibid.
208 Leith, *op. cit.*, 216ff.

acted as a catalyst for the crystallization of the thought of a group who came to be known as the "Cambridge Platonists." These scholars strove manfully to preserve and defend the Christian religion against the attacks of Naturalism, and they did so chiefly by means of serious scientific study and impressive philosophical reconstruction. To combat the criticism of the new naturalism, they projected a view of creation that was the very opposite of the cold mechanism of their opponents. To oppose the imperialistic rationalism of the time, they revived the tenor and tenets of Neo-Platonism. Chief among these men were Ralph Cudworth, John Smith, Henry Moore, and Benjamin Whichcote. These thinkers propounded their positive science and philosophy after being shocked, and spurred, by the atomistic, mechanistic, deterministic philosophy of Hobbes.

Whether they seriously opposed the spirit of the new age, however, is debatable. Whichcote is best remembered for his statement that reason is "the very voice of God."[209] Furthermore, in their efforts to refute Hobbes, these men resorted to a view of man which strongly asserted the independence of his will – its freedom and power to choose the good offered by God – and which carried with it views concerning sin, election, predestination, revelation, etc., utterly contradictory to the expressions of the *Thirty-Nine Articles* (and to the whole Reformation view of Christian doctrine). Their method of dealing with the issues raised by the new currents of thought was, therefore, profoundly different than the course of action adopted by Jonathan Edwards. The doctrines they propounded bear far more affinity to the new liberalism and humanitarianism than they do with the doctrines of classical Anglicanism (as these were expressed at the time of the Reformation, and continue to exist in the *Book of Common Prayer*). The attack these men made on the new cult of Reason and of Nature and of Man cannot really be said to be more than *another variation on the same theme.* Comparing their efforts with the grand self-sufficiency of Descartes and the intellectual currents he set in motion, Professor Willey remarks:

> In all this do we not recognize the Cartesian self-sufficiency, the Cartesian rejection of authority and reliance upon inward certitude? It was the corollary of this century's rejection of the errors of the past, that it should find within the soul the Candle of the Lord, whose beams, if only they were free to shine abroad, would show up a divine universe in a divine light.[210]

---

209 Moorman, *op. cit.*, 255.
210 Willey, *Seventeenth-century Background*, 129.

The "Candle of the Lord" is man's reason, as Whichcote and Smith repeatedly point out, and by following this reason mankind should emerge from darkness and bigotry, and come into the glorious light of truth.[211]

Let us conclude our brief description of the temper of the mind which exercised such influence at the time of Edwards' ministry, and which affected so strongly the thought, and thus the theology, of the age, by recalling a work published in the third decade of the seventeenth-century – Lord Herbert of Cherbury's *De veritate*. This book was one of the earliest, and yet one of the most decisive and enduring, expressions of that rational spirit we are attempting to portray. Lord Herbert was familiar with the findings of the voyages of discovery concerning the manners and morals of the newly-publicized primitive peoples, and he attempted to show that a peaceful solution to the dogmatic and ideological battles of the time could be found through the study of the truth revealed throughout all human cultures and religions. In the "natural instinct" of mankind, he asserted, certain truths have become apparent. Their enduring validity, furthermore, was vouched for by their *universality*, by their acceptance by all people everywhere. In Lord Herbert's own words, "Thus universal consent will be the sovereign test of truth, and there is nothing of so great importance as to seek out these common notions, and to put them each in their place as indubitable truths." Again,

> Universal consent, then, should be regarded ... as the first and sovereign Theology and Philosophy, and to this end divine providence greatly assists, for it has, in these last centuries, so largely revealed what was unknown to the earlier ones, that it seems there remains nothing worthy to be known which has not been declared to us.[212]

But can we trust these "common notions?" Can we really have confidence in the findings of universal man? Lord Herbert's answer is, Yes! We can trust these findings, he says, because we can trust the God-given faculty of reason implanted in man. God in His providence establishes a correspondence between our thoughts and truth.

> Now we derive this universal consent not only from laws, religions, philosophies, and the written remains of all kinds of authors, but we claim that there are certain faculties innate in us by means of which these truths are vouched for. Nevertheless

---

211 Cf. Willey's fine survey in Ibid., 128-141.
212 Ibid., 114-115.

we leave the mad and the foolish to follow any Church, school, or opinion they like ... we say merely that it is easy to establish the general truths which are necessary, and that universal consent (which can only be arrived at by divine providence) is the sole criterion of truth in these necessary things.[213]

Where, then, do we find the clearest expression of these "common notions" whose truth is guaranteed by God's providential working through universal Reason? Through the study of comparative religion, Herbert replies, as well as through retirement into "your own faculties," there to await the still small voice of reason within. By retiring into his own soul, man "will find there God, virtue, and the other universal and eternal truths."[214] Thus will people "establish preambles and foundations of religion by the light of the universal wisdom, to the end that whatever is added afterward at the veritable dictation of faith may resemble the roofs of houses, which rest upon and follow the foundations."[215]

This passage bears study because the "preambles" (that is, the prolegomena), as well as the content (the "foundations") of religion, can be found "by the light of the universal wisdom." Whatever *may* be added later "at the veritable dictation of faith" cannot really be of basic importance. What God *may* say, in other words, cannot seriously add to what He *has already said* through Creation and man's rational capacity to understand and interpret nature, his culture, and the movements of God's "providence," whatever this may mean in such a scheme.

This passage will come to mind later in our study when we hear Edwards explicitly deny that humans may know God from a study of history, nature, or providence. But let us notice here the doctrinal formulation Lord Herbert gave to this "religion by the light of universal wisdom," so that, in later pages, the thought of Jonathan Edwards in relation to the "common notions" of his time may be appreciated.

---

213 Ibid.
214 Ibid., 116-117.
215 Ibid., 118.

As is well known, Lord Herbert summarizes the doctrines found from comparative religion and internal cogitation under five headings:

1. That there is a Supreme Power ...

2. That this Sovereign Power must be Worshipped ...

3. That the Good Ordering or Disposition of the Faculties of Man Constitute the Principal or Best Part of Divine Worship, and that this has always been Believed ...

4. That All Vices and Crimes should be Expiated and Effaced by Repentance ...

5. That there are Rewards and Punishments after this Life.[216]

These were "common notions" of the age in which Jonathan Edwards exercised his ministry. They informed the very atmosphere of his time. They contained within themselves radically new evaluations of the traditional Christian views concerning God, His Spirit, His relationship with mankind and with the world – so that the Christian religion was faced with a whole new mindset, assaulted by a whole new view of truth and of the sources from which it should be gleaned. In short, that a radical attack upon basic Christian dogma was being made became apparent rather early in the development of this new intellectual framework. What place, for instance, could the Christian view of the authority of God's revelation as mediated through the biblical writings find in a scheme such as Toland's? Or Tindal's? What would be the need of the "internal illumination of the Spirit" in the exalted, defied Nature of Shaftesbury? How would the love of God be defined by Lord Herbert; which is to say, how would the traditional interpretation of the Holy Spirit as *the* love of God find a place in Herbert's religion? What becomes of the *holiness* of the Spirit in the Neo-Platonic near-humanism of the Cambridge group? How is the Spirit to receive glory, with the Father and the Son, for working in man that which man, by following his reason and his conscience, can very well work for himself?

What about the notion of history, and particularly, redemption-history, in the new deistic scheme? And what becomes of the old doctrine of Providence in the new concept of nature as a grand, harmonious, self-sufficient Machine? Who needed to be "reborn" within such a world as this age had discovered?

---

216 Ibid., 118-122.

Let us look, then, at Edwards' doctrine of the Holy Spirit of God, emphasizing most those aspects of his program which bear special relevance for his treatment of the Spirit's work in regenerating men, and for Edwards' dialogue with the leading motifs of eighteenth-century Anglo-Saxon thought.

The Holy Spirit of Christ

The foundations for the different – utterly different – view that Edwards had of God and of God's manner of dealing with His creation were not laid in those "common notions" of "universal reason" to which Lord Herbert, John Toland, Matthew Tindal, or Lord Shaftesbury appealed. Nor could they be, Edwards claimed, since, "nature alone is not sufficient for the discovery of the religion of nature ... that is, no means we have by mere nature, without instruction, bring men to the knowledge of God, and our natural relation to and dependence on Him. ..."[217] Differing sharply from the Pelagianism of the Cambridge Platonists, their minimizing of man's sin and exalting of his reason, Edwards continues:

> And as to ... the religion of a *sinner*, or the duties proper for us depraved, guilty, and offending creatures ... the light of nature cannot be sufficient for our information, by any means, or in any sense whatsoever. No, nor is the light of nature sufficient either to prescribe or establish this religion ... it affords no possibility of it.[218]

Lord Herbert had found confirmation for his doctrines in the conclusions of "universal consent," guaranteed by "divine providence," which, he asserted, "is the sole criterion of the truth in these necessary things." Edwards contradicted such a notion:

> God has not given us his *providence*, but his *Word*, to be our governing rule ... The conduct of Divine Providence, with its reasons, is too little understood by us to be improved as our rule ... But God has given us his *Word*, to this very end, that

---

217 *Puritan Sage* (V. Ferm, ed.), 109. See this whole section, which is taken from Edwards' *Miscellaneous Observations*, and printed under the title "The Insufficiency of Reason as a Substitute for Revelation." Part of this may be found in Townsend's *The Philosophy of Jonathan Edwards, From His Private Notebooks*, 219-235. See also Townsend's collection of previously unpublished notes of Edwards' on 210-219, *op. cit.* Finally, see Edwards' sermon on Matthew 5:17 in *Works in Four Volumes*, 4, 438-450.

218 *Puritan Sage*, 109.

> it might be our rule ... And strictly speaking, this is our *only* rule ...[219]

Against those who held up the "evidence" of "common notions" of truth and morality, which were found among various peoples, in different parts of the globe, Edwards asserted that what truth these peoples possessed (he considered their knowledge often to contain truth) came not from their own rational investigations, but from God, through revelation to the most ancient peoples, handed down for generations, or revelation through the historic witness of the Jewish people, and the propagation of their Scriptures; *this* Edwards admitted. He denied, however, that such knowledge of these truths or records of God's dealings constituted personal knowledge of God Himself. God alone, through the gospel of Christ, by the immediate illumination of the Spirit, revealed *Himself* to men. "Where is any people, who to this day have ever delivered themselves by their own reason, or have been delivered without light fetched from the Scriptures, or by means of the gospel of Jesus Christ?"[220] Again:

> We may gather from what has been said, that it is the gospel, and that only, which has actually been the means of bringing the world to the knowledge of the true God. That those are no gods whom the heathens worshipped ... it is the gospel, and that only, which has actually been the means of bringing men to the knowledge of this truth.[221]

Lest we tend to regard this position as but another fallen bulwark of naïve, pre-critical traditionalism, let us hear Edwards' reason for his stance: it is based upon a theology as opposed to the modern as to the eighteenth-century exaltation of the religious truths and moral values of comparative religions:

> This is the main thing that fallen men stood in need of divine revelation for, to teach us how we that have sinned may come to be again accepted of God; or, which is the same thing, how the sinner may be justified. Something beyond the light of nature is necessary to salvation chiefly on this account. Mere natural reason afforded no means by which we could come to the knowledge of this, it depending on the sovereign pleasure of the Being that we had offended by sin ... What is the gospel,

---

219 *Works in Four Volumes*, 1, 188.
220 *Works in Four Volumes*, 4, 30.
221 *History of Redemption*, 265f.

but only the glad tidings of a new way of acceptance with God unto life …?[222]

The real strength of this argument will become apparent when we study Edwards' doctrine of the work of the Spirit in regenerating humans (see the following chapter). It is sufficient at this point to notice that the terms in which Edwards often stated Christian doctrine were identical with the language used by the opponents of that doctrine. This was a favorite device of his sermons, where he instructed his people in the gospel and warned them against prevalent heresy without cluttering his teaching with negative polemic. In his writings, however, he had no such scruples, and would exhaustively tear the reasoning of a Toland, a Chubb, or a Whitby to shreds.[223] Here his common method was (remember the eighteenth-century's idols) to appeal to Scripture *and to reason*, and then, by deadly rational analysis of his opponents' arguments, demonstrate how *contrary to reason* such ideologies as Arminianism, Deism, Arianism, and Naturalism revealed themselves to be.[224] (It is important for us to remember, therefore, that Edwards' rejections of many of the "common notions" of the age sprang, not from the frenzy of anti-intellectual pietism, but from a thorough mastery both of the subject matter of his own field and of the best thought of the age, which, directly or indirectly, attacked or even compromised the doctrine he held to be true.)

The basis for Edwards' ideas of God, His Spirit, and the manner of His Spirit's working with creation and with men is to be found, then, in a source different from the reason of the Cambridge Platonists and the deists, or the "common notions" of naturalists, atheists, or secularized Puritans and Anglican theologians. The foundation for his doctrine of God and His Spirit is the Bible and the Reformation expositions of it. For this reason, his doctrine of God is wholly orthodox, and his exposition of the Trinity breathed the joy, the delight, and the love which we have suggested give his theology a special distinction.[225] Aside from the

---

222 *Works in Four Volumes*, 4, 130.

223 This is his manner throughout much of his *Freedom of the Will*.

224 Ibid., See also his *Original Sin* in *Works in Four Volumes*, 2, 1-190.

225 *Works* (Yale), 1. "We cannot agree, therefore, with Conrad Cherry's statement that Edwards' doctrine of the Trinity is "modeled after his psychology of the faith act." It is drawn from Scripture and informed by traditional Western Trinitarian formulations. Cherry's book is outstanding, however. Conrad Cherry, *The Theology of Jonathan Edwards: A Reappraisal* (Garden City: Anchor Books, 1966), 25.

interesting use of Lockean vocabulary, however, it is strictly an exposition of the traditional Western view of the foundational conciliar decisions of the first five centuries.[226]

Let this sample suffice (it is but one of many that Edwards wrote; discussions of the Trinity fill many, many pages of his notebooks):

> There, even in heaven, dwells the God from whom every stream of holy love, yea, every drop that is, or ever was, proceeds. There dwells God the Father, God the Son, and God the Spirit, united as one, in infinitely dear and incomprehensible, and mutual, and eternal love. There dwells God the Father, who is the father of mercies, and so the father of love, who so loved the world as to give his only begotten Son to die for it. There dwells Christ, the Lamb of God, the prince of peace and of love, who so loved the world that he shed his blood, and poured out his soul unto death for men. There dwells the great Mediator, through whom all the divine love is expressed toward men, and by whom the fruits of that love have been purchased, and through whom they are communicated, and through whom love is imparted to the hearts of all God's people. There dwells Christ in both his natures, the human and the divine, sitting on the same throne with the Father. And there dwells the Holy Spirit – the Spirit of divine love, in whom the very essence of God, as it were, flows out, and is breathed forth in love, and by whose immediate influence all holy love is shed abroad in the hearts of all the saints on earth and in heaven. There, in heaven, this infinite fountain of love – this eternal Three in One – is set open without any obstacle to hinder access to it, as it flows for ever. There this glorious God is manifested, and shines forth in full glory, in beams of love. And there this glorious fountain for ever flows forth in streams, yea, in rivers of love and delight, and these rivers swell, as it were, to an ocean of love, in which the souls of the ransomed may bathe with the sweetest enjoyment, and their hearts, as it were, be deluged with love.[227]

This passage also indicates the major categories under which Edwards discussed the person and work of the Holy Spirit, and it will be helpful now to note the terms by which he denominated the nature and activity of the Spirit, for it is these which will be funded with meaning when we come to examine his doctrine of regeneration. As we mentioned

---

226 See the selection in Faust and Johnson's *Jonathan Edwards*, 375ff. See also Townsend, *op. cit.*, 252f.

227 *Charity and its Fruits* (New York: Robert Carter & Bros., 1852), 327-328. This work is a collected series of Edwards' sermons on 1 Corinthians 13.

before, the doctrine of the Holy Spirit is the *presupposition* for the doctrines of His work in people: Rationalists and enthusiasts, pietists, Methodists, and their formalist opponents differed *basically* because of their different positions on the Person and Nature of the Holy Spirit. To understand Edwards' doctrine of the Spirit's work in regenerating men, therefore, and the differences between his understanding and that of those who favored and those who opposed the Great Awakening, let us note first the major categories by means of which he describes the being of the Holy Spirit. We will select those terms most frequently used by Edwards to describe both the Person and the Work of the Spirit. We shall see, also, that these terms set him in opposition to the position on God's role presented by the movements of thought contemporary to him. These terms are "love," "holiness," "fullness," and "glory." Let us look at each in turn.

Love

In the passage we just quoted, Edwards remarked concerning the Holy Spirit:

> And there dwells the Holy Spirit – the Spirit of divine love, in whom the very essence of God, as it were, flows out, and is breathed forth in love, and by whose immediate influence all holy love is shed abroad in the hearts of all the saints on earth and in heaven ... this glorious God is manifested and shines forth in full glory, in beams of love.[228]

It must be stated at the beginning that each person of the Trinity possesses the attributes ascribed to God: "... all the Divine Perfections are to be attributed to each person of the Trinity."[229] Nevertheless, specific categories are *appropriated* to the Father, Son, and Spirit, respectively, as the Scripture has led the church to note these distinctions. So that, while to the Father as to the Son is all love ascribed, "yet the Holy Ghost is in a peculiar manner called by the name of love – *agape*, the same word that is translated 'charity' in the 13th chapter of 1st Corinthians."[230] Edwards explains:

> The Godhead or the divine essence is one and again said to be love: I John 4:8f ... 16f ... But the divine essence is thus called in a peculiar manner as breathed forth and subsisting in the Holy

---

228 Ibid.
229 *Selections from the Unpublished Writings of Jonathan Edwards*, A.B. Grossart ed., 42. Henceforth, this work will be referred to as *Selections*.
230 Ibid., 42f.

> Spirit ... I John 4:12f ... if we have love dwelling in us, we have
> God dwelling in us ...[231]

The Holy Spirit is the love "breathed forth from the Father and the Son" which is "the divine essence" flowing "in infinite pure love and sweet delight from the Father and the Son. ..."[232] This, of course, is the same Spirit whom "Christ breathed on His disciples" (John 20:22), which proves that this Spirit is *Christ's* Spirit, and thus His to bestow, and, second, that men receive truly the Holy Spirit *of God* when they are drawn to Him through Christ's giving of His own Spirit.[233]

God's love is directed primarily to Himself, within His own Trinitarian fellowship: derivatively, however, His love is directed to those called to be members of the Son. To have fellowship with Christ, therefore, is truly to partake of the inner joy and delight and love of God Himself, in the Spirit. When St. Paul wishes "grace, mercy, and peace, from God the Father and from the Lord Jesus Christ," he does not mention the Spirit because he does not have to do so: "... the Holy Ghost is Himself the love and grace of God the Father and the Lord Jesus Christ. He is the Deity wholly breathed forth in infinite, substantial, intelligent, love ... and so standing forth a distinct personal subsistence."[234]

Because He is the love of God, He comprehends in Himself the happiness of God, which is full and complete in the union of the Father and the Son in the Spirit.[235] This, as we shall see later, is the foundation for the joy and happiness of the saints in their fellowship with God: they are made partakers of God's own Spirit, and thus His own joy, love, and happiness.

No sharper contrast to the humanistic moralism of the eighteenth-century can be imagined than this grounding of the meaning of love in the doctrine of the Holy Spirit. This foundation of ethics will thus

---

231 Ibid.
232 Ibid. Edwards continues, "... and this is that pure river of water of life that proceeds out of the throne of the Father and the Son, as we read at the beginning of the 22nd chapter of the Revelation; for Christ Himself tells us that by the water of life, or living water, is meant the Holy Ghost, John 7:38, 39. This river of water of life in the Revelation is evidently the same with the living waters of the sanctuary in Ezekiel 47:1f; and this river is doubtless the river of God's pleasure, or of God's own infinite delight spoken of in Psa. 36:7f ..."
233 *Works in Ten Volumes*, 8, 270. See also *Selections*, 46f.
234 *Selections*, 7. Cf. *Religious Affections* in *Works in Ten Volumes*, 3, 68f. Also, *Charity and its Fruits*, 37.
235 *Works in Four Volumes*, 3, 183f. See also, 96, 139, 158.

distinguish Edwards from all of his contemporaries who grounded their ethical thought in contemporary reason, nature, or comparative religion. The notions men have of moral obligations and principles are based, of course, on convictions about what they conceive to be really "Real" and truly "True." We shall see later how the basic tenet of Edwards' approach to ethics led him to conclusions at variance with those being accepted by his humanistic and rationalistic – and enthusiastic – contemporaries. His position, of course, is still a valid one for today: he denied, in short, man's right to make up his own definitions as to what is right and what is wrong, as to what love is or is not. He claimed, instead, that – all human learning, science, history, and achievement notwithstanding – *this* was a matter of *divine* prerogative: *God* defines love and *He* defines what we call ethics, and matters in this sphere are illumined by Him, through the Scriptural account which He has given.

Holiness

Another characteristic or attribute approprinted to God's Spirit is that of holiness. The Scripture, Edwards says, often ascribes holiness to the Spirit, "as though 'Holy' were an epithet some way or other peculiarly belonging to Him ..." This is done because, in fact, "the holiness of God does consist in Him." Therefore, "He is called not only the Holy Spirit, but the Spirit of holiness," because the "holiness of the Father and the Son does consist in breathing forth this Spirit."[236] Lest we take these distinctions too rigidly, Edwards reminds us:

> Both the holiness and happiness of the Godhead consists in ... love ... all creature holiness consists essentially and summarily in love to God and love to other creatures; so does the holiness of God consist in his love, especially in the perfect and ultimate union and love there is between the Father and the Son.[237]

His holiness, of course, is "the same with the moral excellency of the divine nature, or his purity and beauty as a moral agent, comprehending all his moral perfections, his righteousness, faithfulness, and goodness. ..."[238] The close connection of the meanings of *God's* love and *God's* holiness is obvious: "In God, the love of what is fit and decent, or the love of virtue, cannot be a thing distinct from the love of Himself."[239]

---

236 *Selections*, 48.
237 Ibid., 47f.
238 *Works in Four Volumes*, 3, 102.
239 *Works in Four Volumes*, 2, 217.

The Spirit of Love is also the Spirit of Holiness, comprehending in Himself the moral beauty, the faithfulness, purity, and righteousness of God. The love of God consists also in the enjoyment of the beauty of His holiness, and this is the love of God which God sheds abroad in our hearts through the Holy Spirit who is given to us.

Basic to Edwards' doctrine of regeneration, therefore, is this view of the Spirit as the Spirit of love and holiness, who comprehends in Himself the righteous beauty and pure faithfulness of the Holy God who loves. *This* Spirit, with *these* attributes, was not really required in the optimistic anthropologies which underlay much of Deistic, Arminian (in the loose sense which this term came to have), and Platonic thought of Edwards' time. In our next chapter we shall further define what Edwards means by "love" and "holiness," and we shall do so in terms of his interpretation of Christ's sacrifice and death for sin. We will only point out here, however, in relation to the position Edwards is taking concerning the foundations of an anthropology, that he selected a pattern for his approach that the Cambridge Platonists, or others who found in nature, reason, or other religions the foundations for their view of man, did not care to follow. The following passage makes Edwards' position quite clear:

> Holiness in man is but the image of God's holiness; there are no more virtues belonging to the image than there are to the original: derived holiness has not more in it than is in that underived holiness which is its foundation: there is no more than *grace* for *grace*, or *grace* in the image answerable to *grace* in the original ...[240]

The true moral beauty God's creatures are meant to manifest consists in the holiness of God dwelling and working in them; which is to say, it consists in the presence among them of God's Holy Spirit.[241] It is in *this* image that people are remade through conversion and sanctification. And this is an image not found in nature or by reason, but only in Jesus Christ. "The Godhead is perceived only by perceiving the Son and the Spirit, for no man hath seen God at any time; He is seen by His image, the Son, and is felt by the Holy Spirit ..."[242]

---

240 *Works in Four Volumes*, 3, 102.
241 Ibid., 102.
242 *Works in Two Volumes*, ed. Hickman (London, 1834), 2, 768.

Fullness

A third decisive term for Edwards' doctrine of the Holy Spirit and His work in men, is "fullness." Let us hear what Edwards means by the use of this word in this connection:

> And as we, by receiving the Holy Spirit from Christ, and being made partakers of His Spirit, are said 'to receive of His fullness, and grace for grace'; and because this Spirit, which is the fullness of God, consists in the love of God and Christ; therefore, we, by knowing the love of Christ, are said 'to be filled with all the fullness of God' (Eph 3:19).[243]

Edwards continues:

> From what has been said it follows that the Holy Spirit is the *summum* of all good. 'Tis the fullness of God. The holiness and happiness of the Godhead consist in it; and in communion or partaking of it consists all the true holiness and happiness of the creature.[244]

The Spirit is "the *summum* of all good" because, being truly God's "fullness," He comprehends in Himself "all the good which is in God." This includes God's "natural" and His "moral" good, His "excellence" as well as His "happiness."[245] When Christ breathes forth His Spirit to His chosen, He communicates to them the priceless gift of the knowledge of God. He gives men knowledge of God as God knows Himself – that is, He grants a true revelation of the Godhead, an "image of God's own knowledge of Himself," though infinitely less in degree.[246]

Secondly, when the Spirit is given to people, they receive with Him God's own virtue and holiness. They receive "God's own moral excellency," for they receive of His "fullness" in the Person of His Spirit. The primary effect of this is love; love to God and love to men. They are filled with the enjoyment God Himself possesses in His own beauty and love. They are filled with praise and admiration for this loving and gracious God who thus gives Himself to them.

Thirdly, in receiving the Holy Spirit believers receive God's "fullness" in that they share in the happiness of the love between the Father and the Son. They are, in effect, drawn into the inter-Trinitarian fellowship

---

243 *Selections*, 48f.
244 Ibid., 49.
245 *Works in Four Volumes*, 2, 204-206.
246 Ibid., 209f.

of God Himself.[247] Explaining this, Edwards summarizes effectively his doctrine of revelation: "What is communicated is divine, or something of God; and each communication is of that nature ..."[248]

Now the implications for such an view of the status of the Holy Spirit for the controversies of Edwards' time are fairly obvious: his age had, in effect, persuaded itself that the functions traditionally ascribed to the Third Person of the Trinity could now be more appropriately ascribed to men, to the "Laws of Nature," and to principles of "Secondary Causation." Traditionally, the Spirit was understood to *effect* God's presence in the world, and to men. Furthermore, He was thought to *enlighten* men to see and hear God's word. Thus, He brought the *effectual lordship* of God over His creatures. But now, after the writings of Galileo, Francis Bacon, Thomas Browne, and others, many were persuaded that God worked *only* by means of secondary causation, according to "laws" once-and-for-all laid down.[249] What need, then, for such a notion of causation which required God's immediate presence and active working in each detail? What need for the Spirit's indwelling and enlightening of people whose minds were not really so disabled by sin as former ages had believed, and whose wills not nearly so powerless as the priests had taught? What need for God's effectual present lordship over His whole creation? Were not the laws He established, the forces He set in motion, supremely sufficient?

In describing the Spirit as God's "fullness," and in defining his meaning as he did, Edwards set himself squarely against those currents of thought which, having taken core elements from His work, were finding little real need for His person. By "fullness" Edwards meant God present and acting as Lord, and, when we get right down to it, the eighteenth-century views which he opposed did not really need a God who was *present*. The consequences of such a divergence of opinion, which are immense, will be more fully explored in later pages.

Glory

The Holy Spirit, said Edwards, is to be glorified equally with the Father and the Son for the work of redemption. This really brings together what we have just said in describing the Spirit as the "Love," "Holiness," and "Fullness" of God. As far as theology and ethics are concerned, this

---

247 Ibid. See also 219, and *Selections*, 55.
248 *Works in Four Volumes*, 2, 210.
249 See Willey, *Seventeenth-century Background*, 26f, 34f, 51f.

emphasis is the actual working out of the principles laid down in the previous assertions.

In the very first work he published, the "Commencement Address" given at Harvard in his twenty-eighth year, Edwards said, commenting on 1 Corinthians 1:29-30:

> So that in this verse is shown our dependence on each person in the Trinity for all our good. We are dependent on Christ the Son of God, as He is our wisdom, righteousness, sanctification, and redemption. We are dependent on the Father, who has given us Christ, and made Him to be these things to us. We are dependent on the Holy Ghost, for it is *of Him that we are in Christ Jesus*; it is the Spirit of God that gives faith in Him, whereby we receive Him, and close with Him.[250]

The substance of this address is indicated by its title, "God Glorified in the Work of Redemption, by the Greatness of Man's Dependence upon Him in the Whole of It." The form of the address consists of an analysis of our dependence upon the Triune God for His working as Father, as Son, and as Holy Spirit. It ends by exhorting people to forsake all forms of religion that detract from God's glory in any aspect of the work of redemption, and to forsake any view that takes from the Father, the Son, or the Spirit, the special functions which Scripture reveals pertain to each in the work of creation, providence, justification, sanctification, and redemption. No better summary of Edwards' whole theology can be imagined, nor a better introduction to his earliest public challenge to the new theologies and ideologies, the new anthropologies and ethics, that were competing with the Puritan heritage he was called upon to defend.

The distance to which Deism and Socinianism, mechanism and Arminianism, had wished to put God is bridged at a stroke by the Church's glorification of the Spirit, with the Father and the Son, for *all* the work of redemption.[251] The Spirit, whose work it was "to bring the world to its beauty and perfection out of the chaos," whose work it is to guide and direct "the wheels of Providence,"[252] is also to be glorified for His divine action in the anointing of the Son of God as the Messiah, and for the work of applying the benefits of the Messiah's death and

---

250 *Works in Four Volumes*, 4, 170. Cf. *History of Redemption*, 25 and 342.
251 Ibid. This piece should be studied in its entirety for any comprehension of Edwards' theology.
252 *History of Redemption*, 350.

resurrection to the redemption of the saints.[253] Neither by appeal to the common notions of mankind, nor to the conscience of "enlightened" Englishmen; neither through the application of one's own innate goodness in works of benevolence, nor by grasping of truth by the exercise of reason; nor through acquaintance with the supposed laws of nature and the forces of causation – through none of these, from none of these, in and by none of these could sinners find God and salvation, said Jonathan Edwards. Redemption, the whole of it, is the work of God. He works in and through humans, but the power of the working and the desire for *good* working is of Him and Him alone.

Let us hear Edwards himself explain the foundation for his teaching on the Spirit's work among the saints through a statement that will also illustrate what we have previously called Edwards' "explicit Trinitarianism," and will thus show his deliberate and systematic reference to the doctrine of the *Person* of the Triune God for an understanding of His *Work*:

> Each *Person* of the Trinity is exceedingly glorified in this work. Herein the work of redemption is distinguished from all the other works of God. The attributes of God are glorious in his other works; but the three persons of the Trinity are distinctly glorified in no work as in this of redemption. In this work every distinct person has his distinct parts and offices assigned him. Each one has his particular and distinct concern in it, agreeable to their distinct, personal properties, relations, and economical offices. The redeemed have an equal concern with and dependence upon each person, in this affair, and owe equal honor and praise to each of them.
>
> The Father appoints and provides the Redeemer, and accepts the price of redemption. The Son is the Redeemer and the price. He redeems by offering up Himself. The Holy Ghost immediately communicates to us the thing purchased; yea, and He is the good purchased. The sum of what Christ purchased for us is holiness and happiness. But the Holy Ghost is the great principle both of holiness and happiness. The Holy Ghost is the sum of all that Christ purchased for men. Gal. 3:13, 14, 'He was made a curse for us, that we might receive the promise of the Spirit, through faith.'
>
> The blessedness of the redeemed consists in partaking of that Spirit, which is given not by measure to Him ... Thus we have an

---

253 *Works in Four Volumes*, 4, 140f; *Selections*, 45; *History of Redemption*, 187-188; *Works in Four Volumes* 3, 311-312, 457.

equal concern with and dependence upon each of the persons of the Trinity, distinctly; upon the Father, as He provides the Redeemer, and the person of whom the purchase is made; the Son as the purchaser, and the price; the Holy Ghost as the good purchased.[254]

This Holy Spirit of God – this Spirit of love and of holiness, this Spirit who comprehends in Himself all the fullness of God and who is, therefore, worthy of equal glory with the Father and the Son for the work of redemption – *this* is the Spirit Christ breathes out upon His followers in every age, and by whom they are born again into a living hope and into a new life in fellowship with God. This is the Spirit promised throughout all of Israel's history, and who, being given to men in unprecedented fullness by the risen Messiah, accomplishes God's eternal will for His creatures, that they might have conscious fellowship with Him.

The whole purpose "which God aimed at in the creation of the world, as the end which he had ultimately in view, was that communication of Himself, which he intended throughout all eternity."[255] He communicates Himself to creatures, not because He needs their fellowship, but because His goodness is such that He wishes them to enjoy Him. This is how God glorifies Himself: by shining forth in all the beauty of His excellency and all the excellence of His beauty. In one of his notes in his *Miscellaneous Observations*, Edwards remarks, (and this passage shows Edwards' understanding of the correspondence between God's own intra-Trinitarian life, and the life of fellowship He gives men through the giving of His Spirit to them):

> God is glorified within Himself these two ways: 1., By appearing or being manifested to Himself in his own perfect idea, or in His Son who is the brightness of His glory. 2., By enjoying and delighting in Himself, by flowing forth in infinite love and delight towards Himself, or in His Holy Spirit.

> So God glorifies Himself towards the creatures also two ways: 1., By appearing to them, being manifested to their understanding. 2., In communicating Himself to their hearts, and in their rejoicing in, and enjoying, the manifestations which He makes of Himself ... God is glorified not only by His glory's being seen, but by its being rejoiced in. When those that see it delight in it, God is more glorified than if they only see it. His

---

254 *Works in Four Volumes*, 4, 141-142.
255 *Works in Four Volumes*, 2, 210. See this entire treatise.

glory is then received by the whole soul, both by the understanding and by the heart.[256]

This passage recalls also what we previously indicated as important characteristics of Edwards' theology: his emphasis 1) on God's beauty and moral excellency, and the consequent joy and happiness the creatures find in fellowship with Him; 2) on the love of God, and in God, between the Father and the Son; 3) on the systematically understood Trinitarian structure of the being of God, and 4) the application of this Trinitarian structure of God's being to the manner of His working in the elect.

Conclusion

Such, then, is the foundation of Edwards' position on the regenerative work of Christ's Holy Spirit. With such a foundation it is not surprising to find him in disagreement with those trends of eighteenth-century thought which we have discussed; nor is it surprising that he should come to different conclusions concerning such issues as the doctrines of providence, election, sin, Christ's sacrifice, and the new birth. The importance of studying Edwards in this context lies in the fact that he was no illiterate defender of Calvinistic traditionalism or bigoted ranter on the side of orthodoxy. He was, on the contrary, one of the finest critical intellects of the century. He had a profound acquaintance with the new ways of thought. He had also a deep appreciation for much in them, as we have seen in his use of Newton and Locke. He was a man of his time who was so perceptive to the deepest feelings of the age as to be able to point out, not just the consequential, but the basic cleavages between the classical Protestant view of God in Christ and that propagated by other leaders of Anglo-Saxon thought.

It must be added that his analysis of the Spirit's work among men (deriving from the fundamentals we have just studied) placed Edwards in opposition not only to the views of the Deists and Arminians but also to the positions of many enthusiastic supporters of the revival movements of the time. We shall study this in succeeding pages, and shall find, again, that the conclusions reached in the matter of the Spirit's *work* will depend on previous decisions concerning the Spirit *Himself* and the authority of the Scriptures as the criterion for discerning His

---

256 Townsend, *op. cit.*, 133. We must disagree with Conrad Cherry when he claims John Locke as the source for Edwards' objections to Charles Chauncy. Scripture – not Locke – is the basis of Edwards' understanding of God and of God's works in men. *Op. Cit.*, 168.

work. What we have sought to do in this chapter is to delineate the foundations upon which Edwards' later conclusions will be seen to rest, and because of which many of his contemporaries had to disagree with him. Edwards' theological assumptions here were, as we have seen, the traditional Western doctrine of the Triune God, as drawn from the biblical witness, and specifically, the properties and activities ascribed in the Scriptures to the person and work of the Holy Spirit of the Lord Jesus Christ.

5

New Birth in the Spirit

So that relation to Christ, whereby believers, in Scripture language, are said to be in Christ, is the very foundation of our virtues and good deeds being accepted of God, and so of their being rewarded; for a reward is a testimony of acceptance. For we, and all that we do, are accepted only in the beloved, Eph 1:6. Our sacrifices are acceptable only through our interest in him, and through his worthiness and preciousness being, as it were, made ours. 1 Pet. 2:4, 5, 'To whom coming, as a living stone, disallowed indeed of men, but chosen of God, and precious, ye also, as lively stones, are built up a spiritual house, a holy priesthood, to offer up spiritual sacrifices acceptable to God by Jesus Christ' ... And hence we are directed, whatever we offer to God, to offer it in Christ's name, as expecting to have it no other way, than from the value that God has to that name. Col. 3:17, 'And whatsoever ye do in word or deed, do all in the name of the Lord Jesus, giving thanks to God and the Father by him.' To act in Christ's name, is to act under him, as our head, and as having him to stand for us, and represent us Godward.

... it is not meet that anything in us be accepted of God, as any excellency of our persons, until we are actually in Christ, and justified through him. The loveliness of the virtue of the fallen creatures is nothing in the sight of God, till he beholds them in Christ, and clothed with his righteousness. 1, Because till then we stand condemned before God, by his own holy law, to his utter rejection and abhorrence. And 2, Because we are infinitely guilty before him; and the loveliness of our virtue bears no proportion to our guilt, and must therefore pass for nothing before a strict judge. And, 3, Because our good deeds and virtuous acts themselves are in a sense corrupt; and the hatefulness of the corruption in them, if we are beheld as we are in ourselves, as separate from Christ, infinitely outweighs the loveliness of that which attends the act of virtue itself, the loveliness vanishes into nothing in comparison of it: and therefore the virtue must pass for nothing, out of Christ.

Jonathan Edwards

Introduction

We saw in the last chapter that Edwards' doctrine of the Holy Spirit's regenerating work was rooted in his view of the biblical witness concerning the Person and work of the Spirit of Christ and that his view of the Person of the Spirit was mediated through traditional Western doctrine and especially through the Calvinistic tradition. (In previous chapters we noted also the intense concern of Puritans generally with the subject of the Spirit and His gracious work in men.) In this chapter, we shall study in some detail his doctrine of the new birth in the Spirit, and we shall do so against the background of his controversy with Arminianism. The inevitable result of Arminian theology, he felt, by blinding people to the basic revelation of God concerning His work for their salvation, robbed them of their inheritance in the Holy Spirit – stripping them of Christ's most precious "purchase" for them, his great "promise" to them, the fruits of the indwelling Spirit which witnessed to their hearts that they were children of God destined to everlasting life with Him. Because of Edwards' conviction concerning the blessings of Christ's gospel, he gave his life to the study and the refutation of Arminian tendencies. His first public address – at Boston in 1731 – challenged the Arminian scheme as a denial of the gospel; his last two major books, written at the end of his life, fought the same fight and maintained the same cause. His writings on the Spirit and conversion have not always been seen in integral relationship to his views on sin and on the sacrifice of Christ, yet it is essential to appreciate the one in order to understand the other. When praying and laboring for a revival – for an outpouring of the Holy Spirit – Edwards preached and lectured on "Justification by Faith Alone," and in doing so publicly confuted Arminian denials of the terrible seriousness of sin, and, by implication, their denials of the real effects of Christ's Sacrifice. In his own words:

> So that relation to Christ, whereby believers in Scripture language, are said to be in Christ, is the very foundation of our

> virtues and good deeds being accepted of God ... For we, and all that we do, are accepted only in the beloved ...

> ... The loveliness of the virtue of the fallen creatures is nothing in the sight of God, till he beholds them in Christ, and clothed with his righteousness.[257]

We shall see in this chapter that Edwards considered regeneration to be that change in man effected by the indwelling of Christ's Spirit through response to the gospel message, whereby they are changed in their minds and hearts, given a new (albeit imperfect) love for God and for others, and guided and empowered to live as children of God and members of Christ. It is the work of the Spirit, through the gospel message.

Let us turn, then, to a consideration of the manner in which Edwards conceived people to come into such a new relationship with God. We will look first at his views on God's promise of His Spirit to believers. Then, we shall examine his view of Christ's work in effecting God's promise; here we shall note his controversy with Arminianism. Finally, we shall study his own expositions of his doctrine of regeneration, or the new birth.

The Promise of the Spirit

In his private notebooks, Edwards wrote that "the great and universal end of God's creating the world was to communicate Himself."[258] This communication of Himself is given only to "intelligent beings." He gives Himself to their understandings and to their hearts or wills (this Edwards calls "the enjoying faculty," by which men receive the joy and pleasure of fellowship with God). "God," he says, "created this world for the shining forth of His excellency and for the flowing forth of His happiness."[259] This doesn't add to His happiness as if He were not fully happy in His Triune life, but it bestows on intelligent creatures the happiness and the glory of a gracious Creator.

In his book *Concerning the End for Which God Created the World*, written in his last years at Stockbridge and published after his death, Edwards spells out in detail his teaching on God's purposes in creation. In all of God's subsequent works, the original intention is served: all He does in the world is coordinated towards the accomplishment of

---

257 *Works in Four Volumes*, 4, 110.
258 Townsend, *op. cit.*, 130.
259 Ibid.

the single purpose for which the world was brought into being. That purpose is the manifestation and exercise of God's glory. His glory is His excellence, His beauty, His purity, and His joy. The manifestation of this excellence, then, is effected by the relating of the glorious nature of this Holy God to the *minds* and to the *hearts* of creatures made for the purpose of enjoying and knowing Him.

> God's work from the beginning of the universe to the end, and in all parts of the universe, appears to be but one. It is all one design carried on, one affair managed, in all God's dispensations towards all intelligent beings, viz., the glorifying and communicating Himself in and through His Son Jesus Christ as God-man, and by the work of redemption of fallen man. So the work of God is one, if we view it in all its parts; what was done in heaven, and what was done on earth, and in hell, in the beginning, and since that through all ages, and what will be done at the end of the world.[260]

The ultimate end of all of God's works in creating and in sustaining and in governing the world is this – the communication of "divine goodness" to His creatures. This "divine goodness," especially characterized by "forgiveness of sin, and salvation," essentially consists in God's own Being being communicated to creatures.[261] In thus giving Himself to creatures He bestows upon things that were not the knowledge and the joy of Him who was from the beginning. This is pure grace. He wills that there be creatures to know and enjoy the indescribable riches and glories of His Being. He wishes that they know His excellence and His greatness, His holiness, and His power. He desires, moreover, that they not only know but love, that which He is. Their minds are to perceive that which their hearts are to love and enjoy.

How, then, is this intention fulfilled? Edwards replies: through "the glorifying and communicating Himself in and through His Son Jesus Christ as God-man, and by the work of redemption of fallen man." Jesus Christ is the objective revelation of the *mind* of God. He is the *Logos*. He is the perfect expression, in human form, of the perfect *idea* God has of Himself. Through Him, and through His work for fallen man, the revelation of God is given to humans. The sum of His work, then, is God's giving of Himself to people, through the Person and work of the God-man. This He does by giving them His Spirit. To recall words we have quoted earlier: "The Godhead is perceived only by perceiving the

---

260 *Works in Ten Volumes*, 10, 33f.
261 *Works in Four Volumes*, 2, 242ff.

Son and the Spirit, for no man hath seen God at any time; He is *seen* by His *image*, the Son, and is *felt* by the Holy Spirit. ..."[262] The manifestation of God's "image" is made effectively real in man, both in his mind and in his heart, through the Holy Spirit:

> ... the Holy Spirit is the *summum* of all good. 'Tis the fullness of God. The holiness and happiness of the Godhead consists in it; and in communion or partaking of it consists all the true loveliness and happiness of the creature ...
>
> What Christ purchased for us, is that we might have communion with God in His good, which consists in partaking or having communion of the Holy Ghost ...
>
> The Holy Spirit is the purchased possession and inheritance of the saints. ...The Holy Ghost is the great subject of all gospel promises, and therefore is called the Spirit of promise (Eph. 1:13). He is called the promise of the Father (Luke 24:49).[263]

In giving men His Holy Spirit to dwell within them, God aims at the fulfillment of His purpose in creating them. The Spirit who is Holy, who comprehends in Himself the love of God, who comprehends also the fullness of the Triune Being, and who, thus, receives equal glory with the Father and the Son for the manifestation of Divine Glory in the work of redeeming fallen men – this Spirit is the gift of the resurrected Son of God and His Father.

> The Holy Spirit, in His indwelling, His influences and fruits, is the sum of all grace, holiness, comfort and joy; or in one word, of all the spiritual good Christ purchased for men in this world, and is also the sum of all perfection, glory, and eternal joy, that He purchased for them in another world.[264]

In earth and in Heaven, the sum of all God intends for His creatures is *Himself!* This is what they receive when they receive the Holy Spirit.

This, of course, is the sum of all that is promised throughout the history of Israel. One of Edwards' finest – and least known – works is a piece he wrote (in answer to the request of men in Scotland) as an *apologia* for a scheme to encourage many Christians to gather regularly to pray for God's Spirit to be outpoured upon them, for the advancement of Christ's Kingdom. Surveying the grand promises of deliverance and restoration, of forgiveness and future glory promised to the chosen

---

262 Grossart, *op. cit.*, 49f.
263 Ibid.
264 *Works in Four Volumes*, 3, 447; *Works* (Yale), 5, 307ff.

people, Edwards declares that "The Holy Spirit is that great benefit, that is the subject matter of the promises, both of the eternal covenant of redemption, and also of the covenant of grace. ..." The Spirit, he says, is "the grand subject of the promises of the Old Testament, in the prophecies of the blessings of the Messiah's kingdom; and the chief subject of the promises of the New Testament ..."[265] Entitled, *A Humble Attempt to Promote Explicit Agreement and Visible Union of God's People in Extraordinary Prayer, for the Revival of Religion and the Advancement of Christ's Kingdom on Earth, Pursuant to Scripture Promises and Prophecies Concerning the Last Time*, this work gathers together the biblical promises of both the Old and the New Testament concerning God's gift of His Spirit to men.[266] Edwards synchronizes with these passages others concerning God's promises to restore Israel and lift up His Holy City as a light to the Gentiles.[267] He concluded this collation of passages and promises by asserting that the Holy Spirit is the sum of *all* the good things promised by God to His people. Nothing less, he said, has been offered us by God, than God Himself. All the temporal blessings are but examples and pale shadows of the real blessing of the presence of God Himself.

So when John the Baptist came preaching that "There cometh one mightier than I after me, the latchet of whose shoes I am not worthy to stoop down and unloose; indeed I have baptized you with water: but He shall baptize you with the Holy Ghost" (Mark 1:7-8), he was merely citing again what the Lord had said to Isaiah: "Fear not, O Jacob my servant; and thou Jeshurun, whom I have chosen. For I will pour water upon him that is thirsty, and floods upon the dry ground: I will pour my Spirit upon thy seed, and my blessing upon thy offspring" (Isaiah 44:2-3). Isaiah had heard what Joel was to hear: "And it shall come to pass afterward, that I will pour out my Spirit upon all flesh; and your sons and your daughters shall prophesy, your old men shall dream dreams, your young men shall see visions" (Joel 2:28). What occurred at Pentecost was prophesied long before.

In the controversies with the rationalists concerning the Great Awakening, Edwards developed, over and over again, the meaning of the many parts of Scripture that refer to God's promise to pour out His Spirit upon His people – individually as well as collectively. Many of Edwards' (and Whitefield's, and the Wesleys') opponents would allow

---

265 Ibid.
266 Ibid., 429-508.
267 Ibid., 447ff.

that the Spirit was given to the Church – *in some sense*. What many opposed (and still oppose) is that the Spirit was also given individually to Christians. The burden of Edwards' exegetical writings and sermons on this issue is that this is just what occurs. Commenting on Christ's words, "If ye then, being evil, know how to give good gifts unto your children, how much more shall your heavenly Father give the Holy Spirit to them that ask Him?" (Luke 11:13) Edwards remarks that "the Holy Spirit is the sum of the blessings that are the subject matter of that prayer about which He had instructed them."[268] The statements of Isaiah (chapters 32, 44, and 59), of Joel (chapter 2), of Ezekiel (chapters16, 36, 37), and of Christ in the Gospels (John 3, 7, 14-17; Luke 11) all find their meaning in what began to be accomplished at Pentecost.[269] The dramatic events Edwards witnessed in his own lifetime, then, were but logical consequences of the type of activity the Holy Spirit had continued to do since the glorification of the Son of God.

God's purpose in creating intelligent beings, therefore, is brought to (partial) fulfillment in their knowledge of and joy in the fellowship they have with Him through the indwelling of the Holy Spirit. Christ, who is full of the Holy Spirit, breathes this same Spirit upon His people. This fulfilled the promise of God. The evidence of Ephesians 1:13-14; Galatians 3:2, 13, 14; 5:22-26; Acts 2; 9:17f; 10; John 7; 14-17, etc., justifies, says Edwards, this conclusion:

> So that all the holiness and happiness of the redeemed is in God. It is in the communications, indwelling, and acting of the Spirit of God. Holiness and happiness are in the fruit, here and hereafter, because God dwells in them, and they in God.[270]

Christians are to pray for nothing less than for God's own Spirit to be given. This is the primary goal of the work of Christ: "What Christ purchased for us is that we might have communion with God in His good, which consists in partaking or having communion of the Holy Ghost. ..."[271]

What God promised throughout Scripture, therefore, was the fulfillment of His intention behind the creation of the world. He promised that He would do what He set out to do – give Himself to creatures,

---

268 Ibid., 3, 452. Edwards deals with this subject innumerable times in his writings, and in reference to many, many passages of Scripture.
269 Ibid., 442ff.
270 *Works in Four Volumes*, 4, 175.
271 Grossart, *op. cit.*, 50.

that they might enjoy Him. Let us conclude this section with a final word from Edwards:

> From Him all creatures come, and in Him their well-being consists. God is all their beginning, and God, received, is all their end. From Him and to Him are all things. They are all from Him, and they are all to be brought to Him. But 'tis not that they may add to Him, but that God might be received by them.[272]

This, then, is the promise – the central promise – of God to men.

The Purchase of the Spirit

> The Importance of all Christian doctrines whatsoever, will naturally be denied, in consequence of denying that one great doctrine of the necessity of Christ's satisfaction to divine justice, and maintaining those doctrines that establish men's own righteousness, as that on which, and for which, they are accepted of God. For that great Christian doctrine of Christ's satisfaction, his vicarious sufferings and righteousness, by which He offered an infinite price to God for our pardon and acceptance to eternal favor and happiness, is what all evangelical doctrines ... have relation to; and they are of little importance, comparatively, any other way than as they have respect to that. This is, as it were, the centre and hinge of all doctrines of pure revelation.[273]

The reason behind Edwards' lifelong struggle against Arminian theology lay in his conviction that this "modern fashionable divinity"[274] withheld from people the only message God had given as a means of saving them – the message, the *gospel*, that the Son of God died for their sin, to release them from its power. The Arminians taught men to depend on *themselves* in areas where the Bible taught men to depend on *God*, said Edwards. Whether in the "modern fashionable" exaltation of human *reason* (which removed the necessity for clinging to the Scriptures), or in the exaltation of man's *virtue* and *power* to follow that which reason indicated to be true (which removed the necessity for believing the "gloomy" anthropology of Scripture, Augustine, the Reformation, and the Protestant Confessions) – in every case the new spirit behind these views inspired people to trust themselves for things which the Protestant churches had formerly taught come directly from the hand of God alone.

---

272 Townsend, *op.cit.*, 133.
273 *Works in Four Volumes*, 3, 542.
274 Ibid.

The mind of "enlightened" eighteenth-century man had been delivered from the restrictions imposed by the Reformation *sola scriptura*; the humiliating *sola gratia* was now seen to be equally unnecessary. Behind the Arminian objections to the Calvinistic views of man's depravity, God's powerful grace, God's choosing men to be in Christ, God's granting men salvation entirely for the sake and merits of Christ (and not for anything they themselves had or would or could do), and God's sure protection of those He chose until their eventual attainment of heaven – behind all the various objections lay the increasingly articulated convictions of Renaissance humanism. These convictions included an estimation of the nature of man which insisted on his power to choose or reject evil, or God, at any moment. The gospel fit into such a scheme, therefore, as a message offered to man in such a way that his acceptance or rejection of it depended not on God but on individual man. (This, of course, explicitly contradicts the crucial biblical views concerning God's *providential control* of His world and its history, and His *electing mercy*.) Such powers as possessed by humans in this "modern fashionable divinity" included a self-determining capacity that made former definitions of grace irrelevant. Man sought *mercy* from God, certainly, but not, as before, *determining and saving gracious power*. Power was one ingredient eighteenth-century definitions of grace did not require.

The implications of such a scheme are immense. "One danger of these Arminian notions is," said Edwards in his work on *Efficacious Grace*, "that they tend strongly to prevent conviction of sin."[275] By teaching that man had within himself the power to alter the direction of his mind and heart, the "modern fashionable divinity" withheld from people that analysis of the human condition which God Himself gave through the Scriptures, as well as the message of God's action in regard to that condition. As Edwards saw the problem, the Arminians were leading souls away from the gospel of Christ and straight into hell.

One would have thought that Puritanism, in England as well as in America, would not have succumbed so quickly to the doctrinal shallowness so characteristic of many expositions of the "new divinity." We must remember, however, that it was the English theologians at the Synod of Dort who were arguing for some valuation to be placed on man's works prior to grace, and it was the stated policy of Laud and the Establishment to root out those men whose zeal for classical theology inclined them towards a stricter Reformation view of theology and

---

275 *Works in Four Volumes*, 2, 561.

parish life. Further, it was the temper of the age to exalt man (and thus, in many ways, to dethrone God).

The "spirit of the age" had been shocked by the determinism of Hobbes' *Of Liberty and Necessity* (1654). Many works had been written to confute this book. Anthony Collins' *A Philosophic Inquiry Concerning Human Liberty* had aroused equally passionate defenses of the glories of man's self-determining power in matters moral and religious. Many thinkers of the time had the acumen to see that this issue was (in the words of Samuel Clarke) "one of the most important truths of moral philosophy that ever was discussed, and most necessary to be known."[276] By "truths of moral philosophy," of course, he meant the Arminian position in this discussion; what *he* wished to be known, was what the Calvinists called a lie of Satan. Attacking Collins' work, Clarke said, "To be an Agent … signifies to have a Power of beginning Motion,"[277] and this power implies the power to initiate moral action in faithful response to the hearing of the gospel. In this power consists the "Essence of Liberty," as he wrote in his book *Being and Attributes of God*.[278] Bishop Butler (who enjoyed immense authority in the field of ethics) argued that the view of man's being bound by sin, and determined by it, or by God's grace, when converted, may be "speculatively true," yet, with regard to practice, it is as if it were false, so far as our experience teaches." To teach such a doctrine would be, he says, "absurd," for it would cut the nerve of all conscience and responsibility and obedience.[279]

The real force of the Arminian (and humanistic) position was felt in the effects of John Taylor's *The Scripture Doctrine of Original Sin Proposed to a Free and Candid Examination*. Published in 1738, this study won many wavering minds away from the scriptural teaching concerning man's true plight. Especially did he proclaim that Adam's fall in no way affected the inner nature of his successors, that men are *not* shaped by a "necessary inclination" to sin, that they have no "natural propensity" to do wrong, and the teaching of the Westminster Assembly's *Catechism* is "false."[280] This work was opposed by a number of writers including

---

276 Quoted in Faust and Johnson's *Edwards*, xliii.

277 *Remarks Upon a Book Entitled A Philosophical Inquiry* (quoted in Faust and Johnson, *op. cit.*, li).

278 See Faust and Johnson, *op. cit.*, lii.

279 *The Analogy of Religion* (Oxford: The University Press, 1848), Part I, Chapter vi, Sections 5-6.

280 John Taylor, *The Scripture Doctrine of Original Sin Proposed to Free and Candid Examination* (Belfast: John Hay, 1738), quoted in Faust and Johnson, *op. cit.*,

Isaac Watts and John Wesley. The tide could not be stopped, however, and the reception of Taylor's book in New England as well as in Old showed the degree to which the original theological positions of the English churches had become uncomfortably restrictive and downright offensive to sensibilities of this generation.

One of the more influential of the New England works espousing the Arminian notion of man's moral freedom to reject or accept good and evil was Samuel Webster's *A Winter Evening's Conversation Upon the Doctrine of Original Sin*, published in 1757. Attack and counterattack followed this book also, and the presses were kept busy with replies to and defenses of this work of Webster, the pastor of Salisbury, Massachusetts. For our purposes, the highest importance attaches to this controversy, for it provoked two of Edwards' major writings, his work on *Original Sin*, and on the current notions concerning man's *Freedom of the Will*. The full title of the former indicates the main target of Edwards' discussion (for Webster was heavily indebted to Taylor's work): *The Great Christian Doctrine of Original Sin Defended; Evidences of its Truth Produced, and Arguments to the Contrary Answered, Containing in Particular, a Reply to the Objections and Arguings of Dr. John Taylor, in his Book Entitled, "The Scripture Doctrine of Original Sin Proposed to Free and Candid Examination, etc."*[281] This work appeared in 1758, the year of Edwards' death, and together with the book on *Freedom of the Will* (1754) constitutes a main source for understanding his objections to the leading themes of the "fashionable new divinity."

Because this controversy over the work of Christ was absolutely basic to consequent views of man, sin, and regeneration, we must present here a summary of Edwards' views on these matters. In Section A of this chapter we studied God's *promise* of His Spirit to men; in Section C we shall study Edwards' view of the *new birth* of man which is effected by the *gift* of the Spirit who gives faith in the gospel; in this middle section we must study Edwards' doctrines of sin, Christ's sacrifice, and election, which constitute the *purchase* for men of the Spirit who is then given to them.

Sin

"One danger of these Arminian notions" – to quote this key sentence of Edwards once again – "is that they tend strongly to prevent convic-

---

lxvi.
281 See *Works in Four Volumes*, 2. See also *Works* (Yale), 1.

tion of sin."[282] By this, he sets himself squarely against Bishop Butler and others who taught that if man were *not* morally free there could be no praising or condemning him for his actions. Obviously, the Bishop and the Puritan had two widely different conceptions of what it means to say "Man is a sinner." What, then, did Edwards mean?

> ... when God made man at first, He implanted in him two kinds of principles. There was an *inferior* kind, which may be called *natural*, being the principles of mere human nature; such as self-love, with those natural appetites and passions, which belong to the *nature of man*, in which his love to his own liberty, honor, and pleasure, were exercised: these when alone, and left to themselves, are what the Scriptures sometimes call *flesh*. Besides these, there were *superior* principles, that were spiritual, holy, and divine, summarily comprehended in divine love; wherein consisted the spiritual image of God, and man's righteousness and true holiness ...[283]

These "spiritual principles" were not part of man's created nature but were, in fact, "divine communications and influences of God's Spirit."[284] Without these, man is "flesh." He is still man, still fully human, still a true and proper creature of God, but he is no longer governed by the Holy Spirit through His indwelling and "communications and influences." Originally, man was made *good*: not morally neutral, as Arminians liked to think, but positively *good*. When he decided to extend himself, however, and to exceed his limits as a good creature, catastrophe followed.[285]

> When man sinned and broke God's covenant, and fell under his curse, these superior principles left his heart: for indeed God then left him; that communion with God, on which these principles depended, entirely ceased; the Holy Spirit, that divine inhabitant, forsook the house ... Therefore immediately the superior divine principles wholly ceased; so light ceases in a room where the candle is withdrawn; and thus man was left in a state of darkness, woeful corruption and ruin; nothing but flesh without spirit. The inferior principles of self-love, and natural appetite, which were given only to serve [the Spirit] being alone, and left to themselves, *of course* became reigning princi-

---

282 *Works in Four Volumes*, 2, 561.
283 *Works in Four Volumes*, 2, 476-477. The emphases, unless otherwise indicated, are Edwards' own.
284 Ibid., 477.
285 Ibid., 287f.

ples; having no superior principles to regulate or control them, they became absolute masters of the heart. The immediate consequence of which was a fatal *catastrophe*, a turning of all things upside down ... Man immediately set up *himself*, and the objects of his private affections and appetites, as supreme; and so they took the place of God.[286]

Man is still man; but he is now improperly ruled – rather, he is *dominated*. He finds himself, through the misuse of his powers and God's favor, left on his own, subject to the spirit of rebellion which tempted his heart to disobey God. Against the Arminian charge that Calvinism made God the author of sin, Edwards stoutly affirmed that it was not God but *man* who sinned. It was *man* who disobeyed, who despised the gracious law of his gracious Creator, and it is man, now, who plans, who desires, who executes, and who rejoices in sin. God does not put sin into man's heart, but now, after Adam's rebellion, God withdraws His Spirit from "rebel man," and leaves him to the service of those gods he now monotonously chooses to enslave him.[287] Sin, in this sense, is "privative" (to use an ancient theological description), in that man is now bereft of the rule of goodness, guidance, and regulation; he is bereft of the rule of goodness and is now ruled by wrong instead. "Divines are generally agreed, that sin radically and fundamentally consists in what is negative, or privative, having its root in a privation or *want of holiness*."[288]

This last point is important: Edwards has sometimes been interpreted in a neo-Platonic sense foreign to his original meaning. Man, without these spiritual principles (i.e., the Holy Spirit) is not less than man; he does not become sub-human or animal. He remains man, fully man. But he is now *sinful man*, and the whole of his humanity is turned now to apostasy, which is "departing from the true God to idols; forsaking his Creator and setting up other things in his room."[289]

What, then, is the consequence of this falling away from fellowship with God, whereby man loses the guiding and regulating presence of

---

286 Ibid.

287 Ibid., 478f.

288 *Works in Four Volumes*, 3, 17.

289 *Works in Four Volumes*, 4, 42. For an example of such neo-Platonizing, see Douglas Elwood's discussion, *op. cit.*, where he seems to equate Edwards' views with those of Paul Tillich in his *Systematic Theology*, 3 vols. (Chicago: University of Chicago Press, 1963). Nothing could be further from Jonathan Edwards' teachings than the writings of Paul Tillich.

the Holy Spirit in his mind and body and heart, and becomes mere *flesh*? There is, says Edwards, a host of terrible consequences of this rebellion. The first point to be noted is the *universality* of this situation: "There is none righteous, no not one ... there is none that doeth good, no not one" (Romans 3:10b, 11b).[290] All men are affected and infected by the power of sin, which rules their hearts in the absence of the Holy Spirit.

> ... mankind are all naturally in such a state, as is attended without fail, with this consequence or issue: that they universally run themselves into that which is, in effect, their own utter, eternal perdition, as being finally accursed of God, and the subjects of his remediless wrath through sin.[291]

Not only is this proved from Scripture, said Edwards, it is quite plain from every history known to man. The study of any people shows that "their nature is corrupt and depraved with a moral depravity that amounts to and implies their own undoing."[292]

Second, the Scriptural indication of the relationship between Adam and all succeeding generations is thus established. When Arminians objected that it was impossible for the sin of the first man to change the nature of his children and that it would be utterly irrational for God to blame later generations for what their forbearers – without their knowledge or consent – had done, Edwards replied: man's reason is not the criterion of the relationship, possible or otherwise, between Adam and later generations. God alone is the judge of such matters. "God, in his constitution with Adam, dealt with him as a public person, and as the head of the human species, and had respect to his posterity, as included in him ..."[293] Mankind is an organic establishment of God's, who has created all people as organically related to all others. The sin of the original man has damaged the cause of all his successors. Adam, in fact, *is* our representative in that he *truly* represents us: he is a sinner, as we are sinners. It is a fact that God's Spirit left Adam, and it is a fact that the majority of mankind live without the indwelling of that same Spirit.[294] Man's "original sin" consists now in the "innate, sinful

---

290 See *Works in Four Volumes*, 4, 505f.
291 *Works in Four Volumes*, 2, 313.
292 Ibid.
293 Ibid., 465.
294 Ibid., 395ff. In view of Edwards' explicit statement of this union of all men with Adam in his sin and fall, it is puzzling to find Elwood denying this; *op. cit.*, 86. Edwards certainly does insist that all men are personally guilty for their own

depravity of the heart," as well as in the guilt he shares with all humans in their common inheritance of the trait so drastically manifested by Adam, their true father.[295]

A third point to be noted is that sin is more than the perversion of individuals and more than their individual or collective sins. Sin is a power, a principality, a malignant kingdom of evil to which men's hearts are bound: "This world is a place where the devil, who is called the god of this world, has influence and dominion, and where multitudes are possessed of his spirit."[296] All people are now enslaved to beings that by nature are no gods, and they give their souls to the service of idols that oppose and despise the living God. "All the sin that men commit, is what they do in the service of their idols: there is no one act of sin, but what is an act of service to some false god."[297]

The fourth point of importance is that we do not wish to renounce the service of these gods. *Man does not wish to cease loving himself or the world.* This is the nature of his problem, which makes all Arminian arguments about free will ridiculous. *Man's will*, said Edwards *is free to serve the cause the man loves*, but it is not free to change its allegiance from loving sin to loving God. The essence of the problem is that man's heart no longer loves God, and no longer wishes to cease loving itself.

> ... for enmity against God reigns in us, and over us; we are under the power and dominion of it, and are sold under it. We do not restrain that which reigns over us. A slave, as long as he continues a mere slave, cannot control his master. "He that committeth sin, is the servant of sin." (John 8:34)[298]

Man now is free to will what he is free to will. He is free to love what he loves. *He is not free to change his love of himself into the love of God.* He has a heart which by corrupted nature *sincerely wishes* to serve only itself: "A man never, in any instance, wills anything contrary to his desires, or desires anything contrary to his will."[299] This is the whole point of the biblical view, Edwards claims: man *wills* to do what God

---

sin. He also says that they are included in Adam's sin and fall, and share in his guilt by the organic relationship they have with him as individual men in the organic whole of mankind. See Edwards' *Works in Four Volumes*, 2, 351ff, 381ff, 391ff.

295 Ibid., 309.

296 *Charity and its Fruits*, 85; *Works in Four Volumes*, 1, 540.

297 *Works in Four Volumes*, 4, 43; see 36ff.

298 Ibid., 54.

299 *Works* (Yale), 1, 139.

does not wish him to will to do. It is because man's deepest desire and inclination go against God's will for man, that he is judged and found wanting. Humans honestly, sincerely and fully will other than God commands. Their basic nature chooses other than what God offers. It is the state of their heart that is at fault, and it is the state of their heart that must be changed, for people cannot change this themselves. They cannot because they will with all their heart *not* to do so.

> ... 'Tis absurd to suppose that a man should directly, properly and sincerely incline to have an inclination, which at the same time is contrary to his inclination: for that is to suppose him not to be inclined to what he is inclined ... If the soul properly and sincerely falls in with a certain proposed act of will of choice, the soul therein makes that choice its own.[300]

Man is now what he chooses most to be. God's judgment is, therefore, absolutely and totally correct: man's heart *is* against God, it *is* filled with pride and self-love, and does not wish to be changed from *this* (though the man may wish to exchange one form of it – say, adultery – for another – say, wealth and respectability). God's condemnation of man for the sin of his heart, and God's outpouring of wrath upon humanity is justified, for all men violate God's will. Contrary to His command, they do *not* love Him above all else, and thus they do not love their neighbors as they love themselves.

> Consider how much *willfulness* there is in your ignorance. Sinners are ready wholly to excuse themselves in their blindness; whereas ... the blindness that naturally possesses the hearts of men is not a merely negative thing; but they are blinded by 'the deceitfulness of sin,'" Heb. 3:13. There is a perverseness in their blindness. There is not a mere absence of light, but a malignant opposition to the light ... Christ observes ... 'this is their condemnation, that light is come into the world, yet men loved darkness rather than light,' John 3:19, 20.[301]

In Edwards' opinion, the Arminian insistence on the will's power to reform itself in response to the gospel message is but a crass example of the blindness of mind and heart caused by the "deceitfulness of sin" (Heb. 3:13). It is man's denial of *God's* analysis of the relationship between them. It is the Devil's lie. "The danger of these Arminian notions is, that they strongly tend to prevent conviction of sin," and

---

300 Ibid., 312.
301 Ibid., 34.

thus man, not being convinced of the real nature and extent of his sin, is not persuaded to fly to God for the remedy God has provided.

Only by the providential action of God's restraining grace is it possible for people to live with as little chaos as they do. Most men may not perform the deeds of the great criminals and conquerors; nevertheless "we are all naturally the enemies of God as much as they. If we have not committed the unpardonable sin, it is owing to restraining grace."[302] We may not duplicate Herod's deeds or Pharaoh's, nor sin in the way of Judas and Saul: yet all of us, in our own way, are filled with pride and enmity against God and His ways. "If one worm be a little exalted above another, by having more dust, or a bigger dung-hill, how much does he make of himself! What a distance does he keep from those that are below him!"[303]

What is the conclusion of all this?

> Now this barbarous ignorance and gross delusion being of such great extent and continuance, shows that the cause is *general*, and that the defect is in the *corrupted nature* of mankind; man's natural blindness and proneness of his heart to delusion.[304]

("Who changed the truth of God into a lie, and worshiped and served the creature more than the Creator ... For this cause God gave them up ... And even as they did not like to retain God in their knowledge, God gave them over to a reprobate mind ...")[305]

Being given over "to a reprobate mind," humans now invent analyses of their situation which bear little resemblance to the analysis God revealed through the Biblical writers. Here we come to the heart of the problem. Wollaston, appealing *to human experience*, claimed that the usual interpretation of the biblical view of man's predicament in sin could not be true. Samuel Clarke had also written in defense of the "Essence of liberty" lying in the will and reason of moral man. Bishop Butler agreed with them and insisted that, theory to the contrary, "*practice*" prevents us from concluding we may teach man that he is bound in sin and morally *un*-free.[306] Jonathan Edwards, obviously, came to different conclusions than did these writers because he began from different premises. Whence, then, come these premises of his?

---

302 Ibid., 53f.
303 Ibid., 181.
304 Ibid., 20.
305 Romans 1:25ff.
306 Cf. above, 202f.

Wherein lies the source for his evidence concerning man's nature? We have seen that his studies of current thought gave him access to all the wealth of information possessed by these other thinkers, and exposed him also to the climate of opinion which influenced them so obviously. Why did such different conclusions than theirs come from his pen?

The answer, of course, lies in his adherence to the biblical witness. Specifically, it is his view of Christ's death under God's law that explains his position. Commenting on Paul's statement, "For by the law is the knowledge of sin" (Romans 3:20b), Edwards says that "that law by which we come to the knowledge of sin, is the moral law chiefly and primarily ..." Again: "I had not known sin but by the law," says Paul (Romans 7:17). The law reveals man's sin, and also, by forbidding it, aggravates "the guilt of the transgressions."[307] What, then, is the content of this law of God which both reveals and provokes the basic inherent in the mind and heart of man?

Negatively, the law may be described as that "one great law of God ... that says, 'if thou sinnest, thou shalt die;' and, 'cursed is every one that continues not in all things contained in this law to do them.'"[308] The positive content of God's law, however, is *love*. The law of the God who is righteous in the beauty of His holy love must be seen in the closest correspondence with the inner nature of His Being (whose law it is). Therefore, "The Scriptures teach us that love is the sum of all that is contained in the law of God, and of all the duties required in His word. This the Scriptures teach of the law in general, and of each table of the law in particular."[309] To be specific: we are called by God in His law to nothing less than to believe with our minds, to love the Lord with all our heart, and with all our souls, and to love our neighbors as ourselves.[310]

This is the very thing we do not do, so we reap the consequence of our sinful un-love of God, which is death. For Adam "died spiritually" even though he still lived on earth; "a dismal alteration was made in his soul by the loss" of the Holy Spirit and His gracious guidance. And he fell under the curse of temporal death – as do all men after him find their

---

307 *Works in Four Volumes*, 4, 82f.
308 Ibid., 100.
309 *Charity and its Fruits*, 11-13. He refers to 1 Timothy 1:5; Matthew 22:37f; Romans 13:9; Galatians 5:14, etc.
310 *Works in Four Volumes*, 1, 116f.

souls dismally altered, and their selves subject to death. But that is not all:

> And besides all this, Adam was that day undone in a more dreadful sense: He immediately fell under the curse of the law, and condemnation to eternal perdition. In the language of Scripture, he is *dead*, that is, in a state of condemnation to death ...[311]

Every man born into the world is born "under the curse of the law, and condemnation to eternal perdition." We are, all of us, in Scripture called "dead." None of us can raise ourselves to a new life with God; none of us can change the basic predilection of our heart towards self-love; worst of all, none of us can pay the price of sin.

The Sacrifice of Christ

The measure of the guilt of man's sin is the measure of the love and obedience he owes to the infinitely good and holy God. Correspondingly, the measure of God's hatred of sin is the measure of His own righteousness, purity, and mercy. Because of this, He instituted the rite of animal sacrifice so that people might come to see the necessity for a "real atonement or satisfaction" being made: "... God did not design, that, in his manner of dealing with mankind, men should be pardoned and accepted without atonement."[312] A crime against an infinitely holy God is itself infinitely heinous. Sacrifices were instituted to show this, and to testify also by their very insufficiency that "a sacrifice of infinite value was necessary, and that God would accept of no other."[313]

No creature could offer such a sacrifice: "Satisfaction for sin must be complete."[314] Not only was the heinous, but the effects of it were far beyond the capacity of man to repair. Nothing man could do could affect the objective situation existing between sinful men and the Holy God: "the defect is in the *corrupted nature* of mankind" and nothing man can do will alter this fact.[315] A bad tree cannot by any stretch of nature produce good fruit. No creature can purchase redemption from such a situation.

---

311 *Works in Four Volumes*, 2, 404.
312 *Works in Four Volumes*, 1, 606f.
313 Ibid.
314 Ibid.
315 See above, 210ff.

But God, in the man Jesus Christ, has done this very thing: "It was a special fruit of the wrath of God against our sins, that He let loose upon Christ the devil, who has the power of death, is God's executioner, and the roaring lion that devours the damned in hell."[316] Christ Jesus took the place of sinful humanity and suffered the infinite wrath of God against evil. He was filled with the sense of God's horror of sin, and God's hatred of it. To a degree no other creature could, He experienced "the clear view of these" dreadful things – human sin and God's hatred and condemnation of it – and endured "immense suffering" on the Cross to pay the price of the sin of the world. The wages of sin is death. The Father hid the face of His mercy from the Son, and so, overwhelmed with God's own full awareness of the hatefulness and horror of sin, uncomforted by the holy fellowship of the Triune Life, Christ died a dreadful death under the moral weight of the world's sin and God's wrath.[317]

The result of His sacrifice is – Redemption! Edwards explains:

> The sacrifice of Christ is a sweet savor, because as such it was a great honor due to God's majesty, holiness and law, and a glorious expression and testimony of Christ's respect to that majesty ... That when He loved man, and so greatly desired his salvation, He had yet so great respect to that majesty and holiness of God, that He had rather die than that the salvation of man should be any injury or dishonor unto those attributes. And then ... it was a sweet savor, as it was a marvelous act of obedience, and ... expression of a wonderful respect to God's authority. The value of Christ's sacrifice was infinite, both as a propitiation, and as an act of obedience; because He showed an infinite regard to the majesty, holiness, etc., of God, in being at infinite expense from regard to those divine attributes.[318]

The contrast between this Man and all other men is thus put in its starkest form: they hate the holiness of God – He loves His Father; they despise the law of the Father – He dies to maintain it; they hate and kill each other – He dies for their salvation; their actions do nothing to alter the situation between Earth and Heaven – His action does everything. Therefore, "the blood of Christ washes also from the filth of sin, as it purchases sanctification; it makes way for it by satisfying, and purchases it by the merit of obedience implied in it."[319] His

---

316 *Works in Four Volumes*, 1, 606f.
317 Ibid., 603.
318 Ibid., 610.
319 Ibid.

blood takes away our guilt; His Spirit overcomes our sin. "What Christ purchased for us is that we might have communion with God and His good, which consists in partaking or having communion of the Holy Ghost ..."[320] By the sacrifice of Christ, the relationship between God and humans is altered, and God's age-old promise to bless men begins to be fulfilled through the outpouring of His Spirit. What man's reason cannot see in the death of Christ is explained to us by the Holy Spirit, by His (internal) corroboration of the biblical witness to the work of the incarnate Son.

> What Christ purchased for us, is that we might have communion with God in His good, which consists in partaking or having communion of the Holy Ghost ... All the blessedness of the redeemed consists in partaking of the Spirit that is given Him not by measure ... All our good is of God the Father, and through God the Son, and all is in the Holy Ghost, as He is Himself all our good. And so God is Himself the portion and purchased inheritance of His people ... The Spirit of God may produce effects upon the inanimate things, as of old He moved on the face of the waters. But he communicates holiness in His own proper nature only, in those holy effects in the hearts of the saints.[321]

Thus sinners on earth find themselves changed – in their hearts – by the power of God, for He who died on earth has ascended to Heaven, whence He pours out upon believers the fruit of His sacrifice and obedience. Thus they find in themselves love to God, which they did not have before, and love of His holiness which they formerly despised. Arminians to the contrary, what men must hear is the message of Jesus Christ who *died* to *deliver* them from *bondage* to *sin*. Only thus will they receive the Word which changes their hearts and fills them with the Holy Spirit.[322]

Election

Christ's purchase of the Holy Spirit, however, did not and will not put into the hands of all people the opportunity or the capacity whereby they might then of themselves change their relationship to God, and attain unto salvation. Neither the *purchase* nor the *gift* of redemption (of the Holy Spirit and His benefits, that is) is a matter within the control of humans: "That is, they which are the children of the flesh,

---

320 Grossart, *op. cit.*, 50.
321 Ibid., 50f.
322 *Works in Four Volumes*, 1, 409ff.

these are not the children of God: but the children of the promise are counted for the seed." And, "it is not of him that willeth, nor of him that runneth, but of God that sheweth mercy" (Romans 9:8, 16).

In his private notebooks, in a section entitled "Miscellaneous Observations on Divine Decrees in General, and Election in Particular," Edwards clarified his view of God's Electing and Providential work.[323] As in his work on *Freedom of the Will*, so here he combats the Arminian objections to Reformation interpretations of Scripture. Against the notion that God has not planned all of His actions that will ever occur in the world, Edwards asserts that He has not only planned, He has *decreed* what will come to pass. He sees it all at a single glance – our past, our present, and ours and the world's future – and all has been foreordained. When the Arminians objected that this makes nonsense of any view of human moral responsibility, Edwards answered that the moral behavior of man is included within God's foreordination in such a way as not to deny his exercise of his faculties. Such an answer, of course, satisfied his opponents no better than had Calvin's. But, like Calvin, Edwards was serious in his affirmation of man's actual responsibility for his behavior. Man's sin, said Edwards, is *man's*; God has foreseen that it would take such a course, and have such consequences, and has decided before the creation of the world what He will do with regard to it. Sin is employed to serve His will. Nothing that occurs frustrates His work. "Even the free actions of men are subject to God's disposal," said Edwards, citing Lamentations 3:37 – "who is he that saith, and it cometh to pass, and the Lord commanded it not?"[324]

When Arminians objected that this also makes nonsense of prayer, Edwards replied:

> When God decrees to give the blessing of rain, He decrees the prayers of His people; and when He decrees the prayers of His people for rain, He very commonly decrees rain; and thereby there is a harmony between these two decrees ... when He decrees striving, then He often decrees the obtaining the kingdom of God; when He decrees the preaching of the gospel, then He decrees the bringing home of souls to Christ ... when He decrees calling, then He decrees justification; and when He decrees justification, then He decrees everlasting glory. Thus, all the decrees of God are harmonious ...[325]

---

323 *Works in Four Volumes*, 2, 513-546.
324 Ibid., 538.
325 Ibid., 514.

The implications of the Arminian scheme were clear: God was not in control of His world, nor of mankind's collective destiny. Edwards' position was, to them, a frightful determinism that denuded man of his glory and his responsibility, and God of His justice and rationality. But from the point of view of Edwards and those others in the Augustinian and Protestant tradition, any other position was a flat denial not only of much of Scripture, but of the central doctrine of justification by *grace* through faith.

> That election is not from a foresight of works, or conditional as depending on the condition of man's will, is evident by 2 Tim. 1:9, "Who hath saved us, and called us with a holy calling, not according to our works, but according to His own purpose and grace, which was given us in Christ Jesus before the world began."[326]

He appealed also to Philippians 2:13, and to Romans 9:15-16: "I will have mercy on whom I will have mercy, and will have compassion on whom I will have compassion. So then it is not of him that willeth, nor of him that runneth, but of God that showeth mercy." From this Edwards concludes that God "determined that He would see to it, that some should perform the conditions of salvation and be saved; or, which is the same thing, that He would cause that they should be surely saved."[327] Such a view, of course, is the only possible complement to Edwards' position on the power and extent of sin, and the degree to which man is bound by it. Nothing short of God's gracious helping power – at each moment – is sufficient to lift deadened creatures from self-love to the love of God. Were election and faith to depend on man's strength or discernment, in response to the message of Christ, then none would be saved.

The usual cry of "Determinism!" does not always take into account a very important qualification in Edwards' argument. In Paul Ramsey's introduction to Edwards' *Freedom of the Will* the point is made, and very well, that Edwards, like Luther, carefully distinguished between *theological* and *natural* causation or determination. The latter form – natural causation – is clearly conceived within a deterministic, mechanistic framework. The former is not. Ramsey quotes from Luther's *De*

---

326 Ibid., 527.

327 Ibid., 529. Edwards refers here to many Biblical texts for his understanding of election: Titus 2:14, Luke 22:22, Psalm 65:4, Isaiah 41:9, Matthew 20:16, 24:24, John 6:37-46, 8:47, 10:3f, 17:6-20, Acts 18:10, Romans 5:9, 11, 1 Thessalonians 5:9, 1 Peter 2:8, 1 John 4:6, etc.

servo arbitrio to illustrate Edwards' meaning, and we might well do the same. Luther says:

> I could wish, indeed, that we were furnished with some better term for this discussion, than this commonly used term, *necessity*, which cannot rightly be used, either with reference to the human will, or the divine. It is of a significance too harsh and ill-suited for this subject, forcing upon the mind an idea of compulsion, and that which is altogether contrary to *will* ... for Will, whether divine or human, does what it does, be it good or evil, not by compulsion, but by mere willingness or desire, as it were, totally free. (Yet God's immutable will rules over all) ...
>
> But by *necessity*, I do not mean *compulsion*, but (as they term it) the *necessity of immutability* but not of *compulsion*; that is, a man void of the Spirit of God, does not evil against his will as by violence, or as if he were taken by the neck and forced to it ... but he does it spontaneously, and with a desirous willingness. ...On the other hand, when God works in us, the *will*, being changed and sweetly breathed on by the Spirit of God, desires and acts, not from *compulsion*, but *responsively*, from pure willingness, inclination, and accord ... All this we do willingly and desiringly, according to the nature of *will*: for if it were forced, it would be no longer *will*. For compulsion is (so to speak) *unwillingness*.[328]

This statement of Luther's correctly represents Edwards' position also at this point. For Edwards, the providential working of God occurs in such a way as to include the (foreseen and fore-allowed and predetermined) actions of men who, *freely following their inclinations and their desires, do what they really wish to do.* How such a correspondence of divine and human plans could occur is a mystery which Edwards (with Luther and Calvin) did not feel called upon to understand or to explain. That such was the case, however, was, to his mind, the clear import of Scripture.[329]

---

328 *Works* (Yale), 1, 41f. See the whole of this illuminating discussion of Paul Ramsey's, 8-47.

329 See Calvin's treatment in *Institutes*, I, 16-18; III, 21-24.

This being so, the question now is, in what way are people brought by God to salvation? How do they qualify for this blessing? Edwards answers, "All elect men are said to be chosen in Christ ..."[330]

> ... Christ, in His election, is the head of all election, and the pattern of all other election. Christ is the head of all elect creatures; and both angels and men are chosen in Him ... i.e., chosen to be in Him.[331]

Election contains two things: foreknowledge and predestination. Commenting on Romans 8 Edwards shows that the former is God's choosing of persons to be in Christ, and the latter is "a destining them to be conformed to the image of His Son, both in holiness and blessedness ... God chose Christ, and gave His elect people to Him; and so, looking on them as His owned them for His own."[332]

> In destining Christ to eternal life, He destined all parts of Christ to it also ... In His being appointed to life, we are appointed to life. So Christ's election is the foundation of ours, as much as His justification and glorification are the foundation of ours.[333]

The Bible, Edwards says, often speaks of Christ as "the ELECT or CHOSEN of God." All the figures of God's revealing action are but types of the true, the real Elect One. Nor is this to be understood in any Docetic sense, but "This election is not for Christ's works or worthiness, for all His works and worthiness are fruits of it."[334] He is truly the Elect of God, and we, by union with Him, are thus ourselves elected to salvation.

Edwards' position is clearly a flat repudiation of the main lines of Arminian doctrine as these were formulated to deny classical Protestant teaching and also to give expression to the "modern spirit." With the Synod of Dort, Edwards affirmed that election is not conditional upon God's foresight of man's future response, but is absolutely unconditional, based only on the free choice of God. Further, the saving benefits of the work of Christ were not intended to be applied to all of mankind, but only to those whom God chose for everlasting life with Him; Third, the state of man – every man – now is such that he is hopelessly deformed in the depths of his heart by sin, and can do nothing to alter his status with God. Fourth, God, acting graciously, does so with

---

330 *Works in Four Volumes*, 2, 537.
331 Ibid., 536f.
332 Ibid.
333 Ibid.
334 Ibid., 535.

power – He *changes* man's heart, *raises* him from the death of sin, and *irresistibly releases* him from the bondage in which he lay. Finally, God has decreed that He will surely bring to salvation those whom He has justified and sanctified in His Son – they shall persevere to the end, for He will see to it.

Edwards' first public address – at the Harvard Commencement, in his twenty-eighth year – furnished the first of but many occasions to oppose the doctrines of "that modern fashionable divinity" which, he believed, obscured from people the judgment of God on their sin, and withheld, therefore, the message of the Cross, and salvation.[335] In 1734, he and others became seriously alarmed at the spread of the Arminian doctrines. Edwards preached a series of sermons which were the occasion of the conversion of many in his congregation, and were, as well, the apparent earthly instigation of the first remarkable "awakening" in Northampton under his ministry. During the Great Awakening of 1740-1743, it was the claim of the New England Calvinists that convictions of sin, and consequent conversions to Christ and growth in sanctification, were not occurring in parishes whose ministers denied both justification by grace as well as the fact of the outpouring of the Spirit.

To the minds of Edwards and the majority of the Congregational ministers, God's Spirit was being given only where the Word of Christ was being preached. Where "free will," "universalism," "reason," and "humanitarianism" were being proclaimed, sinners were not repenting and coming to Christ. The reason, Edwards held, was quite clear: God never did promise to bless the message of those who taught people to depend on themselves instead of on Him for *all* of their salvation. The Spirit, in other words, would come only where Christ was being offered as man's wisdom, righteousness, sanctification, and redemption. Where any of these functions and offices were being taken away from Him, His Spirit was not honoring the (mutilated) gospel that remained.

Let us summarize what we have said in this section: We began by showing Edwards' view of God's promise of His Spirit to men. This, Edwards believed, is God's eternal purpose behind the creation of all His creatures – to give Himself to them, to be known by them and loved and enjoyed by them. These creatures, however, chose, and ever choose

---

335 See again his commencement sermon, "God Glorified in Man's Dependence
    ..." in *Works in Four Volumes*, 4, 169f; or the Banner of Truth edition of *Select Works*, 2, 33f.

to love themselves and their idols rather than their gracious Creator. God withdraws His Spirit from rebels, and they find themselves sunk in sin, ruined by passions and conceits, dreadfully perverted in every aspect of their beings and totally incapable of changing their relationship to God. They live now under the wrath of a righteous God, who will not see His will flouted nor His plan destroyed.

Through the self-sacrifice of Jesus Christ, the Son of God, the situation between God and man is radically changed. But only through Him! The Law of God is upheld, His righteousness is now not betrayed, but is established both in the death of the Messiah and in the restoration of lost sinners to His love and justice. These latter are destined to salvation, being chosen to be in Christ and to live by His power and love.

Throughout this presentation, we saw Edwards' opposition to those doctrines which denied part of the gospel scheme as he understood the Scriptures to teach it. His reason for doing this is plain: life with God comes through union with Christ. The basis of the new birth is the work of the historical Christ. Through the Spirit's persuading people of the truth of the biblical account of what God in Christ had done for them, their hearts are changed through their minds being opened. God's work for men through Christ is all of a piece. In studying these matters, therefore, we have attended to the foundational doctrines of Edwards' specific view of regeneration.

Having discussed his view of God's *promise* and God's *purchase* of the Holy Spirit to and for men, let us turn now to Edwards' doctrine of God's *gift* of His Holy Spirit.

The Gift of the Spirit

Regeneration was a topic of burning interest to Puritans, and the number of sermons and books in which they dealt with this grand theme is legion. This issue gradually became a bone of contention between them and those other Anglicans who fell under the influence of Arminian and humanistic thought. Eventually, the Established Church was able to be characterized as almost solidly Arminian on the subject of regeneration. In plain terms, this included a serious repudiation of the notion of sudden conversion and an insistence upon gradual or nurtured growth in sanctification, logically following ecclesiastical baptism. The latter, indeed, came to be viewed, *in effect*, as a guarantee of grace, *ex opere operato*, however much the Roman term itself might be disallowed.

It is not unfair to characterize the view of later New England Puritanism as "Arminian" in this corrupted sense. As conversions came to be less frequent, the churches adapted themselves to a situation and to a view of church life which accorded more with the apparent realities of current experience. These realities did not, as often as in a previous generation, include decisive, life-changing conversion to Christ. When new birth has occurred or is assumed to have occurred, it is natural that the emphasis should shift then to growth and, therefore, in terms of the Church's task, to nurture. The current massive emphasis on Christian education in the established churches of modern American Protestantism – as contrasted with the overwhelming emphasis even in the nineteenth century on conversion and evangelization – is probably a fair analogy and parallel to the experience and practice of early eighteenth-century New England Protestant church life. For there, too, the emphasis was on "growth." More and more, people were urged to attend the "means of grace" as a way of securing favor with God. Unquestionably, there was a much greater emphasis on God's grace and His work in converting men, than there is today in many Protestant churches: nevertheless, while more theologically explicit, the pattern still boiled down to: "attend the means of grace." In his study, *Revivalism and Separatism in New England*, C.C. Goen wrote:

> ... many ministers, while still holding verbally to the doctrine of election, had taught the necessity for nurture and had fostered a doctrine of preparation. The result was that regeneration, if it came at all, was so subtle as scarcely to be cognizable; and even before the adoption of the Half-Way Covenant, it was generally presumed that those who were faithful in the use of means were assured of salvation. The spread of Stoddardeanism accentuated this kind of thinking, so that by the time of the Great Awakening salvation was thought to come chiefly through the performance of religious duties enjoined by the clergy.[336]

Perry Miller has also underscored the profound shift in emphasis which occurred in the later generations of New England Puritans, and we must comprehend this seismic shift in theological climate in order to appreciate the nature of the controversies which arose because of the revivals of Edwards' time.[337] Solomon Stoddard's practice of admitting professed unbelievers to the Holy Communion on the grounds that the

---

336 C.C. Goen, *Revivalism and Separatism in New England* (New Haven: Yale University Press, 1962), 41.

337 See Perry Miller's chapter, "The Covenant of Grace," in *The New England Mind: The seventeenth-century*.

sacrament was a "converting ordinance" was a prime example of the pass to which Puritan church life had come. Edwards' later decision to reverse his grandfather's policy was based on a different view of God's working and man's responsibility. His adherence to his belief, as we saw, cost him his pulpit.[338]

Nowhere does Edwards display his indebtedness to his Puritan background better than in his exposition of the doctrine of regeneration. Both in his agreements with, and sharp divergences from, the theory and practice of classical Puritanism, we see his relationship with his "fathers in the faith." Let us, then, first examine certain *statements* of his, defining his doctrine. Following this, we shall study in detail his *explanations* of his meaning, in connection with the views of earlier as well as contemporary Puritans.

In his seminal work on *Original Sin* Edwards writes:

> If we compare one Scripture with another, it will be sufficiently manifest that by regeneration, or being *begotten*, or *born again*, the same change in the state of the mind is signified with that which the Scripture speaks of as effected in true *repentance* and *conversion*. I put repentance and conversion together, because the Scripture puts them together, Acts 3:19, and because they plainly signify much the same thing. The word (repentance) signifies a *change of the mind*; as the word conversion means a *change* or *turning* from sin to God. And ... this is the same change with that which is called *regeneration* (excepting that this latter term especially signifies the change, as the mind is *passive* in it) ...[339]

This change in man is what is necessary for him to become a member of Christ and an inheritor of the biblical promises. It is in this transformation "that ... saving *faith* is attained"; quoting John 1:12-13 ("But as many as received him, to them gave he power to become the sons of God, even to them that *believe* on his name, which are *born*, not of blood ... but of *God*.") Edwards comments: "And so it is with a being born again or born of God ..."[340]

---

338 See above, page 74

339 *Works in Four Volumes*, 2, 466. In this section Edwards is showing the biblical foundation for the Christian doctrine of original sin "from what the Scripture teaches of the application of Redemption." Ibid., 466-467. The emphases in this and the following quotations are Edwards' own.

340 Ibid.

"The change that men pass under at their repentance, is expressed and exhibited by baptism. Hence it is called the *baptism of repentance* ... Matt. 3:11; Lk. 3:3; Acts 13:24, and 19:4. And so is regeneration, or being born again, expressed by baptism ... John 3:5, 'Except a man be born of water and of the Spirit.' – Titus 3:5, 'He saved us by the washing of regeneration.'"[341]

It is important to note that for Edwards, and for Puritans generally, none of the sacraments or ordinances were thought to work automatically, *ex opere operato.* God's grace is no prisoner of ecclesiastical management. The baptism of *water* performed by the church is meant to be but a *sign* of the baptism of the Holy Spirit which God alone can work, when and as and how He will. In Edwards' words, "the *sign*, exclusive of the thing signified" is worthless.[342] This understanding was basic to Reformed theology. It lay at the heart of the Church of England's repudiation of the Roman Catholic doctrine of grace. It informs most of the *Book of Common Prayer* – its services, prayers, and Articles of Religion – and it was taken over entire by the English Puritans. Later Anglican writers – notably the Oxford Tractarians – attempted to cite isolated statements from the *Book of Common Prayer* as proof-texts supporting the Roman Catholic doctrine of grace, and of sacraments in particular. The massive fifty-four volume Parker Society edition of the works of the Anglican Reformers demonstrated for all time the essential Protestantism of the Anglican Reformation. English Puritans were steeped in this tradition.

Many who are baptized by water show in their lives that they were never baptized by the Holy Spirit. The rite, however, is nevertheless the sign of the reality – the gift of the Holy Spirit – which God alone can, and which God alone does, give to those whom He has chosen in Christ to be His adopted children.[343] Baptism of believers is meant to be a sign of

341 Ibid., 467.

342 *Works in Four Volumes*, 1, 186.

343 See C.B. Moss' *The Christian Faith* (London: S.P.C.K., 1965) for a modern restatement of the Roman Catholic doctrine introduced into Anglicanism by the Oxford Tractarians. Also, *A General Index* (Cambridge: The University Press, M.DCCCLV, 90-96) to the Parker Society volumes gives exhaustive references to the true Anglican position on this matter. The citations in the writings of Jewel, Cranmer, Tyndale, Hooper, Rogers, Coverdale, and Whitaker are of special pertinence. W.H. Griffith Thomas observes, concerning the true Reformation (rather than Roman) interpretation of the words in the *Book of Common Prayer* "Service of Baptism," "Seeing now that this child is regenerate," "... leading Puritans never objected to the words ... nor did Baxter later on, be-

their prior baptism of repentance. In the case of their children, it signifies the infants' entrance into the visible church, the sphere of God's
gracious saving work, the reality of which must later be acknowledged
when the infants themselves grow and come to a personal acquaintance with the Lord.[344] Ordinances, such as preaching, Holy Communion, and Baptism, are important. The influential Richard Sibbes had
written:

> Attend upon the ordinances of God, the communion of saints
> … and the Spirit of God will slide into our souls in the use of
> holy means …
>
> Will the Spirit work when we neglect the ordinance? It is but a
> pretence … holiness comes from the Spirit, and the Spirit will
> work by His own ordinances."[345]

This, of course, is but the consequence of the Puritans' insistence that
the Spirit refers to God's Word, establishes it, and works according to
it. What the Scripture records as commands of the Word (preaching,
baptizing, communion) must, therefore, of course, be faithfully
observed by the church.

The "means of grace," however, were not to be deified, as the Protestants were convinced Rome had done. Sibbes writes:

> Trust not in the sacraments above their place … the papists …
> attribute too much to the sacraments, as some others do too
> little. They attribute a presence there. They make it an idol.
> …Oh, there is I know not what presence. …there is grace *by
> them*, though not *in* them.[346]

Baptism, therefore, is a *sign* of the *reality* which God only can perform.
The church does its part in prayer and in hope, when it performs the
washing of water. But no man in the church can presume to judge
another's soul, whether on the basis of the Roman Catholic doctrine of
ex opere operato, or whatever.[347]

---

cause Whitgift had said that the Reformers taught that Sacraments did not con-
tain, but only sealed grace." *The Principles of Theology* (London: Church Book
Room Press, 1956), 384. Compare Augustine's treatment in his *On Baptism,
Against the Donatists*, English translation in volume IV of the First Series of the
Nicene and Post-Nicene Fathers (Grand Rapids: Eerdmans, 1956), 411-514. See
especially 456ff.

344 See Nuttall's treatment, *op. cit.*, 90-101.

345 Quoted in Nuttall, *op. cit.*, 91.

346 Ibid.

347 For more on Edwards' doctrine of baptism see *Works in Four Volumes*, 1, 106,

Edwards continues his statement of the doctrine of regeneration by referring to another biblical term:

> The change which a man passes under when born again, and in his repentance and conversion, is the same that the Scripture calls the *circumcision of the heart*. Deut. 30:6, 'and the Lord thy God will *circumcise thy heart*, and the *heart* of thy seed, to love the Lord thy God with all thine heart, and with all they soul.'[348]

It is by this circumcision of the heart that people become "Jews *inwardly*"; this circumcision of heart that must occur for them to become true Christians. This is, simply, conversion, "being the putting off of the body of the sins of the flesh."[349]

Edwards develops his statement of this doctrine even further:

> This inward change, called *regeneration and circumcision of the heart*, which is wrought in *repentance* and *conversion*, is the same with that spiritual *resurrection* so often spoken of, and represented as a *dying unto sin, and living unto righteousness* ...[350]

From Romans 6:3-5 and 11, he concludes that "this spiritual resurrection is that change, in which persons are brought to habits of holiness and to the divine life ..."[351] This "spiritual resurrection" is a "*being born again*" and "*begotten*." As Christ is called "the first-born from the dead" (Colossians 1:18) and "the first-begotten of the dead" (Revelation 1:5), so Christians, in their "*conversion*, or *spiritual resurrection*," are said to be truly "*risen with Christ*, and are *begotten* and born with Him."[352]

Furthermore, this change is no mere option of the Christian life or special work of a spiritual "elite." It is, on the contrary, "the same with that being *born again*, which Christ says is *necessary* for everyone in order to his seeing the kingdom of God" (John 3:3f).[353]

---

160 (for his justification of infant baptism), 111, 130, 185f; *Works in Four Volumes* 4, 120, 171. In this last reference he says: "It is of God that we have ordinances, and their efficacy depends on the immediate influence of the Spirit of God."

348 *Works in Four Volumes*, 2, 467.
349 Ibid., 467f, where he refers to Colossians 2:11-13.
350 Ibid., 468.
351 Ibid.
352 Ibid. He refers also to 1 Peter 1:3 and Acts 26:18.
353 Ibid.

At this point we must refer to Edwards' interpretation of the specific relationship of the converted person to Jesus Christ. In his lectures on *Justification by Faith Alone,* he refers to the new life of a person spiritually resurrected through the gospel and adds:

> The obedience of a Christian, so far as it is truly evangelical and performed with the Spirit of the Son sent forth into the heart, has all relation to Christ, the Mediator, and is but an expression of the soul's believing union to Christ. All evangelical works are works of that faith that worketh by love; and every such act of obedience, wherein it is inward and the act of the soul, is only a new, effective act of reception of Christ, an adherence to the glorious Saviour ... Gal. 2:20 ... Col. 3:17.[354]

In another place, after speaking of Christ's being ingrafted into the stock of David, and thus into the whole church, thereby making all its members participants in the blessings of the "seed of Abraham," and proper children of David, he adds:

> Christ is ingrafted into every believer; every believer is ingrafted into Christ ... For the believer is not only in Christ, but Christ in him. Christ is born in the soul of the believer and brought forth there ... *Grace in the soul is Christ there.*[355]

Christ is thus ingrafted in persons through the propagation, and the reception through faith, of the gospel:

> Christ is ingrafted by the word's being ingrafted, which is able to save the soul. Not only the *written* or *spoken* word is ingrafted, but the *personal* word, which eminently is able to save the soul. Grace in the soul is Christ there.[356]

This, of course, is completely consistent with what John Calvin had written:

> But since Christ has been so imparted to you with all His benefits that all His things are made yours, that you are made a member of Him, indeed one with Him ... We ought not to

---

354 *Works in Four Volumes,* 4, 106-107.

355 *Images or Shadows of Divine Things,* Perry Miller, ed. (New Haven: Yale University Press, 1948), 114-115.

356 Ibid. Compare with Calvin, *Institutes,* III, ii, 1, 6, 7, 8, 24. Neither Calvin nor Edwards meant by this, however, the "mysticism" that is sometimes ascribed to them. See the fine explanation of Calvin's real meaning in Francois Wendel, *Calvin: Origins and Development of His Religious Thought,* translated by Philip Mairet (New York: Harper & Row, 1963), 234ff. Also Niesel, *The Gospel and the Churches,* 184f.

separate Christ from ourselves or ourselves from Him. Rather we ought to hold fast bravely with both hands to that fellowship by which He has bound Himself to us ... Christ is not outside us, but dwells within us. Not only does He cleave to us by an invisible bond of fellowship, but with a wonderful communion, day by day, He grows more and more into one body with us ...[357]

This relationship with Christ, therefore, is the context in which Edwards' statements concerning the change in people effected in regeneration must be read. The change in persons which occurs in regeneration when they are "circumcised in heart," "converted," made "repentant" and spiritually "raised from the dead" is, says Edwards, "the same change which is meant when the Scripture speaks of making the *heart* and *spirit* new, or giving a *new heart* and spirit." He explains, "Conversion is the turning of the heart; which is the same thing as changing it, so that there shall be another heart, or a *new* heart, or a new spirit." It is "a spiritual resurrection ... of the spirit, or rising to begin a *new* existence in life, as to the *mind, heart,* or *spirit*."[358] The emphasis is on the "new existence in life." What Christ described to Nicodemus was what Ezekiel had foretold of the new heart and new spirit – God's own Spirit – which would be given to Israel in the days of the Messiah (Ezekiel 36:25f).

> Here God speaks of having a *new heart* and *spirit*, by being *washed with water*, and receiving the *Spirit of God*, as the qualification of God's people that shall enjoy the privileges of the kingdom of the messiah. How much is this like the doctrine of Christ to Nicodemus, of being *born again of water, and of the spirit*? We have another like prophecy in Ezek. 11:19.[359]

This, of course, is the intent of the biblical statements concerning the "putting off of the *old man*, and putting on the *new man*." The new birth brings forth a new man. The old man of *flesh* (i.e., his heart oriented not to God but to the world), who is born in the image of "the earthly Adam," is put away by the Spirit who makes us to be born "in the image of the *second man*, the *new man*, who is made a quickening spirit, and is the Lord from heaven, and the head of the new creation."[360] A passage

---

357 *Institutes*, III, ii.
358 *Works in Four Volumes*, 2, 469.
359 Ibid.
360 Ibid., 469-470.

from Edwards' private notebooks aptly summarizes this aspect of his belief:

> Hence we learn that the prime alteration that is made in conversion, that which is first and the foundation of all, is the alteration of the temper and disposition of the spirit of the mind. For what is done in conversion is nothing but conferring the Spirit of God, which dwells in the soul and becomes there a principle of life and action. 'Tis this is the new nature, and the divine nature; and the nature of the soul being changed, it admits divine light. Divine things now appear excellent, beautiful, glorious ...[361]

In this sense, Christians are said to be "new creatures," and this is why the emphasis on *creation* is so important. The new birth in the Spirit is such that the person is really "*created again* ... So creating a new heart is called *creating a clean heart*, Ps. 51:10, where the word translated *create*, is the same that is used in the first verses of Genesis." So Paul says, "put on the new man, which after God is *created* in righteousness and true holiness" (Ephesians 4:24; Cf. also 4:22, 23; Colossians 3:9, 10; 2 Corinthians 5:17).[362]

Such a "conferring the Spirit of God" is, as we saw earlier, "the sum of all grace, holiness, comfort and joy; or, in one word, of all the spiritual good Christ purchased for men in this world ..." It is also the sum of "all perfection, glory and eternal joy, that He purchased for them in another world." It is, as well, the sum of all God's promises to His elect people, because the "conferring the Spirit of God" is the *end for which God made the world*.[363] This is just what it means when it is said "God glorifies Himself." He does so by the personal communion with His creatures through His Spirit's dwelling within them, as in a temple, giving them new life from the death of sin, and new love and new dispositions which are appropriate to fellowship with Him. Their minds are changed, and their hearts likewise, by being filled with love to God and joy in His fellowship. As "God is glorified within Himself" in two ways, by His self-manifestation in the Person of the Son, and by "enjoying and delighting in Himself, by flowing forth in infinite love and delight ... in His Holy Spirit," so also,

> ... God glorifies Himself towards the creatures also two ways: 1. By appearing to them, being manifested to their understanding. 2. In communicating Himself to their hearts, and in their

---

361 Townsend, *op. cit.*, 249.
362 *Works in Four Volumes*, 2, 471-472.
363 See above, 194-199.

> rejoicing in, and enjoying, the manifestations which He makes
> of Himself … God is glorified not only by His glory's being
> seen, but by its being rejoiced in. …His glory is then received by
> the whole soul, both by the understanding and by the heart.[364]

This passage is integral to Edwards' thought, for it expresses a determinative concept (as we saw in our previous chapter). The outworking of his positions on God's Word and Spirit, *ad intra* and *ad extra*, therein expressed, will be seen to be basic to his explanations of his doctrine of regeneration, to which we now turn.

Divine Light

"The simile of light," writes G.F. Nuttall in his study of the role of the Spirit in English Puritanism, "… occurs again and again in these writers, and forms the link in their thought between experience and intuitive reason."[365] He supports this statement with a number of quotations from various representatives of the Puritan movement, one of which, from John Owen, is particularly helpful for our study of Edwards:

> The true Nature of Saving Illumination consists in this, that it
> gives the Mind such a direct intuitive insight and prospect into
> Spiritual Things, as that in their own Spiritual Nature they suit,
> please, and satisfie it.[366]

In August, 1733, Edwards preached a sermon to his people in Northampton which so pleased them that they persuaded him to publish it. The following year it appeared under the title, "A Divine and Supernatural Light, Immediately Imparted to the Soul, by the Spirit of God, Shown to be Both a Scriptural and Rational Doctrine."[367] Perry Miller has said, "that the whole of Edwards' system is contained in miniature within some ten or twelve pages in this work." Perhaps this is saying too much, yet this treatise is certainly of utmost importance for comprehending Edwards' theology, and we will look at it now. In doing so, we shall find ourselves in total disagreement with Miller's interpretation. His portrait of Edwards as a "cryptic," "secretive" man hiding what he believes, holding back the inner meaning of truth in his writings which are "immense cryptogram," more a "hoax" than a plain statement of belief, "not to be read but to be seen through" – this we consider a construction of Miller's imagination which is not warranted

---

364 Townsend, *op. cit.*, 133.
365 *Op. cit.*, 40.
366 Ibid., 41.
367 *Works in Four Volumes*, 4, 438-450.

by the evidence he adduces in its support. Such a construction is made possible, we believe by a neglect of the role in Calvinistic and Puritan theology of those terms and categories Miller emphasizes in relation to Edwards' study of John Locke. We consider this important work of Edwards' to be an exceptionally able exposition of the doctrine contained in the words of John Owen which we quoted above. Let us see how this is so.[368]

Edwards bases this work, "A Divine and Supernatural Light," upon Matthew 16:17 where Christ says to Peter, "Blessed art thou ... for flesh and blood hath not revealed it unto thee, but my Father which is in heaven." What had been revealed to Peter was the confession: "Thou art Christ, the Son of the living God." No man – no creature of flesh and blood – could reveal such things. Only the direct, immediate working of God in Peter's mind had shown him the truth of Christ. This was done by "the gracious distinguishing influence and revelation of the Spirit of God."[369] From this Edwards concludes, "that there is such a thing as a Spiritual and Divine Light, immediately imparted to the soul by God, of a different nature from any that is obtained by natural means."[370]

This light must be distinguished from "the convictions that natural[371] men have of their sin and misery," or any feeling they may have of guilt. These "convictions" may indeed be from God, but they are not evidence of His *saving* work, or of His giving Himself in fellowship to these men. The distinction is of absolute importance. Edwards explains:

> He may indeed act *upon* the mind of a natural man, but He acts *in* the mind of a saint as an indwelling vital principle. He acts upon the mind of an unregenerate person as an extrinsic, occasional agent; for in acting upon them, He does not unite Himself to them ... But He unites Himself with the mind of a saint, takes him for His temple, actuates and influences him as a new supernatural principle of life and action. There is this difference, that

---

368 Perry Miller, *Jonathan Edwards*, 44, 46-50, etc. Miller's highly subjective and very questionable construction appears at many points in his provocative study. We think, however, that it renders much of his interpretation of Edwards void. See also 188, 208, 210f, 262, 263, etc. Throughout, Miller really ignores the role of Calvin and Puritanism in Edwards' thought. Compare, for instance, Calvin, *Institutes*, III, ii, 33, with Edwards' doctrine here under discussion.

369 *Works in Four Volumes*, 4, 438-439.

370 Ibid.

371 That is, unconverted.

the Spirit of God, in acting in the soul of a godly man, exerts and communicates Himself there in His own proper nature. Holiness is the proper nature of the Spirit of God. The Holy Spirit operates in the minds of the godly, by uniting Himself to them, and living in them, and exerting His own nature in the exercise of their faculties. ...So that the subject is thence denominated spiritual.[372]

Employing the classical distinction between "common" and "special" grace, he says: "Common grace differs from special in that it influences only by assisting of nature; and not by imparting grace, or bestowing any thing above nature."[373] In other words, God raised up Cyrus to do His will, and to be moved with compassion for the plight of the Jews. But this does not mean, necessarily, that in thus moving Cyrus' heart God was also giving Himself in fellowship to him. God *works on* and *upon* and even *within* unconverted men. He does not give Himself in fellowship to them.

Edwards then underscores the common Puritan theme, that the "Spiritual Light" God gives men by His Spirit does not contain "any new truths or propositions not contained in the word of God ..." What the Spirit does is to enforce the truth and power to which the Word witnesses.[374]

This "Spiritual Light" therefore is not to be equated with natural man's "conscience," as Lord Herbert and others wished to do. God may move men's consciences without giving Himself to them. Nor is a person's zeal for religion any sign of the indwelling Spirit's work. Mere natural man is often able to be affected with the story of Christ's dying love, and other matters. An eloquent speaker can move men's hearts with "an affecting view of divine things ... but God alone can give a spiritual discovery of them."[375]

What, then, is this "Spiritual Light" which is given by God to the newborn Christian? It is, says Edwards, "a true sense of the divine excellency of the things revealed in the word of God, and a conviction of the truth and reality of them thence arising."[376]

To appreciate this point we refer back to the previous discussion concerning God's two ways of glorifying Himself: through His Word,

---

372 Ibid., 440.
373 Ibid., 439.
374 Ibid., 441.
375 Ibid.
376 Ibid.

and through His Spirit, *ad extra* and *ad intra*. Hear now what he says in another sermon concerning the role of man's understanding in conversion. This sermon is entitled, "The Importance and Advantage of a Thorough Knowledge of Divine Truth," and was preached in 1739. In this, he says:

> Such is the nature of man, that nothing can come at the heart, but through the door of the understanding: and there can be no spiritual knowledge of that of which there is not first a rational knowledge. It is impossible that any one should see the truth or excellency of any doctrine of the gospel, who knows not what that doctrine is. A man cannot see the wonderful excellency and love of Christ in doing such an such things for sinners, unless his understanding be first informed how those things were done. He cannot have a taste of the sweetness and divine excellency of such and such things contained in divinity, unless he first have a notion that there are such and such things.[377]

Now let us turn back to his sermon on "A Divine and Supernatural Light," and see there his development of the proposition that this light is "a true sense of the divine excellency of the things revealed in the word of God, and a conviction of the truth and reality of them thence arising."[378]

"A spiritual and saving conviction of the truth and reality of these things, arises," says Edwards, "from such a sight of their divine excellency and glory; so that this conviction of their truth is an effect and natural consequence of this sight of their divine glory." A person who receives this is not only rationally convinced, but he has "a real *sense* of the excellency of God and Jesus Christ, and of the work of redemption, and the ways and works of God revealed in the gospel." He is made to see and to feel and to know the "divine and superlative glory in these things" – to *sense* them more strongly than he senses honey with his mouth, or the ground with his feet. He has more than a "merely rational belief that God is glorious"; he has a heartfelt sense and appreciation, a moving and powerful awareness of the "loveliness" and "holiness" and "gloriousness of God" implanted in his heart.[379]

The epistemological basis for this is found in what Edwards describes as a "two-fold understanding or knowledge of good that God has made the mind of man capable of." The first he calls "merely speculative or

---

377 Ibid., 5.
378 Ibid., 441.
379 Ibid., 441-442.

notional." The second is "that which consists in the sense of the heart ... the will, or inclination, the heart, is mainly concerned."[380] This distinction was, of course, a favorite one with the Reformers, in their controversies with Rome. Emphasizing the need for the second, heartfelt knowledge, Calvin says, "Whoever is moderately versed in Scripture will understand ... that when we have to do with God, nothing is achieved unless we begin from the inner disposition of the heart."[381] This clear distinction and the consequent emphasis not only on the intellectual but also on the heartfelt, personal acquaintance with the Lord through the faithful hearing of the doctrine of Christ, became a hallmark of Puritan preaching. With all due respect to the influence of John Locke on Edwards, we must disagree with Perry Miller at this point: the importance of the "sense of the heart" in his theology is a plain development of Calvinistic, and especially Puritan, thought and preaching. Let us hear once again its expression through John Calvin as he speaks of the right reception of the Gospel:

> For it is a doctrine not of the tongue but of life. It is not apprehended by the understanding and memory alone, as other disciplines are, but it is received only when it possesses the whole soul, and finds a seat and resting place in the inmost affection of the heart ... We have given the first place to the doctrine in which our religion is contained, since our salvation begins with it. But it must enter our heart and pass into our daily living, and so transform us into itself that it may not be unfruitful for us ... its efficacy ought to penetrate the inmost affections of the heart, take its seat in the soul, and affect the whole man a hundred times more deeply than the cold exhortations of the philosophers![382]

Edwards, therefore, was clearly in the line of succession from Calvin through Puritanism when he placed such an emphasis on the necessity for a "two-fold understanding or knowledge of" God and the Gospel.[383]

When the Holy Spirit imparts to a person this twofold form of knowledge of Him, giving a "true *sense* of the divine excellency of the things revealed in the word of God ...," then that person is really *convinced* of the "truth and reality" of these things.[384]

---

380 Ibid., 442.
381 *Institutes*, III, iii, 16.
382 Ibid., III, vii, 4. See Nuttall, *op. cit.*, 38ff.
383 See Edwards' treatment of this in Townsend, *op. cit.*, 113-126.
384 *Works in Four Volumes*, 4, 442.

This "conviction of the truth" of the gospel is brought about in several ways: a person's prejudices against God's revelation are removed, he hears the word with new ears, and he sees God's world with new eyes. His mind is opened "to the force of arguments" which formerly he despised. Furthermore, his mind is positively inclined towards the doctrines of Christ, and actively assisted by the Spirit in learning and understanding God's revelation. His attention is called more often to it, the power of his mind enlarged in the study of it, and his judgment assisted in understanding its truth. From this, his enjoyment of God's revelation is vastly increased in such studies: Edwards says, "The beauty and sweetness of the object draws on the faculties, and draws forth their exercises; so that reason itself is under far greater advantages for its proper and free exercise."[385] The "superlative beauty" of God and His ways with men is powerfully impressed upon the Christian's mind and heart, and he needs no proof that such things are of God:

> There is a beauty in them that is so divine and godlike, that is greatly and evidently distinguished of them from things merely human, or that men are the inventors and authors of; a glory that is so high and great, that when clearly seen, commands assent to their divinity and reality.[386]

God's ways, being revealed in this way, plainly commend themselves as *God's* ways. "This evidence that they that are spiritually enlightened have of the truth of the things of religion is a kind of intuitive and immediate evidence. They believe the doctrines of God's word to be divine because they see divinity in them ..."[387]

This, then, is that type of conviction of the truth of the gospel which the Spirit imparts to men in giving them saving faith. Unconverted persons have nothing of this.

In the second part of the sermon, Edwards considers in more detail the manner by which this "Divine and Supernatural Light" is given to people. He begins by showing that man's "natural faculties" are made use of. Indeed, these faculties are the "subjects of this light" and in such a way "that they are not merely passive, but active in it; the acts and exertions of man's understanding are concerned and made use of in it." To the complete surprise of those who claimed Calvinism to be but a deterministic system in which men were shoved about as if they were stones, Edwards insisted that "God, in letting this light into the soul,

---

385 Ibid., 442-443.
386 Ibid.
387 Ibid., 443.

deals with man according to his nature, or as a rational creature; and makes use of his human faculties."[388]

Not only that, but God also makes use of "outward means" in order to convey this "Supernatural Light" to men. This "Light" is not given as it once was to prophets and apostles; it is, on the contrary, given through the use of their testimony. So "it is not given without the word. The gospel is made use of in this affair: this light is the light of the glorious gospel of Christ. 2 Cor. 4:4."[389]

The use of "means" does not, however, alter the fact that the giving of this light is an immediate, direct work of God Himself. None of the means He uses have any power in themselves. There are *no* self-operating causes in the entire universe, not even preaching or the Bible. Speaking of the biblical writings, he says, "The word of God is no proper cause of this effect; it does not operate by any natural force in it. The word of God is only made use of to convey to the mind the subject matter of this saving instruction ..."[390] Repeating a previous emphasis, he insists that "a person cannot see the excellency of any doctrine, unless that doctrine be first in the mind. ..." The seeing of it, however, is "immediately from the Spirit of God; though the conveying of the doctrine or proposition may be by the word." He summarizes, "So that the notions that are the subject matter of this light, are conveyed to the mind by the word of God; but that due sense of the heart, wherein this light formally consists, is immediately by the Spirit of God."[391]

In the third part of this sermon, Edwards shows, by many references to Scripture, that this doctrine is biblical. He cites 1 John 3:6, 3 John 11, John 14:19 and 17:3 to show that God gives to men through Jesus Christ a knowledge of Himself not granted to the world. He quotes Matthew 11:25-27, 2 Corinthians 4:6, Galatians 1:15-16, Psalm 119:18, and Psalm 25:14 to prove that this special revelation of God to His chosen people is a direct act of His power, an immediate revealing by "arbitrary operation" and by "gift."[392]

---

388 Ibid.

389 Ibid.

390 Edwards shows himself at this point to be clearly opposed to certain forms of "fundamentalism" that grant to the Bible a power and efficacy Roman Catholicism gives to the sacraments.

391 Ibid., 444.

392 Ibid., 444-445.

What God gives to Christians, then, is something unconverted men have nothing of. It is "a true and saving belief" in the gospel of Christ, in the redemption the Son wrought for the elect. The knowledge of this is given directly by the Holy Spirit at the direction of the Son, whose "sole prerogative" it is to breathe forth His Spirit.[393] The "Divine and Supernatural Light" thus imparted by the presence of the Spirit has its proper correspondence in man's response to it, which is *faith*.

Let us turn now to Edwards' presentaion of *faith* and the role it plays in the regenerating work of the Holy Spirit.

Faith

"Faith," says Edwards, in a brilliant definition of his own view, "is a sensibleness of what is real in the work of redemption." It is the total dependence of the total person on God, believing in and trusting in Him alone for salvation and all that pertains thereto. "Faith abases man, and exalts God, it gives all the glory of redemption to God alone."[394] It is a *belief* in God in Christ, a belief given by the direct action of the Holy Spirit.[395] Hypocrites may *profess* belief in the redemption wrought, but only true Christians can do this *from the heart*, for this is the effect of saving grace in the heart and mind.[396] Faith, therefore, should not be called (as many theologians mistakenly have called it) a "condition" of justification, nor should repentance be so called; both are the work of God Himself, in converting a person to Himself. In fact, "*Conversion* is the condition of justification, because it is that great change by which we are brought from sin to Christ, and by which we become believers in Him ..."[397] In conversion, "our minds" are "changed, that we may believe, and so may be justified."[398]

"Faith unites to Christ, and so gives a congruity to justification, not merely as remaining a dormant principle in the heart, but as being and appearing in its active expressions."[399] All of God's decrees are harmonious, and so also is God's relationship to those who are members of His Son, who are clothed in the Son's righteousness, indwelt by His

---

393 Ibid.
394 Ibid., 178.
395 *Works in Four Volumes*, 1, 131-132.
396 Ibid., 111.
397 *Works in Four Volumes*, 4, 118.
398 Ibid., 119. Edwards departs from the order of discussion favored by Calvin in *Institutes*, III, ii, 1-9.
399 Ibid., 106.

Spirit, and moved to love God and do His will. *This* is the sense in which there can be said to be a "congruity" between man's faith and his justification at the hand of God, a congruity, not of man's deserving, but of the harmony of God's action in relationship with him. It *is* congruous for God to give faith to those whom He has predestined to salvation, and to justify those to whom He gives faith, and for whose account Christ died and rose. By faith in the work of Christ, and by our inclusion in the benefits of His work, we are "made accepted in the beloved" (Ephesians 1:6).

We are justified through faith because our faith is our trustful acceptance and heartfelt appreciation for the union with God given us through the sacrifice of Christ. We are, through faith in the gospel, made members of Christ's body, the people of God. United to Christ, we receive, with Him, His inheritance. "God does not give those that believe a union with or an interest in the Saviour, in reward for faith, but only because faith is the soul's active uniting with Christ, or is itself the very act of union, on their part."[400] Because the saints are truly united with Christ, they are therefore included in His justification and made to be partakers with Him of salvation: "What is *real* in the union between Christ and His people, is the foundation of what is *legal* ..."[401] God pronounces Christians to be justified because they are truly united in fellowship with His Son. Faith is, in essence, "receiving Christ into the heart."[402] Faith has to do, not with a new gift of supernatural power that then becomes a permanent part of man's created nature, but rather with the new direction in which his completed nature is now orientated. Edwards makes here a distinction that drew the ire of many Calvinists in his own time, and in succeeding generations: man, he says, has power to love. What he lacks is the desire, the will to love God with this love he has. Nothing is required of man which is beyond his natural capacity, considering the powers of his human nature. What is required is the proper employment of these capacities in the love and service of God. He explains:

> 'Tis very true that God requires nothing of us as condition of eternal life but what is in our own power, and yet 'tis very true at the same time that it's an utter impossible thing that ever man should do what is necessary in order to salvation, nor do the least towards it, without the almighty operation of the Holy

---

400 Ibid., 70.
401 Ibid., 70-71.
402 *Works in Four Volumes*, 2, 602.

> Spirit of God – yea, except everything be entirely wrought by the Spirit of God.[403]

Faith, then, is not a power or capacity of nature that must be added to what man has. It is rather the new characteristic and determination of mind and heart, the new orientation and inclination that animates him because of the active indwelling of Christ's own Spirit. Through faith, man's heart and will are completely altered. He lives now, for the first time, for Christ.

This distinction, as we said, was not pleasing to many Calvinists, and one might wonder why Edwards employed it. It does serve a useful purpose at this point, however, because it introduces us to the serious claims made by Edwards for man's *personal* change in his conversion. (It serves, as well, to preserve intact the full humanity of man – distorted in his life though it be – as well as point up the true nature of the work of the Spirit in reorienting those called to Christ.) People are fully active in faith, insists Edwards. The Spirit works, and we work, in such a way that "all that men do in real religion is entirely their own act and yet every tittle is wrought by the Spirit of God."[404] Living through faith in Christ, "everything they do, they themselves do, which I suppose none will contradict. 'Tis the exertion of their own power."[405] Through faith their power is exerted in love to God and to men; through their commitment to the gospel of God's Son their hearts are drawn in love and service to Him. Through faith, therefore, Christ reigns as Lord in their hearts.

Edwards describes this in various ways: Faith, he says, "is a belief of a testimony," "the proper act of the soul towards God as faithful," "a belief of the truth, from a spiritual taste and relish of what is excellent and divine ... Believers believe the truth in the love of it. ... The object of faith is the Gospel, as well as Jesus Christ."[406] "Faith is a receiving of Christ"; it is, indeed, "a receiving of Christ into the heart ... it is called obeying the gospel ... It is obeying the doctrine from the heart." It is also "a committing ourselves to Christ," "a being reconciled with God." "To believe in Christ is to hearken to Him as a prophet; to yield ourselves subject to Him as king; and to depend upon Him as a priest."[407]

---

403 Townsend, *op. cit.*, 155.

404 Ibid., 156.

405 Ibid.

406 Note again the classical Protestant insistence that Christ is known only through the knowledge and reception of His redeeming work for us.

407 See his *Treatise* in *Works in Four Volumes*, 2, 601-641. See especially 601-605.

Drawing all these statements together, Edwards says that the essential meaning of the New Testament term *pistis*, faith, is as follows:

> ... the best and clearest and most perfect definition of justifying faith, and the most according to Scripture ... is this, faith is the soul's entirely embracing the revelation of Jesus Christ as our Saviour. The word *embrace* is a metaphorical expression; but I think it much clearer than any proper expression whatsoever ... it is the whole soul according and assenting to the truth, and embracing of it ... It is the soul's entirely acquiescing in this revelation, from a sense of the sufficiency, dignity, glory and excellency of the author of the revelation.[408]

In this connection also faith is a "submitting to the righteousness of God ... It is a receiving the truth with a love to it. It is receiving the love of the truth ..."[409]

The interesting thing about this complex of definitions and explanations is the degree to which Edwards finds himself removed from both the merely notional, intellectualistic views of some of the seventeenth and eighteenth-century Protestant orthodoxy as well as from the subjectivity of contemporary Enthusiasm. With the orthodox, he places the heaviest possible emphasis on the intellectual reception and appropriation of the gospel as well as the accompanying doctrine of Christ. With the enthusiasts he places immense emphasis on the personal, truly loving relationship given in faith between the Christian and the Lord of the church. He was deliberately opposed to those of his contemporaries who settled in either of these two camps, to the detriment of the truth witnessed to by the other. As we shall see in the next chapter, he struggled through preaching and through writing to make each side see the full and intimate relationship between man and Christ given in faith, which must include knowledge *and* love, doctrine *and* the "soul's entirely acquiescing in this revelation, from a sense of glory and excellency of the author of the revelation."[410]

What the Holy Spirit does through the Word, therefore, is to give men this faith in God through Christ. Let us hear Edwards explain once again why this word "faith" is the best term to describe the New Testament view of "the cordial reception of Christ and the truth."

> *First*, this revelation of things spiritual, unseen, strange, and wonderful, is exceedingly remote from all the objects of sense,

---

408 Ibid., 606.
409 Ibid., 605.
410 Ibid.

and those things which we commonly converse with in this world, and also exceedingly alien from our fallen nature; so that it is the first and principal manifestation of the symphony between the soul and these divine things, that it believes them, and acquiesces in them as true. And, *Secondly*, the Lord Jesus Christ, in the gospel, appears principally under the character of a Saviour, and not so much of a person absolutely excellent; and therefore, the proper act of reception of Him, consists principally in the exercise of a sense of our need of Him, and of His sufficiency, His ability, His mercy and love, His faithfulness, the sufficiency of His method of salvation, the sufficiency and completeness of the salvation itself, of the deliverance and of the happiness, and an answerable application of the soul to Him for salvation; which can be expressed so well by no other word but faith, or affiance, or confidence, or trust, and others of the same signification; of which faith, is much the best ... *Thirdly*, we have these things exhibited to us, to be received by us, only by a divine testimony. We have nothing else to hold them forth to us.[411]

This faith is the gift of God the HolySpirit.[412] "No man can say that Jesus is the Lord, but by the Holy Ghost ... Whosoever shall confess that Jesus is the Son of God, God dwelleth in him, and he in God" (1 Corinthians 12:3, John 4:15).

Let us turn now to a consideration of Edwards' exposition of the manner in which God dwells within the hearts of believers, giving such a faith in Christ and in His gospel as has been described. We shall study in this connection the little-known but vitally important, posthumously published *Treatise on Grace*.

Grace

This *Treatise* is perhaps one of the most beautiful of all Edwards' writings, although there is no certain internal or external evidence to indicate when it was written. It was among the manuscripts taken to Scotland by Alexander B. Grossart and published in 1865 with some other short pieces under the title, *Selections from the Unpublished Writings of Jonathan Edwards*. Both the structure and the content of this work are so helpful to our understanding of Edwards at this point that we will follow Edwards' own argument, as we continue to explore his doctrine of regeneration.

411 Ibid., 608.
412 Ibid., 549.

Grace "in the heart," according to the Scriptures, is "no other than the Spirit of God itself dwelling and acting in the heart of a saint ..."[413] Thus Edwards concludes the third and final section of this *Treatise*. We must now see how he reached this conclusion, by what means he supported it, and how he explained it.

The first part of the work is entitled "That Common and Saving Grace Differ, Not Only in Degree, But in Nature and Kind." We recall what was said about "common" and "special" grace in the preceding pages, and the different "spiritual light" given to Christians, of which unregenerate men have nothing. Here Edwards develops the same point from a study of the New Testament passages that tell of the necessity of a "new birth." From John 3:6f, Galatians 5:17f, 6:8, and 1 Corinthians 3:1, he concludes:

> ... it is manifest ... that men that have been the subjects only of the first birth, have no degree of that moral principle or quality that those that are new born have, whereby they have a title to the kingdom of heaven. This principle or quality comes to them no otherwise than by birth, and the birth that it must come by is not, cannot be, the first birth, but must be a new birth.[414]

This new birth is the birth in the Holy Spirit, effected by His application of Christ and His saving work to the mind and soul of the saints. The elect are then said to belong to Christ in a sense that cannot be applied to the unregenerate:

> Rom. 8:9 – 'Now if any man have not the Spirit of Christ, he is none of His'; *and also those that have the Spirit are His.* 1 John 3:24 – 'Hereby we know that He abideth in us by the Spirit which He hath given us.'[415]

This distinction is necessary, Edwards says, from the fact that the Spirit indwells Christians. By His coming, He makes them partake of fellowship with the Triune God. He dwells in them, their lives are changed to conform to Him, and they bear fruits appropriate to their new life. This the unregenerate cannot do. However much he may imitate the "fruits of the Spirit," he cannot really possess and manifest them because the source of them, the Spirit of Christ Himself, does not dwell in him and inform his life (1 Corinthians 2:10-15). The man who has not the Holy Spirit, therefore, is without a "sense of spiritual" things, he is "perfectly

---

413 Grossart, *op. cit.*, 52. See the excellent new edition edited by Paul Helm, *Treatise on Grace* (Cambridge: James Clarke & Co., 1971).
414 Ibid., 10.
415 Ibid., 21.

destitute of any sense, perception, or discerning of the things of the Spirit ... he knows nothing of the matter any more than a blind man of colours." The reason he has no knowledge of spiritual things, of course, is that he has not the Spirit Himself who gives these things, dwelling in him.[416] He has no fellowship with Christ, no communion with God.

> The communion of saints with Christ does certainly very much consist in that receiving of His fullness and partaking of His grace spoken of, John 1:16, 'Of His fullness have we all received, and grace for grace;' and in partaking of that Spirit which God gives not by measure unto Him. Partaking of Christ's holiness and grace, His nature, inclinations, tendencies, love, and desires, comforts and delights, must be to have communion with Christ. Yea, a believer's communion with the Father and the Son does mainly consist in his partaking of the Holy Ghost, as appears by 2 Cor. 3:14 – 'The grace of the Lord Jesus Christ, and the love of God, and the *communion* of the Holy Ghost.'[417]

This communion with Christ, this receiving the Holy Spirit in a new, a spiritual birth, is the result of *saving* grace. *Common* grace is merely the working of God on, or even within, unbelievers; all man's good and happiness in the natural state is the result of this gracious working of God. But this is not the conferring of union with Christ and His salvation; that is what *saving* grace is. The Bible clearly shows, says Edwards, "that those that are in Christ are actually in a state of salvation, and are justified, sanctified, accepted of Christ, and shall be saved."[418]

This saving grace, then, is the coming of the Spirit in such a way as to awaken men from their death in sin, to new life in fellowship with God. It is "a work of creation" on God's part, a "work of resurrection." He calls persons from death to life, and by giving them new ears they are made able to hear and to respond to the call. Regeneration, therefore, is a *sudden* thing, for

> ... there is no medium between being dead and alive. He that is dead has no degree of life: he that has the least degree of life in him is alive ... *conversion is wrought at once.* That knowledge, that reformation and conviction that is preparatory to conversion may be gradually carried on, yet the work of grace upon the soul whereby a person is brought out of a state of total

---

416 Ibid., 21-22.
417 Ibid., 23.
418 Ibid., 23-24. He cites Philippians 3:8-9, 2 Corinthians 5:17, 1 John 2:5, 3:24.

corruption and depravity into a state of grace, to an interest in Christ, and to be actually a child of God, is in a moment.[419]

This passage is important. It shows Edwards' insistence that a person is really born again, spiritually, through regeneration. A new thing is really, effectually brought to pass. Before, a person was dead; now, he is alive. Contrary to what later Puritans had come to think concerning the efficacy of the means of grace and the (probable) obligation God was under to reward those who faithfully attended them, Edwards shows that there is no bridge between Heaven and Earth except that which comes from above. No work of man can cross this gap; without Christ and His Spirit, men are dead in sin. With Him, they are alive. The new life in Christ is a creation *ex nihilo*, as was Christ's raising of a cripple. Commenting on Christ's words upon this occasion, "Verily, verily I say unto you, the hour is coming, and now is, when the dead shall hear the voice of the Son of God, and they that hear shall live" (John 5:25), Edwards remarks:

> ... which words must be understood of the work of conversion. In creation, being is called out of nothing and instantly obeys the call, and in the resurrection the dead are called into life: as soon as the call is given the dead obey.[420]

This, says Edwards, is why conversion is sometimes "spoken of in Scripture" as "calling."[421]

By calling through the Word, the Holy Spirit brings men into new life in Christ and into the fellowship of His people; the called man is not thereby made perfect, but he is made new – he is now activated by a new nature, through a new seed or principle of desire and action implanted in mind and heart. The company of such persons is no longer called the company of sinners but the company of saints. Though sin remains, and struggles with the indwelling Spirit throughout a Christian's entire life on earth, the predominate power and characteristic by which he is now activated are the Holy Spirit. He is, therefore, now called "spiritual."[422]

What, then, is the essence or chief characteristic of this new "principle" or "seed" that distinguishes those who know Christ from those who do

---

419 Ibid., 24f.
420 Ibid.
421 Ibid. He cites Romans 8:28-30, Acts 2:37-39, Hebrews 9:15, 1 Thessalonians 5:23-24, Matthew 4:18-22, 9:6.
422 Ibid., 24f.

not? In the second part of this *Treatise on Grace* Edwards shows that "That principle in the soul of the saints, which is the grand Christian virtue, and which is the soul and essence and summary comprehension of all grace, is a PRINCIPLE OF DIVINE LOVE."[423] With all of its manifold manifestations, it is but one seed, one principle in the heart; it is Divine Love.

The Scripture clearly shows, says Edwards, that "*Divine Love is the sum of all duty.*"[424] And in 1 Corinthians 13 Paul shows that "Divine Love ... is the essence of all Christianity ..."[425] For here Paul makes the crucial distinction between the "*gifts* of the Spirit and the *grace* of the Spirit," the latter being a love "which has God for its object." The love Christians have for other people is a function of their love for God, and derives from it. The love they have for God is, of course, the work and effect of the presence of the Holy Spirit dwelling within their minds and hearts. (Recall what was said in the first part of this chapter concerning the Holy Spirit as being "in a peculiar manner called by the name of love ... The Godhead or the Divine essence is ... said to be love ... But the divine essence is thus called in a peculiar manner as breathed forth and subsisting in the Holy Spirit ..."[426] Because the Spirit Himself is the Spirit of divine love, those whom He indwells are made into the image of the Son of God through whom the Spirit of Love is given to men. They are filled with divine love, and they respond with their own love for God and for men.[427]) In short, the love that indwells and inspires the minds and hearts of Christians is God Himself, the Holy Spirit, who is Love. In one of his sermons on 1 Corinthians 13, Edwards explains how he understands this:

> It is from the breathing of the same Spirit that true Christian love arises, both toward God and man. The Spirit of God is a Spirit of love, and when the former enters the soul, love also enters with it. God is love, and he that has God dwelling in him by His Spirit, will have love dwelling in him also. The nature of the Holy Spirit is love, and it is by communicating Himself, in His own nature, to the saints, that their hearts are filled with divine charity. Hence we find that the saints are partakers of the divine nature, and Christian love is called the 'love of the Spirit' (Rom. 15:30), and 'love in the Spirit' (Col. 1:8), and the

---

423 Ibid., 30. See also *Charity and its Fruits*, 1-25.
424 Ibid., 31f. He cites Romans 13:8, 10, 1 Timothy 1:5, Matthew 22:37f, James 2:8
425 Ibid.
426 See Grossart, *op. cit.*, 43.
427 Romans 5:5; Colossians 1:8; 2 Corinthians 6:6, Philippians 2:1.

> very bowels of love and mercy seem to signify the same thing
> with the fellowship of the Spirit (Phil. 2:1). It is that Spirit, too,
> that infuses love to God (Rom. 5:5); and it is by the indwelling
> of that Spirit, that the soul abides in love to God and man ...[428]

By the indwelling of this divine love, the disastrous effects of man's Fall
begin to be overcome. The dreadful enmity man had for God is taken
away; the unregulated chaos of man's human capacities – apart from
the Spirit – is restored to more order and graciousness, as man himself
is restored to the image of the Son of God. "Flesh" remains, even to the
end of man's life on earth. It remains, *but it does not rule.* "Spirit" now
rules. The Holy Spirit dwells in men as in His temple. This is their new
birth, a birth from sin into a new life with God in Christ. "The first
effect that is produced in the soul," through this new birth, "whereby it
is carried above what it has or can have by nature, is to cause it to relish
or taste the sweetness of the Divine relation ..."

Edwards continues:

> When once the soul is brought to relish the excellency of the
> Divine nature, then it will naturally, and of course, incline to
> God every way. It will incline to be with Him and to enjoy Him.
> It will ...be glad that He is happy. It will incline that He should
> be glorified, and that His will should be done in all things. So
> that the first effect of the power of God in the heart in REGEN-
> ERATION is to give the heart a Divine taste or sense; to cause
> it to have a relish of the loveliness and sweetness of the supreme
> excellency of the Divine nature; and indeed this is all the imme-
> diate effect of the Divine Power that there is, this is all the Spirit
> of God needs to do, in order to a production of all good effects
> in the soul.[429]

Again, Edwards insists that man is not perfected through this regeneration, nor is he removed from the sphere of temptation, error, or sin.
His new nature of love to God is regarded as good and not wicked,
therefore, entirely "from the nature of the object loved rather than
from the degree of the principle in the lover. The object beloved is of
supreme excellency ... worthy to be chosen and pursued and cleaved
to and delighted [in] far above all."[430] Man is accounted righteous not
because *he is very righteous*, but because the very God of righteousness Himself is his only hope and trust, and is the object of his feeble

---

428 *Charity and its Fruits*, 4-5.
429 Ibid., 4f.
430 Townsend, *op. cit.*, 205-206.

love and gratitude. Though there is but "little grace in the hearts of the godly, in their present infant state, to what there is of corruption," yet Scripture shows that this principle of grace is that which "reigns and predominates in the heart of a godly man in such a manner that it is the spirit that he is of, and so, that it denominates the man."[431] However feeble he may be, the new born Christian is a feeble *member of Christ*. He is marked out by God as His own, and the divine love that indwells his heart begins to reform his whole being in conformity to Christ's image.

In the third part of this *Treatise on Grace*, Edwards gathers together all he has said previously by showing that grace in the heart of men is simply the Holy Spirit there. It is God, in the person of the Spirit, dwelling within them in fellowship and power.[432] He shows what the Scripture means by calling this *"holy and Divine principle in the heart as not only from the Spirit, but as being* spiritual." He states that "Thus saving knowledge is called spiritual understanding, Col. 1:9 ... So the influences, graces, and comforts of God's Spirit are called spiritual blessings: Eph. 1:13 ..." As a matter of fact, "the imparting of any gracious benefit is called the imparting of a spiritual gift: Rom. 1:11 ... And the fruits of the Spirit which are offered to God are called spiritual sacrifices, 1 Peter 2:5 ..." Furthermore, a "spiritual person signifies the same in Scripture as a gracious person, and sometimes one that is much under the influence of grace: 1 Cor. 2:15."[433]

Two important conclusions follow from this evidence, Edwards says: first, *"this Divine principle in the heart is not called spiritual, because it has its seat in the soul or spiritual part of man, and not in his body."* This would be a complete misunderstanding of the biblical teaching concerning God and man. Rather, "it is called spiritual, not because of its relation to man, in which it is, but because of its relation to the Spirit of God, from which it is."[434]

The second conclusion to be drawn is this: this principle of Divine Love is in the Scripture called "spiritual" not, primarily, because it is *"from the Spirit of God,"* but because *"it is of the nature of the Spirit of*

---

431 Ibid.

432 Grossart, *op. cit.*, 39f. He cites John 3:5, 6:53, Titus 3:5, Ezekiel 36f, 2 Thessalonians 2:13, Romans 5:16, 1 Corinthians 6:11, 1 Peter 1:2, Galatians 5:22f, Ephesians 5:9, Hebrews 10:29.

433 Ibid., 40f.

434 Ibid., 41.

God."[435] (We shall see in the following chapter that the heart of Edwards' opposition to the skeptical attitude the rationalists took concerning the Great Awakening had to do with this doctrine. What rationalistic Christians were willing to accept was a *working* of the Spirit in man, along prescribed lines, carefully within certain boundaries. Edwards' point was that the *Lord* the Spirit came to *dwell within*, and create His own boundaries. Edwards' opposition to the opposite extreme of the enthusiasts was based on the same principle: the *Lord* the Spirit dwelt within men, all right, but along lines prescribed by *the Word* in the Scriptures. It was the *Lordship* of God that was at stake in these controversies. Edwards wrote: "*The Scripture does sufficiently reveal the Holy Spirit as a proper Divine Person*; and thus we ought to look upon Him as a distinct personal agent."[436] Edwards was opposing both extremes for denying, in effect, the Lordship of God, each in its own way.)

We find in Edwards' doctrine of regeneration, therefore, not only the strongest possible emphasis upon the *being* of God, in all His objectivity, present in His saving work in man, but also the strongest possible emphasis on the *abiding humanness* of the man called to receive the Holy Spirit. As Edwards' defense of God's objectivity and Lordship offended many enthusiasts, so also did his assertion of man's subjective appropriation and experience of God's revelation shock the rationalists. Never did Edwards renounce the absolute, unbridgeable distinction between God and man. Saving grace, he said, is the Spirit of God dwelling within and acting upon man. But it is the Spirit of *God*, and He dwells within and acts through and with *man*. Man's own spirit is not obliterated; rather, it is called to and established in freedom in God's service. There is fellowship too close to be conceived, but God remains God and man remains man, and each always will. What occurs, therefore, is a real rebirth of creatures; creatures who formerly hated or despised God, now love Him. The image of the God-man Jesus Christ is the pattern after which God begins to fashion the saints through the indwelling of His Spirit.[437] It is *men* who become living "temples of the Holy Ghost." The joy they receive is thus God's own holy joy, His own "infinite delight" in Himself, which is given to them to become their "delight" also. This is the sense in which they come to possess "the

---

435 Ibid., 42.
436 Ibid., 42-43.
437 *Charity and its Fruits*, 278f.

fullness of God" (Ephesians 3:19), through the indwelling of that Spirit who comprehends in Himself "all the fullness of God."[438]

This "fullness of God" is perceived by Christians in several aspects: they find that through Christ they partake of divine knowledge, through their reception of the revelation of God's being and work in the person of Christ; they partake of God's own holiness and virtue, as He gives Himself to them and works in them; and they partake of His happiness, His own rejoicing, and love in the Triune life, and thus they enjoy His glory.[439] Therefore, Edwards concludes,

> Hence our communion with God the Father and God the Son consists in our possession of the Holy Ghost, which is their Spirit. For to have communion or fellowship with either, is to partake with them of their good in their fullness and union and society ...[440]

Again, Edwards insists that Christians do not perfectly and fully receive the "fullness of God" through the Holy Spirit, at least not in this life. Rather, they receive the "earnest" of that Spirit who is to be given in full in the next life. But "that little of" the Spirit "which the saints have in this world is said to be the earnest of the purchased inheritance (Eph. 1:13, 14; 2 Cor. 1:22; 5:5)."[441] They receive the "earnest" of "that which we are to have a fullness of hereafter." Thus this Spirit is called "the Spirit of Promise," and He fills the church with trust and hope in the outpouring of Himself and His blessings in the next life.[442]

How does the Spirit unite Himself to the souls of humans? Or, to put it into other words, what is saving grace? Edwards replies that it is, in fact, the Holy Spirit "uniting Himself to the soul of a creature, as a vital principle, dwelling there and exerting Himself by the faculties of the soul of man, in His own proper nature, after the manner of a principle of nature ..." He comes and works in man in such a way that the man himself is freed from that which bound the proper exercise of his capacities, and can now freely, joyfully, gratefully, and zealously work for God with all of his being. Man works, as God works in him. God works in him, and man fully and freely works. "That love, which is the very native tongue and Spirit of God, so dwells in their souls that

---

438 Ibid. In this connection Edwards was fond of Proverbs 8:30, 36:8, John 7, and Hebrews 1:9.
439 See above, 106-107
440 Grossart, *op. cit.*, 48f.
441 Ibid., 50f.
442 Ibid.

it exerts itself in its own nature in the exercise of those faculties, after the manner of a natural or vital principle in them."[443] In further explanation he says:

> And herein lies the mystery of the vital union that is between Christ and the soul of a believer, which orthodox divines speak so much of – that is, His Spirit is actually united to the faculties of their souls. So it properly lives, acts, and exerts its nature in the exercise of their faculties. By this Love being in them, He is in them (John 17:26), and so it is said, 1 Cor. 6:17 – 'But he that is joined to the Lord is one Spirit.'[444]

This is the sense in which "the saints are said to be made 'partakers of God's holiness,' not only as they partake of the holiness that God gives, but partake of that holiness by which He Himself is holy."[445]

This also is the sense in which "the saints are said to live, 'yet not they, but Christ lives in' them" (Galatians 2:20). "So that they live by His life, as much as the members of the body live by the life of the root and stock: 'Because I live, ye shall live also,' (John 14:19). And again, 'For ye are dead, and your life is hid with Christ in God' ... 'When Christ, who is our life shall appear ...'"[446]

Against the Arminians, Edwards maintained the basic Calvinistic thesis that God's grace is, of course, "irresistible" in that it is the sovereign God Himself acting graciously towards an intended end. The Spirit *frees* man, through the gospel, literally *frees* man from bondage to error and from the power of sin in the heart. The superior power of God delivers men from the vicious power of Satan. It is a victory over an evil power that is achieved in regeneration. The power of grace in the heart is not just the moral suasion of the gospel story, as many Arminians maintained. It is, rather, the powerfully determining force of the liberating Spirit giving life to the dead.

> ... God gives such assistance to virtuous acts, as to be properly a *determining* assistance, so as to determine the effect; which is inconsistent with the Arminian notion of liberty. The Scripture shows that God's influence in the case is such, that He is the cause of the effect; he causes it to be: which shows that His influence determines the matter, whether it shall be or not.[447]

443 Ibid., 53f. Cf. *Works in Four Volumes*, 3, 378.
444 Grossart, *op. cit.*, 53f.
445 Ibid., 54.
446 Ibid.
447 *Works in Four Volumes*, 2, 559f.

But, the "matter" that is determined is the freeing of man's mind and heart, so that he may freely give himself to the life of love with God for which he was created. This is what it is to be born again from the dead.

The conscious personal activity of persons in this new relationship is pointed to, ultimately, in two ways, says Edwards. First, this union is "from Christ, and is the very Spirit and life and fullness of Christ"; secondly, "as it acts to Christ." Explaining the second point, Edwards says that "the very nature of" this new relationship "is love and union of heart to Him."[448] People are delivered from self-love and inspired to follow Christ, to serve and honor Him in all that they do. Their consciences become more and more sensitive to Him and to his will, to what honors or what dishonors Him. This direction of the Christian life to Christ corresponds to the inter-Trinitarian love of the Father for the Son, which is manifested in the workings of God in world history in the signal outpourings of the Spirit. This points up the significance for Edwards of the outpourings in his own time. The connection of God's work in human history, in individual conversions, and in His own inter-Trinitarian life is central to Edwards' view. Speaking of the Great Awakening in New England, Edwards writes:

> When God manifests Himself with such glorious power in a work of this nature, he appears especially determined to put honor upon His Son, and to fulfill the oath that he has sworn to him, that He would make every knee to bow, and every tongue to confess to Him. God hath had it much on His heart, from all eternity, to glorify His dear and only begotten Son; and there are some special seasons that he appoints to that end ... and these are times of remarkable pouring out of his Spirit, to advance His kingdom; such a day is a day of His power, wherein His people shall be made willing ...[449]

They are made willing to do joyfully what the Father also does joyfully: to pour out honor and blessing and glory unto the Son, in their hearts and in their lives, to the best of their abilities. This union of the heart between Christ and Christians is foreshadowed by Ezekiel's story of the bringing to life of dead bones and revealed in Christ's breathing out His breath to His disciples (John 20:22). "And therefore Christ Himself

---

448 Grossart, *op. cit.*, 54.

449 *Works in Four Volumes*, 3, 312f. He cites Isaiah 28:16 and 8:14-15, as these are combined in 1 Peter 2:2, 7-8, and Romans 9:33. He cites also Isaiah 24:14, Acts 13:41, and Zechariah 9:9-11.

represents the communication of His Spirit to His disciples by His breathing upon them, and communicating His breath ..."[450]

This last point has an important consequence, one which caused Edwards to object to the Roman Catholic and to the degenerate Puritan interpretation of a "habit of grace." Such language is impossible, he says, for Christ remains Lord over His breath!

> Indeed the first exercise of grace in the first light [in conversion] has a tendency to future acts, as from an abiding principle, by grace and by the covenant of God, but not by any natural force [i.e., of human, or ecclesiastical nature or power]. The giving one gracious discovery or act of grace, or a thousand, has no proper natural tendency to cause an abiding habit of grace for the future; not any otherwise than by Divine constitution and covenant. But all [are communicated] ... as much from the immediate acting of the Spirit of God on the soul as the first; and if God should take away His Spirit out of the soul all habits and acts of grace would of themselves cease as immediately as light ceases in a room when the candle is carried out.[451]

Now, this might be taken to contradict what Edwards had insisted as to the abiding change of nature effected in regeneration. Let us see how he explains this, for he is convinced there is no inconsistency here:

> ... no man has a habit of grace dwelling in him any otherwise that as he has the Holy Spirit dwelling in him ... and being in union with his natural faculties, after the manner of a vital principle. So that when they act grave, 'tis , in the language of the Apostle, 'not they, but Christ living in them.' Indeed, the Spirit of God, united to human faculties, acts very much after the manner of a natural principle or habit. So that one act makes another and so settles the soul in a disposition to holy acts ..."[452]

Then Edwards states the difference between his and the views he rejected: *"but that it does, so as by grace and covenant, and not from any natural necessity."* The Spirit of God remains the Lord, and the manner of His continual working in Christians remains the manner of personal fellowship, not mechanistic determination, nor deifying the creatures in whom He dwells. They remain creatures, justified each moment by grace, knowing it, praying for it. At no point have they reason to cease thanking God for all the work of redemption. They

---

450 Grossart, *op. cit.*, 55.
451 Ibid.
452 Ibid.

live *in* Christ by living *to Him* as *Lord*. His Church never attains sovereignty over His grace.

Edwards began this *Treatise on Grace* by distinguishing between the work of God's Spirit *on* unregenerate people, from His dwelling in personal fellowship within the hearts and minds of those called to believe the gospel of Christ. He showed that this coming of God's Spirit is an immediate divine act, an immediate awakening of man from death in sin to life in Christ. In the second part of this *Treatise* he showed that the essence of this new principle of life in the soul of Christians is simply divine love dwelling within and acting throughout the whole person. That is, it is the Holy Spirit bringing God's own loving Person to man, and working to restore him to the image of Christ. The third and final part of this work presented in more detail just how God's own Spirit dwells within believers, without ceasing to be God, and without forcing men to cease being totally dependent creatures of grace, living each moment by grace, joyfully and thankfully and consciously striving to do so for the sake of Christ whom they love, with all of the human capacities with which they were endowed, and which have now been liberated for His service.

Fellowship

In our first chapter, we noted the intense concentration upon the fellowship of Christians that was a characteristic of Puritan life and theology. To them, the church of God was a living institution, indwelt by His Spirit, powerfully supported and guided by Him every moment. The clerical absenteeism characteristic of Anglicanism, and the apparent irrelevance of the church's scholarship for the daily life of ordinary Christians was a scandal and offense to the Puritans. The most eminent Puritan theologians were practiced in preaching to plain people in plain terms and were renowned also for their practical books aimed at guiding Christian families in their daily lives.

This intensely high doctrine of the church was not shared by many of their Establishment contemporaries. Ministers and laymen of Puritan sympathy braved fines, imprisonment, torture, and death to come together for study and for prayer, for preaching and for the hearing of sermons. Their view of the Spirit's regenerating work was set in the context of the Holy People of God through whom the Word and the Spirit came to men. So important was this matter to Jonathan Edwards that he was (as we have seen) dismissed from his parish for attempting to promote that high doctrine of the church formerly held by Puritanism, but, by this time, renounced by many descendants of the original settlers.

We must conclude our presentation on Edwards' doctrine of the new birth, therefore, by noting his view of the human fellowship that formed the context of conversion and sanctification. We began our exposition of this doctrine in the framework of the fellowship of God: Father, Son, and Spirit. We conclude it with Edwards' remarks upon the fellowship of believers to which and through which life with God is given to individuals. Edwards writes:

> This matter may be best understood, if we consider that Christ and the whole church of saints are, as it were, one body, of which He is the Head, and they members, of different place and capacity: now the whole body, head and members, have communion in Christ's righteousness; they are all partakers of the benefit of it ..."[453]

The Church of Christ is the God-elected community that has succeeded the Old Israel. By the indwelling of the Holy Spirit, the members are united to God and to each other. Through the ordinances of worship – baptism, communion, preaching, prayer, etc. - God's Word enlightens Christians' minds and His Spirit fires their hearts and souls for His cause. The proper education of ministers and teachers was of outstanding importance, for how could people hear the gospel without its being preached? And *properly* preached, as Scripture witnessed to it? Though scattered throughout the whole earth, the church is yet one great society: "… it is the glory of the church of Christ, that she, in all her members, however dispersed is this one society, one city, one family, one body ..."[454]

External order is vital to the proper life of the Church. Contemporary Anglicanism was content to have hundreds of parishes vacant, thousands of parishioners without shepherds, with little spiritual guidance and less spiritual discipline. Not so with the Puritans. The "order" desired by many Anglicans was so irrelevant to Christian nurture, as the Puritans understood this responsibility, that there was little to choose from between the established church on the one hand, and the enthu-

---

453 *Works in Four Volumes*, 4, 116.
454 *Works in Four Volumes*, 3, 463.

siasts who wanted to abolish all forms and structure, on the other. On the contrary, consistent with his Calvinistic heritage, Edwards writes:

> Without order there can be no general direction of a multitude to any particular desired end ... If a multitude would help one another in a regular subordination of members, in some measure as it is in the natural body; by this means they will be in some capacity to act with united strength: and thus Christ has appointed that it should be in the visible church, as 1 Cor. 12:14, to the end, and Rom. 12:4, 5, 6, 7, 8. Zeal without order will do but little, or at least it will be effectual but a little while ... Order is one of the most necessary of all external means of the spiritual good of God's church ..."[455]

Edwards opposed strongly the disorder that came when individuals left their jobs, took upon their shoulders the office of preachers, evangelists, or "exhorters," and invaded parishes, disrupting whole congregations by their pretension to spiritual authority. The business of being a pastor was too weighty a matter to entrust to persons untrained and unschooled in its requirements, he believed.

Unlike many of his contemporaries, Edwards did not claim divine authority for any one form of church order. He began his ministry in a Presbyterian pulpit, exercised most of it in a Congregational church (the type into which he had been born), and died as president of a Presbyterian College. Whatever the form chosen, some order was essential to the Christian life. For Christians, he said, are drawn by God into a fellowship of love, and are expected to order and discipline themselves for the mutual benefit of themselves and their neighbors. People are not called to be lonely Christians, but to be members of a godly army, whose Captain is Christ. They are led by His guidance, through the Spirit and the Scriptures, and through leaders whom He has appointed, the pastors and teachers who expound God's Word and instruct His people in discipline and service, and the elders who rule the flock for Christ. The whole body is commanded by God to strive for a union of "heart and soul" in the Christian life.[456] The members are to uphold each other in their hope of the coming of Christ and their own future glory with Him. They are a fellowship of hope and they encourage each other by their acts of love and discipline, so that the

---

455 Ibid., 379f. Much can be learned of Edwards' view of the church in his works against Solomon Williams; see *Works in Four Volumes*, 1, 85-292.
456 *Works in Four Volumes*, 1, 142f.

whole body of Christ lives in confident expectation of the vindication of Christ's cause.[457]

To this end, Edwards inspired many of his people to meet regularly in each others' homes for Bible study, prayer and mutual exhortation. Quite often, he was asked to attend these meetings and speak and preach. Such occasions were especially frequent at the times of the revivals. The family, of course, was the basic Christian unit and had always been so considered in Puritanism. The young people and the elders were also encouraged to come together for mutual growth and instruction.

To Edwards' mind, therefore, new birth in the Spirit brought persons into the closest personal fellowship with other Christians and with the Lord. It ushered them into an organized society that provided for the teaching and preaching of God's Word, for mutual help in trouble and need, for organized worship as well as for informal prayer, and for the initiation by baptism of those whom the Spirit had touched (or their children, as a sign of hope in God's grace). Persons found fellowship at the Table of the Lord in the company of other Christians and were expected to take their share of responsibility in the organized and disciplined body of Christ. New birth, then, was the beginning of a new life, a new life with God and with men.

Conclusion

We have completed our presentation of Edwards' doctrine of the new birth. In our next chapter, we must show just how Edwards sought to test and to discern the work of the Holy Spirit among humans, to delineate His work from the work of other spirits of the time. We shall see the intense controversy into which he was drawn in his attempt to apply his doctrine of regeneration to the pastoral problems of his own, as well as of other, congregations, and we shall note also his variation from traditional Puritan understandings of the order of the Spirit's working in the stages of conversion.

Before turning to this study of his application of his doctrine, it will be useful to summarize the material we have examined so far in this present chapter.

This chapter was divided into three main sections: The Promise of the Spirit, The Purchase of the Spirit, and The Gift of the Spirit. It will be recognized at once that this structure is meant to conform to Edwards'

---

457 *Works in Four Volumes*, 4, 36-37.

explicit Trinitarian reference, as this is most clearly set out in his address, "God Glorified in the Work of Redemption, by the Greatness of Man's Dependence Upon Him in the Whole of It." Here he refers the whole of the Christian life to the various workings appropriated to the Father, to the Son, and to the Holy Spirit.[458] He shows in detail how men are dependent upon God for *all* of their good and for the *whole* of their salvation, and he concludes by warning them to shun any theology that tends to dissuade people from total trust in God. He says, "... those doctrines and schemes of divinity that are in any respect opposite to such an absolute and universal dependence on God, do derogate from God's glory, and thwart the design of ... our redemption."[459] In the whole work of redemption, in all its parts, "all of the glory evidently belongs to God, all is in a mere, and most absolute, and divine dependence on the Father, Son, and Holy Ghost." Indeed, "all is of the Father, all through the Son, and all in the Holy Ghost."[460]

Applying this to the structure of our chapter, we see at once that the titles of our three sections might have been: "The Father's Promise," "The Son's Purchase," and "The Spirit's Gift," for in each of these sections we indicated Edwards' insistence upon the total sufficiency of God in this work and the total insufficiency of man in any part of it. Therefore, the very existence of the creature is the consequence of God's intention to manifest His glory and blessedness to beings who are to know and enjoy Him. The sum of the prophetic witness, we saw, was God's promise to give Himself to His people. The disastrous effects of sin were overcome through the work of the God-Man, the Son, in His sacrifice. By union with Him, by incorporation in His election, people are drawn forth from wickedness to a foretaste of eternal blessedness, and to a promise of the same in future glory. Through this work and message of the work of the Son, persons' minds are enlightened, when Christ's Spirit applies the gospel to their hearts. Through the light of human understanding, the power of the gospel is applied to human hearts. They are filled with love for that which they now know to be true, and love for Him in whom love and truth are embodied, and in whose Spirit love and truth are given to them. They trust themselves to Him whom they love, for they find that His working in them is the fruit of His presence in them. They find themselves, therefore, in an inconceivably intimate union with God, and in deep spiritual commu-

---

458 *Works in Four Volumes*, 4, 169f.
459 Ibid., 177.
460 Ibid.

nion with other followers of Christ. God is all their portion and all their joy and good, and from Him, they receive all that they need or wish, in this life and the next.

> God Himself is the great good which they are brought to the possession and enjoyment of by redemption. He is the highest good, and the sum of all that good which Christ purchased. God is the inheritance of the saints; He is the portion of their souls. God is their wealth and treasure, their food, their life, their dwelling-place, their ornament and diadem, and their everlasting honour and glory. They have none in heaven but God; he is the great good which the redeemed are received to at death, and which they are to rise to at the end of the world. The Lord God, he is the light of the heavenly Jerusalem; and is the 'river of the water of life' that runs, and 'the tree of life that grows, in the midst of the paradise of God.' The glorious excellencies and beauty of God will be what will forever entertain the minds of the saints, and the love of God will be their everlasting feast.[461]

Edwards' doctrine of regeneration is but a function of his doctrine of the whole work of redemption. That is, it is a function of his doctrine of God the Father, God the Son, God the Holy Ghost, one God. We have sought in this chapter to show this connection. Regeneration, therefore, speaking subjectively, is the reception by man of God Himself in his mind and soul and heart and body; it is the reception of intimate fellowship with God, in the Person of His Holy Spirit through faith in the Son. Grace in the soul is God there indwelt.

---

461 Ibid., 174.

6

On Discerning the Spirit

Introduction

Speaking of the paramount theological problem facing the New
England churches during the Great Awakening, C.C. Goen, in his
Revivalism and Separatism in New England writes:

> It was not enough to settle the theological problem of salva-
> tion by grace, or even the ecclesiological question of personal
> conversion as prerequisite to church membership – the prac-
> tical problem still remained of discerning accurately who were
> converted. What were the assurances of one's own salvation,
> and by what evidences could others be judged? These were
> dangerous and difficult questions, but they were raised inescap-
> ably when the revival disrupted the comfortable complacency
> of the old order.[462]

"Grace in the soul is Christ there," said Jonathan Edwards.[463] But how
was grace to be recognized? What are the signs of the Spirit's regenerating work in men? What does Christ do when He gives Himself in
fellowship to the saints? Or, in eighteenth-century vocabulary, what
is "true religion" and how might its presence be discerned? "Beloved,
do not believe every spirit, but test the spirits to see whether they are
of God; for many false prophets have gone out into the world" (1 John
4:1). What is necessary for every generation was especially necessary
for the New England Christians of the eighteenth-century revivals; so
much so, in fact, that Jonathan Edwards postponed his extensive works
against Arminian theology until he had given some attention to this
pressing theme.

---

462 C.C. Goen, *op. cit.*, 44. His own discussion of Puritan piety is poor, however.
463 *Images of Shadows of Divine Things*, Perry Miller (ed.), 114-115.

We recall that the task of discerning the Holy Spirit's work in the souls of the saints had always been of special interest to the Puritans.[464] They fully shared the Protestant Reformers' hatred of the Roman church's teaching concerning the impossibility of a Christian's ever really knowing whether God was truly gracious to *him*, and would save *him*. They preached and taught the doctrine of assurance of salvation through the participation in Christ God gives by His Spirit. The Puritans trained their congregations to search the Scriptures for knowledge concerning the works of the Spirit within the hearts of the saints, that they might know for themselves the joy of His presence, and rejoice in the tokens of His love that He gave.

Jonathan Edwards was familiar with many of the most important Puritan works dealing with this theme. He had, furthermore, the incalculable advantage of having lived in his father's parsonage during several revivals there.[465] In addition, therefore, to his father's experience of ordinary, less remarkable conversions throughout the whole of his ministry, the advice of his father concerning the more dramatic revivals was of inestimable benefit, for it was to be his lot to participate in even more startling and widespread outpourings. The same is to be said for the benefits he received during his two years under the experienced Solomon Stoddard.

It is not surprising, therefore, that Jonathan Edwards' doctrine of regeneration, and his understanding of the ways of guiding persons under "affliction," "conviction," and "conversion" were firmly settled in his mind before the time of the first revival under his own ministry in 1733. Perhaps no one else in all New England was so well prepared or equipped to give guidance under the amazing outpourings that were to occur. His first revival work, the *Faithful Narrative* (1737), carried so much weight because of the careful discrimination it displayed, and the scholarly and serious effort it represented to separate the wheat from the chaff in the dramatic revival in the Connecticut Valley. With increasing experience and reflection, his succeeding studies revealed even finer powers of discernment. His final revival work, the *Treatise Concerning Religious Affections* (1746), was hailed on both sides of the Atlantic as a classic in the field and a model guide for Christian pastors.

How sorely a guide was needed during the years following the Great Awakening of 1740! Long unused to "experimental religion," the

---

464 See above, 37ff.
465 Dwight, *Works in Ten Volumes*, 1, 58.

churches reacted to this revival with tremendous enthusiasm and, increasingly, equally misguided zeal. While the majority of the pastors stemming from the Puritan tradition accepted the revival as an outpouring of God's Holy Spirit, a minority, after a period of cautious silence, began to attack first the "excesses" and, finally, the whole of the revival. By 1743, therefore, the controversy was so intense that the paramount practical problem facing New England churches was seen to be their paramount theological problem as well. That was, How may the Spirit of God be discerned in His saving work among men? For over a decade of New England life, pastors, elders, deacons, teachers, Christian magistrates, and families were forced to take sides in the critical debate. Willingly or unwillingly as they may have been in the face of this notoriously difficult problem, every pastor nevertheless had to give his people some guidance on this score. Jonathan Edwards was responding to this, the most pressing cultural problem of his time when he wrote the works that made him famous in this field.

The problem was compounded by the very simplicities that the extremists on both sides offered as solutions. The opponents of the revival justified their opposition to it by all references to 1) the "enthusiasm" (i.e., fanaticism) of those who claimed to be savingly affected, 2) the "antinomianism" they asserted was implicit in such a state of raised "passions," and 3) the strife and antagonism engendered by the so-called revival. These, in general terms, were basic planks in the platform of the opposers. An effective presentation of this position was provided by Benjamin Doolittle's *An Inquiry Into Enthusiasm* (Boston, 1743), wherein he defined enthusiasm as "strong Fancy, Imagination or Conceit of having large Communications from or Participations with the Deity."[466] The term "enthusiasm" itself was a smear word in eighteenth-century ears and had connotations not only of rational and moral but also of doctrinal error. It was an effective polemical term.

The man who was destined to become the chief antagonist of the revival was the Reverend Charles Chauncy of Boston. At the beginning, he accepted the events as the work of God's Spirit; later, when excesses began to abound, he withdrew his approbation and began to criticize, albeit anonymously. By 1743, he considered the whole thing a work of the devil himself, allowed by God as a punishment on New England. An honest man, and a complete rationalist who later embraced first Arminianism and finally Unitarianism, Chauncy penned a major attack on the Awakening in the four hundred and twenty-four pages

---

466 Quoted in Gaustad, *op. cit.*, 78.

of his *Seasonable Thoughts on the State of Religion in New England*, published in 1743. This was a direct, point by point refutation of Edwards' important and influential *Some Thoughts Concerning the Present Revival of Religion in New England*, that had appeared a few months before Chauncy's counter-attack. Consistent with the tactics of the opponents of the Awakening, three-fourths of Chauncy's work were devoted to cataloging the evils and "excesses" that he had seen, heard, and had heard of, in the revival. Repelled by many instances of "*swooning away* and *falling to the Ground ... bitter Shriekings and Screamings; Convulsion-like Tremblings and Agitations, Strugglings and Tumblings,*"[467] Chauncy used case after case of such events to discredit the whole of the revival. Passion ran riot, he said. Passions subdued reason and thereby proved the satanic source of the whole movement.

How, then, might such a phenomenon as the Great Awakening be judged? At one pole were those who were ready to grant every "Conceit" or "Fancy" of the imagination to be a direct illumination from the Holy Spirit of God. At the other pole were those for whom the mere articulation of joy, love, or "affection" in the Lord indicated satanic delusion and necessitated the conclusion that passion gone amok. The first group was ready to justify any action or claim of one thought to be regenerate; the others came to disbelieve all who testified to having received comforts, joys, or assurance from God. Between these two extremes stood a large number of clergy for whom Jonathan Dickenson and Jonathan Edwards were the chief spokesmen. At the heart of the controversy, of course, were basically irreconcilable opinions concerning both the nature of man and the manner in which God's Spirit worked in him. Crucial to the whole debate were totally opposed views concerning the *criteria* by which the work of God's Spirit was to be discerned in His regenerating work. It is to this problem that we must now turn.

Criterion

"The height of Virtue is this," said Henry More, "constantly to pursue that which to Right Reason seems best." With this, Richard Fiddes, in his *A General Treatise of Morality* (1724) agreed: "I proceed, everywhere, upon this principle, that Reason is the proper Rule of human

---

467 Chauncy, *Seasonable Thoughts* (Boston: Rogers and Fowle, 1743), 77.

Judgment, and Action." Six years later the Dissenting theologian Isaac Watts wrote:

> ... it is still Reason exercising itself, and judging of the fitness and unfitness of things, by and according to these native and essential Principles of Reasoning which I have spoken of, that is the only Rule or Test of *what is Vice* and *what is Virtue*.[468]

Expounding his version of the Quaker position, Robert Barclay, in his *Theses Theologicae* of 1675, wrote that "divine inward revelations" give men illumination for "the building up of the true faith," and that such illuminations, while they will not contradict the Scripture, are yet not to be judged by Scripture:

> ... for this divine revelation and inward illumination is that which is evident and clear of itself, forcing, by its own evidence and clearness, the well-disposed understanding to assent, irresistibly moving the same thereto ...[469]

William Penn attempted to secure the Quaker view from mere rationalism by arguing that:

> It is not our Way of Speaking to say the Light within is the Rule of the Christian Religion; but that the Light of Christ within us is the Rule of true Christians, so that it is not our Light but Christ's Light that is our rule.[470]

This offers really no specific help in solving the controversy between Chauncy and Edwards, between Puritan and Quaker, between conservative-rationalist and revivalist. In fact, Jonathan Edwards' criteria for distinguishing the Holy Spirit and His gracious and saving work in people from the work of other "spirits" entailed a rejection not only of the doctrine of revelation as held by either Chauncy or Fox and Penn, but also of the doctrine of man as conceived by either rationalist or Quaker. What essential difference is there really between the "Rule" discovered by Quakers to dwell "within" through the "Light of Christ," and the rationalism of Cambridge Platonism as expressed by John Smith's statement that "To follow Reason is to follow God"?[471] What a confidence in human opinions is thereby expressed by both positions! What a valuation of man is therein proclaimed – a valuation of his

---

468 Quoted in Faust and Johnson, *Edwards*, lxxvi.
469 From the Second Proposition. See *Creeds of the Churches*, Leith (ed.), 325.
470 Quoted in Nuttal, *op. cit.*, 44.
471 Quoted in Willey, *The Seventeenth-century Background*, 71.

rational powers and his capacity to know through thinking the deep matters pertaining to salvation.

In contradiction to the criteria employed by Charles Chauncy, John Smith, or George Fox, Jonathan Edwards began his *Some Thoughts Concerning the Present Revival of Religion in New England* by observing that "the error of those who have had ill thoughts of the great religious operations in the minds of men" in the New England churches "seems fundamentally to lie in three things …." These are,

First: In judging of this work *a priori*.

Secondly: In not taking the Holy Scriptures as a whole rule whereby to judge of such operations.

Thirdly: In not justly separating and distinguishing the good from the bad.[472]

Critics judge of God's work *a priori* by applying to it their preconceived notions as to what He can or will do or not do.[473] By "not taking the Holy Scriptures as a whole" they apply perhaps a part of the Christian revelation to their own particular secular anthropology. Specifically, the rationalists fought the Great Awakening on the basis of their dogmatic adherence to the medieval faculty-psychology, with its tripartite division of man's soul into mind, passions, and will, or some such. Rather than take God's revelation in Scripture as their guide, they preferred to employ philosophy, "particularly the philosophical notions they entertain of the nature of the soul, its faculties, and affections."[474] Against such a view, Edwards insisted that it is "false philosophy" to think of man's "soul" and "will" as superior to his "affections" (as the rationalists maintained), and it is "false religion" to think of a man being a Christian without having his "affections" drawn powerfully to God in love, joy, and peace. "All acts of the affections of the soul are in some sense acts of the will, and all acts of the will are acts of the affections."[475] In

---

472 *Works in Four Volumes*, 3, 277; *Works* (Yale), 4, 291ff.

473 For a modern example of this *a priori* approach to God's works, see the assertions of Rudolph Bultmann in his epoch-making essay, "New Testament and Mythology" in *Kerygma and Myth* (London: S.P.C.K., 1957), 3ff.

474 *Works in Four Volumes*, 3, 279. Again, Rudolph Bultmann's use of an "existentialist" analysis of man, as the basis for his apologetic exposition of the New Testament *kerygma* is a modern case of what Edwards was trying to refute.

475 Ibid., 279-280.

his early notebooks, under the *Notes on the Mind,* he had written down for later consideration the following:

> ... Concerning speculative understanding and sense of heart; whether any difference between the sense of the heart and the will or inclination; how the Scriptures are ignorant of the philosophical distinction of the understanding and the will; and how the sense of the heart is there called knowledge or understanding.[476]

His later studies confirmed this early insight, and henceforth his repudiation of the scholastic anthropology adopted by Enlightenment Protestantism, with its dim view of human affections. Its mistaken exaltation of the intellect and the intellect's supposed control over the will was a constant feature of Edwards' opposition to the rationalists.

Thirdly, by their not "distinguishing the good from the bad" in the revival, opponents allowed themselves to throw out the baby with the bath, to ignore the gracious working of God because of the stench of the concomitant activity of Satan and of human sin. Even the best saints, Edwards insisted, remain infected by sin, and Christians who know their hearts and the Scriptures should not be surprised at the evil that appears even in the church of God. Witness the excesses that accompanied the Reformation!

No, the criterion by which God's church must seek to discern the regenerating work of the Holy Spirit in her members can only be the criterion God Himself has given. That is because the Spirit does not reveal new doctrines, nor does He work differently in people at this age than He did when first He drew men into fellowship with God through the risen Christ. The Spirit always works according to the Word. Specifically, He operates according to the manner of His working as described in the written Word, the Bible.[477] We discern the work of regeneration, therefore, not by applying our *a priori* views of God's way of acting, nor our philosophical notions concerning the possible ways "modern" man can be acted upon by God, nor by reference to instances of excess and sin in those claiming to be followers of Christ. On the contrary, we are to let ourselves be guided in such matters by God Himself through His written Word. He has revealed in Scripture the manner of His action in regenerating men; there He shows the effects He will have upon men

---

476 Townsend, *op. cit.,* 71.

477 *Works in Four Volumes,* 3, 364f. See also 116. Cf. Calvin, *Institutes,* I, 9, 1, which Edwards quotes in this connection.

by the indwelling of His Spirit. By this and by this alone are we to be guided. The Scripture is sufficient for our knowledge of this matter.[478]

We must not mistake Edwards' meaning here: he does not regard the Bible as a book of canon law dropped from heaven. There are, within its pages, he says, a variety of materials with varying degrees of relevance to, and thus authority for, the Christians of later ages. The task of a systematic biblical study is to differentiate between these materials and their applicability to the lives of succeeding generations. There are in the Bible "primary truths, and others more remote," and "the Scripture requires we distinguish between them."[479] It is the office of the Spirit to guide men in this task, so that we can trust Him to instruct us when, in faith and prayer, we attend to His written witness. Edwards concludes this discussion of the criterion by which we discern the work of regeneration by saying:

> And why cannot we be contented with the divine oracles, that holy, pure word of God, that we have in such abundance, and such clearness, now since the canon of Scripture is completed? Why should we desire to have anything added to them by impulses from above? Why should not we rest in that standing rule that God has given to His church, which the apostle teaches us is surer than a voice from heaven? And why should we desire to make the Scripture speak more to us than it does? Or why should any desire any higher kind of intercourse with heaven, than that which is by having the Holy Spirit given in His sanctifying influences, infusing and exciting grace and holiness, love and joy, which is the highest kind of intercourse that the saints and angels in heaven have with God, and the chief excellency of the glorified man Jesus Christ?[480]

It is not by reason (blinded and perverted by sin as it is), nor by imaginations or affections or feelings (likewise perverted, and often inspired by Satan) humans can be guided in seeking to discern the regenerating work of God. Edwards repudiated both the rationalists and emotionalists as groups who idealized and exalted only one aspect of man's capacity and thus rejected the scriptural revelation concerning the extent of his sin and desperate need, and the extent of God's actual guidance through the prophetic and apostolic testimony. The "signs" of the working of God as He regenerates men are described by God in the Scripture, and evidenced in the present life of the church. Let

---

478 See *Works in Four Volumes*, 1, 182, 188; 3, 366f, 383f, 388.
479 *Works in Four Volumes*, 3, 544f.
480 *Jonathan Edwards*, 169. ???

us turn now to Edwards' description of the "signs" he finds in God's written word.

The Signs of the Spirit

In 1741, the Great Awakening was at its height and Yale University invited her now - famous son to give the September Commencement Address. Edwards took this opportunity to suggest to the assembled pastors and leaders certain "marks" or "signs" by means of which the church might be better able to distinguish the good from the bad in the current revival. This address was later published under the title, *The Distinguishing Marks of a Work of the Spirit of God*, and Perry Miller says, concerning this important piece,

> ... it appeared in Boston with a preface by Cooper [who had done the same for Edwards' Harvard Address of 1731], was reprinted in Philadelphia by Benjamin Franklin, in London with a recommendation by Isaac Watts, in Glasgow and Edinburgh ... and again in London, 1744 and 1745, with an endorsement by John Wesley. Letters now began to flow from Great Britain to Northampton bearing the signatures of the greatest of Dissenters and addressed to a recognized master.[481]

The Distinguishing Marks

Edwards begins this work by quoting 1 John 4:1, "Beloved, believe not every spirit, but try the spirits whether they are of God."[482] This whole chapter of the first letter of John was written, Edwards says, to guide the early Christians in the outpouring of the Holy Spirit in the Apostolic Age, and it can serve as well to show us "what are the true, certain, and distinguishing evidences of a work of the Spirit of God, by which we may safely proceed in judging of any operation we find in ourselves, or see in others."[483] Asserting first that "the *Scriptures*" are to be "our guide" in such a matter, he then announces the three parts of his address: in the first he discusses "What are *no* signs" by which we can certainly judge of the Spirit's work in men; in the second he studies "What *are* distinguishing Scripture evidences," and in the third part he draws "Practical Inferences" for the church's immediate use.[484]

---

481 *Jonathan Edwards*, 169.
482 *Distinguishing Marks*, in *Works in Four Volumes*, 1, 525f; *Works* (Yale), 4, 215ff.
483 Ibid., 526.
484 Ibid. Our subsequent exposition will follow Edwards' own, which is found in pages 525-562 of Volume 1 of his *Works in Four Volumes*.

The first "sign" that cannot be considered a conclusive evidence of the Spirit's saving work is that "it is carried on in a way very unusual and extraordinary ..." God certainly does work extraordinary effects on humans through the preaching of His word, and He did so in biblical times, but other spirits can also affect people powerfully, so that this in itself is no sure proof.[485]

Second, the production of "any effects on the bodies of men; such as tears, trembling, groans ... or the failing of bodily strength" is also no certain sign. Scripture is filled with accounts of men's bodies being overwhelmed both by divine and by natural or satanic instigation. This too is no conclusive evidence either way.[486]

Third, the fact that people who claim the regenerating influences of God speak at length about the things of religion is also no certain sign. It is inconceivable, he says, that a group of persons who have been brought to a saving knowledge of Christ would *not* think and speak much about it. But much "religious" talk is of itself no sign.[487]

Fourth, against the rationalistic opponents of the revival, Edwards asserted that "It is no argument that an operation on the minds of a people is not the work of the Spirit of God, that many who are the subjects of it, have great impressions made on their imaginations." Human experience shows, he says, that when persons are strongly affected by some object or reality that engages their attention, then their imaginations are also fired with the same theme: but this constitutes no sure proof of *God's* working in such cases.[488]

Fifth, against those who argued that the revival was simply the result of one person catching another's madness and thus seeking to imitate him, Edwards asserted that "It is no sign that a work is not from the Spirit of God, that example is a great means of it." Scripture shows that God used and intends to use the example of witnesses to inspire others to come to Him (Matthew 5:16, 1 Peter 3:1, 1 Timothy 4:12, Titus 2:7). "There is a language in actions," he writes, and many people have in fact come to know the living God through the examples of other Christians. This, then, is no sign that the revival is not of God.[489]

---

485 Ibid., 526. He cites Acts 2:13, 26:24, and 1 Corinthians 4:10.
486 Ibid., 527f He refers to Acts 16:29f, Psalm 32:3-4, Matthew 14:26, Canticles 2:5, 8.
487 Ibid., 530. He refers to Acts 17:6.
488 Ibid.
489 Ibid., 532.

Sixth, "It is no sign that a work is not from the Spirit of God, that many, who seem to be the subjects of it, are guilty of great imprudence and irregularities in their conduct." A knowledge of the Biblical revelation concerning man's sin, and the barest acquaintance with the New Testament discussions of the problems that arose in the apostolic church, should discredit such an objection as this. That true saints err should not surprise us at all, for we know of "the exceeding weakness of human nature, together with the remaining darkness and corruption of those that are yet the subjects of the saving influences of the Spirit of God and have a real zeal for God."[490]

Seventh, "Nor are many errors in judgment, and some delusions of Satan intermixed with the work, any argument that the work in general is not of the Spirit of God."[491] The saints themselves may be deluded somewhat by the devil, "in the present state, where grace dwells with so much corruption, and the new man and the old subsist together in the same person; and the kingdom of God and the kingdom of the devil remain for a while together in the same heart."[492] This seventh sign is closely allied to the one preceding, and yet the distinction is necessary.

Eighth, that some "who were thought to be wrought upon" savingly by the Holy Spirit, "fall away into gross errors, or scandalous practices," is again no sign that the revival itself is not God's work.[493] Church history abounds with instances of persons who were at first considered by the church as true members of Christ, but who later fell away and thus revealed the spuriousness of their faith. The church does not have a capacity to judge for certain the hearts of professing believers. The saints may be deceived by persons in their midst. Here again, Edwards refers to the history of the early church, and to the Reformation.

His ninth point is interesting. Many opposers of the revival had pointed with horror at the powerful, vivid preaching then being practiced by promoters of the Awakening, charging that the ministers were trying to scare men into heaven by picturing graphically the frightfulness of hell. Edwards, who, because of his doctrines of election and of conversion and of God's free grace, held it impossible for anyone to scare a

---

490 Ibid., 534.
491 Ibid., 535.
492 Ibid. 536.
493 Ibid.

soul into heaven, yet defended this vivid manner of preaching. To the pastors he said:

> If any of you who are heads of families saw one of your children in a house all on fire, and in imminent danger of being consumed in the flames, yet seemed to be very insensible of its danger, and neglected to escape after you had often called to it – would you go on to speak to it only in a cold and indifferent manner? Would you not cry aloud, and call earnestly to it, and represent the danger it was in, and its own folly in delaying, in the most lively manner of which you was capable?[494]

This raises an important point for the interpretation of Edwards' theology. Certain teachings of his that repelled the humanitarianism of nineteenth-century scholars now seem to be in danger of a twentieth-century fad. That is, doctrines that an earlier generation of scholars simply rejected as false and unworthy of the gospel are now liable to be subject to the process of "reinterpretation" or "demythologizing." The danger is a real one. One interpreter writes that Edwards' statements concerning the everlasting torments of the damned in hell should be regarded as an "experiment in evangelism, the extremes of which he himself acknowledges in the treatise on religious affections." On this interpretation, Edwards' stated view of hell is called only a "limiting concept" in his "philosophy," a "symbol of nothingness."[495] We assert on the contrary that Edwards sincerely believed in the existence and the horror of hell and, therefore, like his contemporary George Whitefield, for love of men's souls he strove to warn men of it, that they might turn to Christ. "If there really be a hell of such dreadful and neverending torments ... of which multitudes are in great danger ... then why is it not proper for those who have the care of souls to take great

---

494 Ibid., 537.

495 Elwood, *op. cit.*, 80. How Elwood arrived at these conclusions is difficult to conceive, for Edwards' writings abound with explicit affirmations of the very opposite position. See Edwards' *On the Endless Punishment of Those Who Die Impenitent*, in *Works in Four Volumes*, 1, 612-642. See also the sermon, "The Final Judgment," in *Works in Four Volumes*, 4, 202-225, and especially the remarks on 214f, concerning eternal punishment. Again, cf. the sermons, "The Justice of God in the Damnation of Sinners," "The Future Punishment of the Wicked Unavoidable," and "The Eternity of Hell Torments" – all of which are found in *Works in Four Volumes*, 4, 226ff. And – of course! – the Enfield sermon, "Sinners in the Hands of an Angry God" in *Works in Four Volumes*, 4, 313f.

pains to make men sensible of it?"[496] We must understand his defense of this type of preaching, therefore, as being absolutely consistent with his view of the facts of the case as they affected the destiny of men.

Edwards was in thorough agreement with those who objected to the suddenly popular practice of untrained, unqualified laymen dropping their work and spreading throughout neighboring parishes as "evangelists" or "exhorters." The fervency of preaching of authorized ministers and the power with which they moved men to think of heaven and hell and the wrath and mercy of God were certainly not, however, he insisted, a sign that the whole revival, that occasioned this intensity, was not a work of God.

In listing these nine "signs," and in discussing them from a biblical, theological, and experimental basis, Edwards provided a far more effective check to the extremes of fanatics than any of the broadsides of the rationalists. None of these signs in themselves, he said, could prove *or* disprove that the current operation was or was not a work of the Spirit of God. Neither the evidence of strong effects on men's minds, or on their bodies, nor much religious talk, nor powerful impressions on men's imaginations, nor the effect of others' examples, nor the fact of imprudence in the conduct of the saints, nor their errors of judgment, nor the falling back into sin of some who were thought to have been converted, nor the fervent and zealous way of preaching adopted by many pastors – none of these things, in themselves, proved or disproved the work of the Spirit of God to be present in the current revival.

Having thus antagonized some of the enthusiasts and out-reasoned the rationalists (by his really basic and biblical criticism of the things they merely despised and condemned), Edwards turned to a positive exposition of what he considered to be the Scriptural signs of the Spirit's work in regenerating men. From an analysis of 1 John 4, he found five chief positive signs of the Spirit's gracious, saving work.[497]

---

496 *Works in Four Volumes*, 1, 537. Here, Edwards' defense of fervent preaching is based on his oft-stated conviction as to the reality of the dreadful and eternal punishments awaiting those who die apart from Christ. Elwood's interpretation is clearly untenable.

497 Ibid., 539ff.

First, a "sure sign" of the saving work of the Spirit within men is evidenced:

> When the operation is such as to raise their esteem of that Jesus who was born of the Virgin, and was crucified without the gates of Jerusalem; and seems more to confirm and establish their minds in the truth of what the gospel declares to us of His being the Son of God, and the Saviour of men ...[498]

The second, third, and fifteenth verses of this chapter of John's Epistle show this confession of Christ as come in the flesh, and as the Son of God and Saviour, to be a sure work of the Spirit. And the word "confess" means more than merely "allowing"; it means declaring with total conviction and fervent love that what is asserted in the gospel is true. It includes being filled with joy and praise in the knowledge of the truth of this news of God's Son. The emphasis on Jesus as come in the *flesh* is to be heavily underscored, said Edwards; the Spirit speaks of no "mystical" Christ, no "light within," in His stead. The Spirit testifies to that Son of God come in the flesh, whom the devil hates and always slanders and towards whom Satan never raises man's affections in love, gratitude, and trust.[499]

This is the first evidence of the saving work of the Holy Spirit: the conviction that Jesus Christ as the Scriptures describe Him is the Son of God come in the flesh for the salvation of the sons of men.

Second, "When the Spirit ... at work operates against the interests of Satan's kingdom," opposing sin and all forms of worldly lust, then we can be sure that this Spirit is truly of God.[500] Satan does not fight against himself. When people are led to resist his kingdom, to strive to cleave to Christ and the things He wishes for them, then they can be sure that the Spirit that inspired them thus to struggle against sin is God's own.

> It is not to be supposed that Satan would convince men of sin, and awaken the conscience; it can no way serve his end to make that candle of the Lord shine the brighter and to open the mouth of that vicegerent of God in the soul ...
>
> And therefore, if we see persons made sensible of the dreadful nature of sin, and of the displeasure of God against it; of their own miserable condition as they are in themselves, by reason of sin, and earnestly concerned for their eternal salvation, and

---

498 Ibid., 539.
499 Ibid. He cites Matthew 10:32, Romans 15:9, Philippians 2:11, 1 Corinthians 12:3.
500 Ibid., 540.

sensible of their need for God's pity and help, and engaged to seek it in the use of the means that God has appointed, we may certainly conclude that it is from the Spirit of God, whatever effects this concern has on their bodies; though it cause them to cry out aloud ... or to faint; or though it throw them into convulsions, or whatever other way the blood and spirits are moved.[501]

It is the Spirit of God that draws people away from their former lusts and sins, and He does so "by the sense they have of the excellency of divine things, and the affection they have to those spiritual enjoyments of another world, that are promised in the gospel."[502]

Third, a sure sign of the Spirit's gracious work is when people are caused to have "a greater regard to the Holy Scriptures," and a greater conviction of their "truth and divinity."[503] "We are of God; he that knoweth God heareth us" (1 John 4:6). This, says Edwards, applies also to the works of all the prophets and apostles: those who know God hear their testimony to be the testimony of God's own faithful and authoritative witnesses.[504] Such a love and high regard for God's message to men would not be inspired by the Adversary. "To the law and to the testimony, is never the cry of those evil spirits that have no light in them ..."[505] God alone gives such a love for the things contained in His written word. It is the sign of those who do not know Him that they seek other sources than His for their doctrine.[506] When people find in themselves, therefore, an increasing love for this holy book and for its doctrines, they can thank God's Spirit for working this within them. Satan would not and does not do such a thing: "Would the prince of darkness, in order to promote his kingdom of darkness, lead men to the sun?"[507]

---

501 Ibid., 540-541. He cites Matthew 12:25-26.
502 Ibid.
503 Ibid.
504 Ibid. He cites Ephesians 2:20.
505 Ibid., 542. He cites Isaiah 8:19-20, and Revelation 19:15.
506 This point is not the least of the contributions Edwards might make to modern Protestant theology.
507 Ibid., 542.

Fourth, the sixth verse of this chapter of John's Epistle gives us another sign in the words, "The spirit of truth and the spirit of error." Edwards explains:

> ... if, by observing the manner of the operation of a spirit that is at work among a people, we see that it operates as a spirit of truth, leading persons to truth, convicting them of those things that are true, we may safely determine that it is a right and true spirit.[508]

If they become convinced of the reality of God, and of His holiness and His hatred of sin, and of the brevity of their lives on earth, but eternal accountability of their souls in the life to come; and if they become convinced of their sin and guilt and of their desperate needs of Him – then, as this teaching is true, they have been led to it by the Spirit of Truth Himself. God and God alone makes men "sensible of things as they really are." When this occurs in a person, his "duty is immediately to thank God for it ..."[509] The Spirit of truth leads people into the truth as it is in Jesus.

Fifth, "If the spirit that is at work among a people operates as a spirit of love to God and man, it is a sure sign that it is the Spirit of God." This, says Edwards, is stressed throughout the rest of this chapter from John.

> In these verses (12 and 13) love is spoken of as if it were that wherein the very nature of the Holy Spirit consisted; or, as if *divine love* dwelling in us, and the *Spirit of God* dwelling in us, were the same thing; as is also in the last two verses of the foregoing chapter. Therefore this last mark which the apostle gives of the true Spirit he seems to speak of as the most eminent: and so insists much more largely upon it, than upon all the rest; and speaks expressly of both love to God and men ...[510]

When "the Spirit that is at work among a people" fills them with profound awareness of and enjoyment in God's "glorious perfections; and works in them an admiring, delightful sense of the excellency of Jesus Christ," showing Him to be "altogether lovely, and makes Him precious to the soul," and wins and attracts their hearts and minds to Him and "the wonderful free love of God in giving His only-begotten Son to die for us," then we can be sure that it is the Holy Spirit of God that so works among this people, and not another spirit.[511]

---

508 Ibid.
509 Ibid., 543.
510 Ibid.
511 Ibid.

This is not to say that hypocrites, or deluded persons, may not manifest an imitation of such love; indeed they may, as the history of the Christian church amply demonstrates. But true Christian love is that which "arises from apprehension of the wonderful riches of the free grace and sovereignty of God's love to us, in Christ Jesus ..." It is, furthermore, "attended with a sense of our own utter unworthiness, as in ourselves the enemies and haters of God and Christ, and with a renunciation of all our own excellency and righteousness." The chief characteristic of this true Christian love, therefore, is humility: a humility that really "renounces, abases, and annihilates what we call self. Christian love, or true charity, is a humble love. 1 Cor. 13:4, 5."[512] It is a love that fills us with a sense of our "littleness, vileness, weakness, and utter insufficiency; and so with self-diffidence, self-emptiness, self-renunciation, and poverty of spirit; these are the manifest tokens of the Spirit of God." This Spirit makes Christ to be our example; we are led to love not only friends but enemies. Edwards concludes: "Love and humility are two things the most contrary to the spirit of the devil, of any thing in the world; for the character of that evil spirit, above all things, consists in pride and malice."[513]

Summary: these five things, then, are "sure signs" of the work of the Spirit of God in His regenerating and saving action among men: 1) a love for Jesus Christ as the Son of God who came in the flesh for our salvation; 2) an increasing war against sin, and a dread and hatred of it, brought about through a powerful consciousness of the glory of "divine things" revealed in the gospel of Christ; 3) a high esteem of the Holy Scriptures as the written revelation of God to men, and a love of the doctrines concerning our salvation and our Savior therein contained; 4) a being taught the truth of God and man, as it is revealed in the gospel of Christ – a being led from darkness into light, from ignorance of God into His truth; and 5) a love of God and of men that is marked by humility and self-renunciation, and total dependence on God for all that pertains to this life and the next.

Edwards concludes his *Distinguishing Marks of a Work of the Spirit of God* with a section entitled "Practical Inferences." He discusses here the correspondence between the biblical marks or signs as he has just enumerated and their manifestation in the Great Awakening. He shows also common elements in the cases of many persons of his acquaintance who had come to know Christ, and who manifested the signs in

---

512 Ibid., 544.
513 Ibid.

their lives. We will not follow his argument further, except to note one very important point that he makes in his conclusion, and that is, the distinction between *gifts* and the *grace* of the Spirit. This distinction is important in Reformed theology, and it is central to Edwards' view. He says:

> Some of the true friends of the work of God's Spirit have erred in giving too much heed to impulses and strong impressions on their minds, as though they were immediate significations from heaven to them, or something that it was the mind and will of God that they should do, which was not signified or revealed anywhere in the Bible without those impulses. These impressions, if they are truly from the Spirit of God, are of a quite different nature from His gracious influences on the hearts of the saints: they are of the nature of the extraordinary *gifts* of the Spirit, and are properly inspiration, such as the prophets and apostles and others had of old: which the apostle distinguishes from the *grace* of the Spirit, 1 Cor. 13.[514]

People were confusing these two things, he says, partly because of a misunderstanding concerning the biblical witness about them. They thought that in the last days the Spirit would restore to His church the "*extraordinary gifts* of the Spirit" such as characterized apostolic and prophetic times. These were given chiefly to serve the *grace* of the Spirit, which is divine love in the soul.

> God communicates His own nature to the soul in saving grace in the heart, more than in all miraculous *gifts*. The blessed image of God consists in *that* and not in *these*. The excellency, happiness, and glory of the soul immediately consists in the former ... Salvation and the eternal enjoyment of God is promised to divine grace, but not to inspiration. A man may have these extraordinary gifts, and yet be abominable to God, and go to hell ... Many wicked men at the day of judgment will plead, 'Have we not prophesied in thy name, and in thy name cast out devils?' The greatest privilege of the prophets and apostles, was not their being inspired and working miracles, but their eminent holiness. The grace that was in their hearts, was a thousand times more their dignity and honor, than their miraculous gifts ... The influences of the Holy Spirit, or divine charity in the heart, is the greatest privilege and glory of the highest archangel in heaven; yea, this is the very thing by which the creature has fellowship with God Himself, with the Father and the

---

514 Ibid., 556.

> Son, in their beauty and happiness. Hereby the saints are made partakers of the divine nature, and have Christ's joy fulfilled in themselves.[515]

It is the "ordinary sanctifying influences of the Spirit of God" which are the "*end*" of all miraculous gifts, and the purpose for which the latter are given. It is the saving grace in the heart that is the divine love shed abroad by the indwelling of the Holy Spirit. Miraculous *gifts* were given in prophetic and apostolic times to serve the *grace* of God in the establishing of the church, Edwards thought. Edwards cautions New England Christians from giving heed uncritically to strong mental impressions or claiming that they were revelatory.: "I have seen them fail in very many instances ..." Not only that, but he knows by "experience that impressions being made with great power and upon the minds of true, yea, eminent saints ... are no signs of their being revelations from heaven."[516] So that "They who leave the sure word of prophecy [i.e., Scripture] – which God has given us as a light shining in a dark place – to follow such impressions and impulses, leave the guidance of the polar star, to follow a *Jack with a lantern*."[517]

The *grace* of the Spirit, therefore, is to be preferred to all the miraculous *gifts* He may give. For the grace of the Spirit is Himself, in the hearts of the saints.

The Religious Affections

In 1742 and 1743, the Great Awakening was enjoying its most pronounced effects, and Edwards gave a series of lectures in his parish to guide his people during this momentous time. These lectures were later prepared for publication and appeared in Boston in 1746 under the title, *A Treatise Concerning Religious Affections*. This work was reprinted in Boston and in London in the 1760s and again in the 1770s, was published in Edinburgh in 1777, frequently abridged (once by John Wesley), translated into Dutch, and published in Utrecht in 1779 and put into Welsh the following century. This was unquestionably Edwards' most popular publication, many thousands of copies appearing well into the nineteenth century; it was also his most thorough attempt to expound the biblical witness to the signs of the Holy Spirit's saving work in men.[518]

---

515 Ibid., 557.
516 Ibid., 557f.
517 Ibid., 559.
518 See pages 74ff of the excellent editor's introduction to the Yale edition of *Reli-*

The *Religious Affections* is divided into three parts: part one is a general defense (against the rationalists in the church) of the biblical witness concerning the fact that when men are called by God into fellowship with Him they really are *"affected."* To those who threw up their hands in horror at any element of real personal change in those professing to be Christians, Edwards demonstrated that "True religion, in great part, consists in holy affections ..." and not primarily in the merely intellectual cogitations by means of which many churchmen wished to describe it. Scripture, he says, shows that the "affections" most evidenced by those whom God has called to Himself are those of "fear, hope, love, hatred, desire, joy, sorrow, gratitude, compassion and zeal."[519]

> The Scriptures place much of religion in godly fear ... hope in God and in the promises of His word ... love, love to God, and the Lord Jesus Christ, and love to the people of God, and to mankind ... hatred also, as having sin to its object ...[520]

"Affections," he continues, are "... no other than the more vigorous and sensible exercises of the inclination and will of the soul." God has given man's soul "two faculties" chiefly – *understanding* and the *affections*. The former, the *understanding*, is the faculty by means of which we rationally perceive, speculate, discern, and judge of matters. It is to this faculty that the gospel of Christ is addressed, expounding to our minds the revelation of God in Christ Jesus. The second faculty, the *affections*, is that by means of which the soul not only perceives but is drawn to, or repelled by, an object presented to the understanding. It is the inclination of the heart either for, or against, that which impinges upon the consciousness of rational creatures.

> This faculty is called by various names: it is sometimes called the *inclination*; and as it has respect to the actions that are determined by it, it is called the *will*; and the *mind*, with regard to the exercise of this faculty, is often called the *heart*.[521]

The complexity of this definition should warn us against the common error (against which Edwards himself was fighting) of simply opposing the one faculty to the other, the "head" to the "heart," the "understanding" to the "passions," as has been so popular in theological polemics. To the rationalists in the church, all "affections" were

gious Affections, the second volume in the Yale *Works* project.
519 Ibid., 102.
520 Ibid., 102-104. Edwards here cites many, many biblical passages to support this fundamental point.
521 Ibid., 96.

regarded as "passions." To many enthusiastic followers of the revivals, the intellectual element of Christian faith was badly misunderstood and erroneously condemned. Edwards repudiated the one-sidedness of each of these extremist positions. As he understood the meaning of the biblical term "heart," it signified the whole person in action, his mind and his will included, being attracted to or repelled by something presented to him through his consciousness. So that "the affections are no other than the more vigorous and sensible exercises of the inclination and will of the soul."[522] The "affections," further, are to be distinguished from the "passions" in that the latter describe the strong motions or inclinations that are "more sudden, and whose effects … more violent, and the mind more overpowered and less in its own command."[523] The "affections," on the contrary, are the settled, prevailing dispositions and attitudes of the whole man – his mind, heart, will, and soul. (It will be recognized what difficulties of psychological vocabulary hindered eighteenth-century discussion. We can best understand Edwards by tracing out in his own examples the meanings he wishes to assign to these terms. In this way some of the apparent difficulties found in his synthetic definitions may be resolved.)

In the second part of the *Religious Affections*, Edwards discusses twelve signs that, of themselves, "Are No Certain Signs that Religious Affections are Truly Gracious, or that They Are Not."[524] This section is quite similar to the first part of the *Distinguishing Marks*, but there are additions here that are of some importance.

In the first three signs, Edwards – similar to the manner of the other treatise – shows that neither proof nor disproof that a work among men is from God's own Spirit is offered by the strength of the effects or "affections"; nor by bodily manifestations, nor by the persons involved speaking a great deal about the things of religion.[525] In the fourth sign, he says that nothing is proved either way by the fact that a person did not himself provoke or inspire within himself the desire to set his "affections" on the things of religion. If the affections are truly Christian, then *of course* they are not self-motivated, but they may have been provoked by another agent – Satan, for example. That "persons did not

---

522 Ibid.
523 Ibid., 98.
524 Ibid., 125.
525 Ibid., 127-137.

make 'em themselves, or exite 'em of their own contrivance ..." is no certain sign either way.[526]

The fifth sign is interesting. Many persons claimed comfort from the fact that Bible verses were often brought remarkably to their minds. This, they said, must be the supernatural action of God within them.[527] Edwards agreed that God often worked in this way in the saints, but he reminded his readers that the temptations of Christ in the wilderness were provoked by Scriptural verses being brought to mind by Satan! What the devil did then to the Lord he can certainly do now to weak men.[528]

Sixth, "'Tis no evidence that religious affections are saving, or that they are otherwise, that there is an appearance of love in them." What Satan cannot *produce* – real love – he can nevertheless *imitate*.[529]

Seventh, even though a variety of signs of religious affections appear in a person's character and manner, this gives no conclusive proof that these affections are Christian and from the indwelling of Christ's Spirit. Though false religion is usually "maimed and monstrous," yet "when false affections are raised high, there are many false affections that attend each other."[530] It is natural for a person's whole character to be somewhat conformed by his giving strong allegiances to some object or ideal. No sure sign is thereby given that these various affections are from Christ's regenerating work.

The eighth sign is important: "Nothing can certainly be determined concerning the nature of the affections by this, that comforts and joys seem to follow awakening and convictions of conscience, in a *certain order*."[531] Edwards' treatment of this problem – the *ordo salutis* – is significant, and reveals a depth not always found either among his contemporaries or among those claiming his influence. First, he asserts that God, when saving men, saves them from a dreadful fate; not only so, He makes them know the dreadfulness of their situation, and to call upon Him for mercy and forgiveness. Edwards here appears to lay emphasis on the Lutheran insistence that the Law is presented

---

526 Ibid., 138.
527 Ibid., 142.
528 Ibid., 144f. See his discussion of the great use God makes both of Scripture, and of heretical teachers in the church.
529 Ibid., 146.
530 Ibid., 147f. He cites 1 Samuel 24:16-17, 26:21; Romans 10:2; 2 Kings 17:32-33; Psalm 106:12; Matthew 13:20; Acts 22:3, etc.
531 Ibid., 151. See also 418.

before the Gospel. It is with the individual soul today, he says, as it was with Israel of old, who,

> ... before God heals them, are brought to acknowledge that they have sinned, and have not obeyed the voice of the Lord, and to see that they lie down in their shame ... and that only God can save them ...[532]

Ordinarily, therefore, God makes people *know* – to *see* and *sense* and *feel* – the horror of sin and of His wrath from which they must be delivered before He actually does save them.

And yet – here Edwards departed from much popular thought in Puritan circles – for people to have terrors of conscience through conviction of sin, and then to have peace in the promise of the gospel (in that order), is no proof that this sequence is from the gracious working of the Holy Spirit. The devil also works to accuse men's consciences by the use of God's law – and he also gives persons a false peace after such convictions of sin. Further, the "unmortified corruption" of man's own "heart may quench the Spirit of God ... by leading men to presumptions; and self-exalting hopes and joys ..."[533]

The point is that if the *work* of the Spirit can be imitated, the *order* of that work can also be counterfeited.

But, more important, "the Spirit is so exceeding various in the manner of His operating, that in many cases it is impossible to trace Him, or find out His way."[534]

The ninth sign is self-explanatory: "'Tis no certain sign that the religious affections ... dispose persons to spend much time in religion, and to be zealously engaged in the external duties of worship."[535]

Tenth, that people praise God frequently with their mouths is no sure sign of saving grace within their hearts. This is similar to the third and ninth signs, but, because of the prevailing confusion on this score, Edwards had to deal with it repeatedly. He cites the praise the multitudes gave Christ – and how these same zealous mouths cried a short time later, "Crucify Him, crucify Him!"[536]

---

532 Ibid., 152f. He cites Deuteronomy 32:36-37, Exodus 2:23, 5:19, Luke 8:43-44, Matthew 15:22, 2 Corinthians 1:8-10, etc. He quotes also from the works of Stoddard, Perkins, and Shepherd.

533 Ibid., 157.

534 Ibid., 162. See the discussion that begins on 160.

535 Ibid., 163.

536 Ibid., 165f.

Eleventh, "'Tis no sign that affections are right, or that they are wrong, that they make persons that have them, exceeding confident that what they experience is divine, and that they are in a good estate."[537] This is not meant to negate the biblical doctrine of assurance, says Edwards: Scripture promises assurance to the saints, and the Reformers fought Rome on this score.[538] But men can deceive themselves in this matter; the devil can also mislead them, and give them false confidences. A good test is this: "The comfort of the true saints increases awakening and caution," while the other kind merely puts men's minds at ease with the comfortable conviction that they are right with God, and may thus "rest assured"; their view of God's holiness and majesty becomes dim, and likewise their sense of their own sin and corruption.[539]

Certainty, however, is of itself no conclusive sign. The true faith that men have in God is that faith "by which men are *brought into* a good estate," and not their mere "believing that they are *already in* a good estate."[540] More signs than the mere *feeling* of assurance are needed.

And yet, says Edwards, when true saints fall into despair, it is often because their love for God has grown cold. God, at such times, withdraws the comforts of His Spirit so that they might come to fear for their souls and stir themselves again to gratitude and obedience. In giving in to their lusts, they are bound to lose the comforts of God's love; and He means that they should, until they repent and seek again His forgiveness, and pursue thorough reformation. When He comes again with power, their hearts are flooded with love: "Fear is cast out by the Spirit of God, no other way than by the prevailing of love: nor is it ever maintained by His Spirit, when love is asleep."[541] It is wrong to comfort the saints with a remembrance of their conversion or other experiences, when they are currently indulging in sin or sloth, and thus have fear for their relationship with God. God *intends* that they fear and tremble in such a situation so that they might be moved to repent and receive again His peace.

---

537 Ibid., 167.
538 Ibid., 167f. He cites Job 19:25; 2 King 20:3; John 15:11, 16:33; Galatians 2:20; Philippians 1:21; 2 Timothy 1:12; Hebrews 6:17-18, 9:9; 2 Peter 1:5-8; 1 Corinthians 2:12, 9:26; 1 John 2:3, 5, 3:14, 19, 24; etc.
539 Ibid., 172. See his whole discussion of that false faith that rests on a conviction of its own *belief*, and that true faith that actually rests upon Jesus and His saving work, *op. cit.*, 167-181.
540 Ibid., 178.
541 Ibid., 180.

Twelfth, it is no certain sign that persons are subjects of the regenerating work of the Spirit, that other newborn Christians consider them so to be.[542]

This is a point of critical importance: *no one but God Himself can surely judge another's soul*. All of the signs Edwards gives are stated with the proviso that they are chiefly intended for the use of individuals in judging their own hearts with regard to their relationship with God: "The true saints have not such a spirit of discerning, that they can certainly determine who are godly, and who are not." They cannot see into the hearts of others.[543] Persons must not rest content merely because others consider them to be true followers of Christ. The only guide given for the provisional estimations of others is the biblical one, "By their fruits ye shall know them."[544] Nowhere are we guaranteed infallibility in the application of this principle!

To summarize, Christians cannot judge whether they have been born again in the Spirit by any such signs as the twelve listed above, although many of these signs *are* worked by the Holy Spirit in His regenerating operations among men. Other agents can produce signs such as these, however, so in and of themselves they offer no decisive help in discerning the saving work of the Spirit of God.

What, then, are the more positive signs by which the Holy Spirit's work may be distinguished from the work of other spirits and other causes? Let us turn now to the third and concluding section of Edwards' *Religious Affections* for his extensive answer to this question.

This third part of his book is headed by the statement, "Shewing What Are Distinguishing Signs of Truly Gracious and Holy Affections."

Edwards begins this section by reminding his readers again that no signs can be given to make infallible judgment possible. God alone sees our hearts.[545] Furthermore, he stresses (again) that these positive signs will not be likely to help a regenerate person who has fallen into "a dead, carnal and unchristian frame." The work of grace is so small in such a case, and the person's spiritual vision so clouded with sin and ingratitude, that the Scriptural signs cannot by such persons be applied

---

542 Ibid., 181.
543 Ibid., 181f. Edwards here quotes from a number of the Puritan writers, showing their agreement with the view he is maintaining. He refers also to 2 Samuel 6:7; Isaiah 11:31; Matthew 13:26; Revelation 2:17; etc.
544 This point will be stressed in subsequent pages.
545 Ibid., 193f. See *Works in Four Volumes*, 1, 169, 173.

with much success; nor did God intend that they be in such situations. Edwards explains:

> And therefore many persons in such a case spend time in fruit-less labor, in poring on past experiences, and examining themselves by signs they hear ... when there is other work for them to do, that is much more expected of them; which, while they neglect, all their self-examinations are like to be in vain ... The accursed thing is to be destroyed from their camp, and Achan to be slain; and till this be done they will be in trouble. It is not God's design that men should obtain assurance in any other way, than by mortifying corruption, and increasing in grace, and obtaining the lively exercises of it. And although self-exam-ination is a duty of great use and importance, and by no means to be neglected; yet it is not the principal means, by which the saints do get satisfaction of their good estate. *Assurance is not to be obtained so much by self-examination as by action ...* 1 Cor. 9:26.[546]

With these two things in mind, let us turn now to his treatment of the biblical evidences for discerning the regenerating work of the Holy Spirit.[547] Edwards lists twelve positive signs.

First, "Affections that are truly spiritual and gracious, do arise from those influences and operations on the heart that are *spiritual, super-natural*, and *divine*."[548]

This, of course, refers to that indwelling of the Holy Spirit discussed in the previous chapter. The nature of the affections is "spiritual" in that they are the fruit of the Holy Spirit's presence and work in the heart. They are "supernatural" in that they are *His* work (operating through a new and newly-made-willing human heart) and are what a person could never do of himself, by his own powers; and they are "divine" in the sense previously discussed.[549] This sign, therefore, is really the

---

546 Ibid., 195f. The emphases are the author's.

547 We mention again that these "signs" were first presented to Edwards' congrega-tion in the form of lectures, and they thus presuppose thorough knowledge of the matters discussed in the five positive "marks" of his *Distinguishing Marks* (i.e., a love of Christ as God's Son come in the flesh for our salvation, increas-ing power over sin and increasing hatred of it, increasing love for the Scriptures and the things of God therein revealed, growth in the truth and disengagement from error, and, finally, increasing love for God and men.)

548 Ibid., 197. Edwards' emphases.

549 Edwards here makes a careful distinction, in order to guard against the error of supposing that God is exhausted in this, His self-giving, and that "no more"

foundation of all the others, and the grounds for their possibility. This condition comes about by a person's being supernaturally persuaded that the gospel of Christ is true, and truly spoken by God to him. A sinner is thereby "convinced of the veracity of God, and that the Scriptures are His Word," and he then needs no new revelations or dramatic invitations to accept the proffered mercy of God.[550] What is effected here is a "spiritual application of the Word of God ..." Edwards explains:

> A spiritual application of the Word of God consists in applying it to the heart, in spiritually enlightening, sanctifying influences. A spiritual application of an invitation or offer of the gospel consists in giving the soul a spiritual sense or relish of the holy and divine blessings offered, and also the sweet and wonderful grace of the offerer, in making so gracious an offer, and of His holy excellency and faithfulness to fulfill what He offers ... so leading and drawing forth the heart to embrace the offer ... And so a spiritual application of the promises of Scripture, for the comfort of the saints, consists in enlightening their minds to see the holy excellency and sweetness of the blessings promised, and also the holy excellency of the promiser ... thus drawing forth their hearts to embrace the promiser, and things promised; and by this means, giving the sensible actings of grace, enabling them to see their grace, and so their title to the promise.[551]

The first thing to be said of truly gracious affections, therefore, is that they are the fruit of the indwelling of the Holy Spirit, and of the new life of joy and trust and gratitude in God and His word thereby bestowed. Men are thus inspired to serve Him, to do His gracious will.

Second, "The first objective ground of gracious affections, is the transcendentally excellent and amiable nature of divine things, as they are in themselves; and not any conceived relation they bear to self or

---

of Him remains in heaven. He says, "Not that the saints are made partakers of the essence of God, and so are 'Godded' with God, and 'Christed' with Christ, according to the abominable and blasphemous language and notions of some heretics; but, to use the Scripture phrase, they are made partakers of God's fullness (Eph. 3:17-19; John 1:16), that is, of God's spiritual beauty and happiness, according to the measure and capacity of a creature; for so it is evident the word 'fullness' signifies in Scripture language." Ibid., 203. Edwards defends the *extra Calvinisticum.*

550 Ibid., 222-223. See his use of the prominentPuritan writer Thomas Shepard, at this point.

551 Ibid., 225.

self-interest."[552] God *is* truly glorious and excellent and lovable, and the Spirit gives men a love for *this* God, for who He is, as He is in Himself. The Spirit makes people see and sense and know His surpassing majesty and beauty and holiness, and the joy of fellowship with *this* kind of Being. Certainly, people come to know Him only through the gracious gospel of Jesus Christ and His sacrifice and resurrection for them. Certainly, they are made joyful and grateful by the magnitude of the gifts received in this affair. But the *basis* of the saints' love to God is not His being the "answer" given to man's desperate "questioning," or His being the most perfect "satisfaction" for the articulated "needs" of the natural man. The basis of the saints' love to God *is the real conscious-ness and awareness they are given of the glorious nature of the Being who also gives Himself to them.* The object of Christian sight is therefore not "my salvation"; it is "My God." The distinction is decisive.[553]

"Hypocrites," Edwards says, rejoice primarily in "themselves," admiring their own experiences, "and what they are primarily taken and elevated with, is not the glory of God or beauty of Christ, but the beauty of their experiences ..." They thus "put their experiences in the place of Christ, and His beauty and fullness," and they "take more comfort in their discoveries than in Christ discovered ..."[554] Truly gracious and saving affections, by contrast, are based on a foundation that is "out of self, in God and Jesus Christ ..."[555]

Third, "Those affections that are truly holy, are primarily founded on the loveliness of the moral excellency of divine things. Or ... a love to divine things for the beauty and sweetness of their moral excellency ..."[556] By "moral," Edwards explains, he does not mean what the term "morality" usually implies. Rather, he refers to "that which is contrary to sin, i.e., holiness or virtue."[557] He is speaking not of some code of ethics, but of the living God of Israel and the church. He distinguishes between *natural* and *moral* evil, and *natural* and *moral* good. Natural good, in reference to God, describes His attributes of power, knowl-edge, etc. The moral attributes are His holiness, beauty, righteousness, etc. It is by the exercise of His moral attributes that God opens to His people His mind and His heart, showing His goodness and faithful-

---

552 Ibid., 240f.
553 Ibid., 244f.
554 Ibid., 251-252.
555 Ibid., 253.
556 Ibid., 253-254.
557 Ibid., 254.

ness, His holiness and love. The basis of truly gracious affections, then, is the view humans receive of the moral beauty of God. It is the love of divine things for their holiness and moral excellency (as defined in the gospel) that is "the beginning and spring of all holy affections."[558] From loving God in this way men are drawn to love Him for all His work and for the whole of His Being. The Spirit, in regenerating a person, gives him a "sense" and a "taste" of the glorious beauty of God's holiness and faithfulness and love.

Fourth, "Gracious affections do arise from the mind's being enlightened, rightly and spiritually to understand or apprehend divine things."[559] This is one of the most important sections of the *Religious Affections* and we must recall what was said earlier about the "Divine and Supernatural Light" that God manifests to the saints by His word and Spirit (see above, 188 ff.). "Holy affections are not heat without light; but evermore arise from some information of the understanding, some spiritual instruction that the mind receives, some light or actual knowledge."[560] The Christian is made to "see and understand something more of divine things than he did before, more of God or Christ and of the glorious things exhibited in the gospel ... Knowledge is the key that first opens the way for men into the kingdom of heaven ..."[561] Gracious affections lead believers into more and more knowledge of and love for Christ and cause them to busy themselves in learning about Him. The knowledge gained is "certainly a kind of understanding, apprehension or discerning of divine things, that natural men have nothing of, which the Apostle speaks of ... 1 Cor. 2:14 ..."[562] This apprehension is also a love of God and of the gospel, a love of the loveliness of divine things therein revealed. So that "spiritual understanding," Edwards says,

> ... consists of a sense of the heart, of the supreme beauty and sweetness of the holiness or the moral perfection of divine things, together with all that discerning and knowledge of divine things of religion that depends upon, and flows from such a sense. Spiritual understanding consists primarily in a sense of heart of that spiritual beauty.[563]

---

558 Ibid., 256. This is quite concrete: it is no *mysterium tremendum*; it is the revealed Triune God, in all His moral and natural beauty, who is adored by Christians.
559 Ibid., 266.
560 Ibid.
561 Ibid.
562 Ibid., 270.
563 Ibid., 272.

Against the one-sided emphases of both rationalists and enthusiasts, Edwards underscored the point that both the mind and the heart of man are caught up in this spiritual sense that God gives through His word and Spirit.

> ... nor can there be a clear distinction made between the two faculties of understanding and will, as acting distinctly and separately in this matter. When the mind is sensible of the sweet beauty and amiableness of a thing, that implies a sensibleness of sweetness and delight in the presence of the idea of it: and this sensibleness of the amiableness or delightfulness of beauty, carries in the very nature of it, the sense of the heart; or an effect and impression the soul is the subject of, as a substance possessed or taste, inclination and will.[564]

This, then, is the nature of that spiritual apprehension or understanding of divine things that the Spirit gives in regeneration. A lack of this "sense of the heart," therefore, indicates a lack of the regenerating work of God:

> Well therefore may the Scriptures represent those who are destitute of that spiritual sense, by which is perceived the beauty of holiness, as totally blind, deaf and senseless, yea, dead. And well may regeneration, in which this divine sense is given to the soul by its Creator, be represented as opening the blind eyes, and raising the dead, and bringing a person into a new world ... 2 Cor. 5:16-17.

Edwards continues:

> ... He that sees not the beauty of holiness, knows not what one of the graces of God's Spirit is; he is destitute of any idea or conception of all gracious exercises of soul, and all holy comforts and delights, and all effects of the saving influences of the Spirit of God on the heart ... and in effect is ignorant of the whole spiritual world.[565]

Having received this "taste" and "sense" of holiness, a Christian is enabled to discern what is pleasing to God and what is not, to know what is right for him to do, and what is wrong. The soul is thus helped in its obedience to God's word.[566]

---

564 Ibid.
565 Ibid., 274-275.
566 Ibid., 275.

Fifth, "Truly gracious affections are attended with a reasonable and spiritual conviction of the judgment, of the reality and certainty of divine things."[567]

"All those who are truly gracious persons have a solid, full, thorough and effectual conviction of the truth of the great things of the gospel."[568] Their minds are persuaded of the truth of God's word. There is no *sacrificium intellectualis* here; the saints are really convinced, and their minds are spiritually opened to the sight of God's revelation in the gospel of His Son.[569]

Rational persuasion alone, of course, is not enough. The devils in hell are so persuaded. The intellectual persuasion true Christians have is a conviction accompanied with the "sense of the heart" described in the previous sign. It is a persuasion of the mind and of the heart, with the spiritual "sense" and "taste" of the beauty of the holiness and love therein revealed.[570] "A sense of the true divine beauty being given to the soul, the soul discerns the beauty of every part of the gospel scheme." It is, therefore, a "reasonable solid persuasion and conviction of the truth of the gospel, by internal evidences of it," and not merely by external or historical arguments.[571] It comes, rather, by the sight of God's glory and truth given in the new spiritual apprehension. People are really convinced.

Sixth, "Gracious affections are attended with evangelical humiliation."[572] Edwards defines this "evangelical humiliation" as a "sense that a Christian has of his own utter insufficiency, despicableness, and odiousness, with an answerable frame of heart,"[573] and this "evangelical humiliation" is to be distinguished from "legal" humiliation. The latter is often effected in unregenerate men by the Holy Spirit, whereby they are convinced of their sin and guilt, and of the wrath of God, and of His natural attributes. The former, however, is "from the special influences of the Spirit of God, implanting and exercising supernatural and divine principles" and giving a "discovery of the beauty of God's holiness and moral perfection."[574] Above all, by "evangelical humiliation" believers'

---

567 Ibid., 291.
568 Ibid.
569 Ibid., 291-292.
570 Ibid., 297. See the discussion beginning on 293.
571 Ibid., 302f.
572 Ibid., 311.
573 Ibid.
574 Ibid.

hearts are changed, and they "are brought sweetly to yield, and freely and with delight to prostrate themselves at the feet of God."[575] This is that "brokenness" of heart, and "poverty of spirit" and childlikeness, of which the Gospels often speak. The whole of the gospel is calculated to bring sinners to this sort of humiliation.[576] Such evangelical humiliation is one of the "most essential things pertaining to true Christianity." It is the major part of Christian self-denial, of his self-denial of his own "natural self-exaltation" and pride.[577]

This problem of pride was one of the major causes of chaos during the Great Awakening, and Edwards was convinced it was the chief enemy of the revival, that caused more Christians to stumble and fall, and more unbelievers to turn from the gospel being offered at that time.[578] This pride, which masqueraded as humility, wrecked the good work of the Spirit, and revealed, more than anything else, "the deceitfulness of the heart of man ..."[579] It manifested itself especially 1) by its inclination to magnify one's own spiritual attainments, and 2) by its claiming to possess great humility. Against these two tendencies, true evangelical humiliation makes a Christian really aware of his spiritual poverty, of the incalculable extent of his own corruption, of the unimaginable degree of his failure to love and thank God as much as he ought.[580]

Seventh, "Another thing, wherein gracious affections are distinguished from others, is, that they are attended with a change in nature."[581] This is almost a summary of his doctrine of regeneration.

> Therefore if there be no great and remarkable, abiding change in persons, that think they have experienced a work of conversion, vain are all their imaginations and pretenses ... Conversion ... is a great and universal change of the man, turning him from sin to God ... thenceforward he becomes a holy person, and an enemy to sin.[582]

If this abiding change of nature and of disposition, or prevailing inclination and habit, does not occur, then a person may be sure he has not been converted to God.

---

575 Ibid., 312.
576 Ibid.
577 Ibid., 314-315.
578 *Works in Four Volumes*, 3, 363f.
579 *Works* (Yale), 2, 319.
580 Ibid., 320f.
581 Ibid., 340.
582 Ibid., 340-341.

Edwards again adds a very important qualification:

> Indeed allowances must be made for the natural temper: conversion don't entirely root out the natural temper: those sins which a man by his natural constitution was most inclined to before his conversion, he may be most apt to fall into still. But yet conversion will make a great alteration even with respect to these sins. Though grace, while imperfect, don't root out an evil natural temper; yet it is of great power and efficacy with respect to it, to correct it.[583]

Sin remains, therefore, but it no longer rules. Edwards makes another clarification:

> And a transformation of nature is continued and carried on ... to the end of life; till it is brought to perfection in glory. Hence the progress of the work of grace in the hearts of the saints, is represented in Scripture, as a continued conversion and renovation of nature ... Rom. 12:1-2 ... Eph. 1:1 ...[584]

Eighth, "Truly gracious affections differ from those affections that are false and delusive, in that they tend to, and are attended with the lamblike, dovelike spirit and temper of Jesus Christ ..." Which is to say, "they naturally beget and promote such a spirit of love, meekness, quietness, forgiveness and mercy, as appeared in Christ."[585] Edwards illustrates this from many passages of Scripture that refer to these qualities in Christ and in Christians.[586] The point, of course, is that

> Christ is full of grace; and Christians will receive of His fullness, and grace for grace: i.e., there is grace in Christians answering to grace in Christ ... such kind of graces, such a spirit and temper, the same things that belong to Christ's character, belong to theirs. That disposition wherein Christ's character does in a special manner consist, therein does His image in a special manner consist.[587]

This spirit, however, in no way militates against Christian fortitude. "The whole Christian life is compared to a warfare, and fitly so." Christians are called to be steadfast in their war against sin, but this must not be mistaken as if to mean brutality to others. "True Christian fortitude," he says, "consists in strength of mind, through grace, exerted in

---

583 Ibid., 341.
584 Ibid., 343f.
585 Ibid., 344-345.
586 Ibid., 345f.
587 Ibid., 347.

two things: in ruling and suppressing the evil ... of the mind ... and in resolutely following Christ, in the face of all manner of opposition."[588] The chief opposition is tis found within our own hearts. Therefore:

> The strength of the good soldier of Jesus Christ, appears in nothing more, than in steadfastly maintaining the holy calm, meekness, sweetness, and benevolence of his mind, amidst all the storms and injuries ... and surprising acts and events of this evil and unreasonable world ... 'He that is slow to anger is better than the mighty; and he that ruleth his spirit, than he that hath taken a city' (Prov. 16:32).[589]

Ninth, "Gracious affections soften the heart, and are attended and followed with a Christian tenderness of spirit."[590] This is quite similar to the previous sign. What Edwards wishes to emphasize here is the "tenderness" and sensitiveness of a Christian, regarding both God and sin. The Christian dreads to sin against the gracious God of the gospel, yet thinks this reverential fear in no way militates against the joy and trust he has in the God who has made him an adopted son.

Tenth, "Another thing wherein those affections that are truly gracious and holy, differ from those that are false, is beautiful symmetry and proportion."[591] This does not mean that every Christian will naturally excel in every virtue. Rather, it means that they will be drawn to that end, and will be continually reshaped by the Spirit towards such a symmetry of character and disposition. Perfection will be achieved only in heaven. Until then, all Christians are beset with errors of judgment and of character and of knowledge. These flaws render them less than perfect vessels of grace. The image of Christ that has been implanted in them by the Holy Spirit is true to the original, however; "there is feature for feature and member for member."[592] The Spirit continually works for the thorough reformation and perfecting of every Christian. Violent inconsistencies will gradually be subdued, and the whole of

---

588 Ibid., 350f.
589 Ibid., 350.
590 Ibid., 357.
591 Ibid., 365. See the quotation from John Owen, ibid., 372-373, as well as Edwards' whole discussion, 365-376. The important thing to remember here is that, as grace in the soul is God Himself in the Person of the Spirit dwelling and working therein, the whole of a Christian's personality comes to be altered by His sanctifying influences, and, given the inequalities of individual temperament and capacity, certain of the "signs" will be more readily discernible in certain persons, and in greater degree, than in others. The converse is also true.
592 Ibid.

one's character led continually towards a symmetry that fulfills that "entire sanctification" that is our destiny in heaven. All of the signs of the Spirit's regenerating work are thus related and should become increasingly apparent in the individual life.

This point is an important one, and we thus must take issue with Professor Smith's remarks on page 24 of his excellent introduction to the Yale edition of the *Religious Affections*, where he seems to miss the significance of this tenth sign. We do not agree that Edwards "nowhere considers the relations between the signs." On the contrary, we feel that the tenth sign is an explicit attempt to discuss this very problem.

Professor Smith's objection may show but another example of the difficulty under which current Edwards scholarship labored before a critical edition of the whole of Edwards' works became available. As we mentioned above, *Religious Affections* must be understood in the context of all of his writings. The *Treatise on Grace*, for example, together with *Charity and its Fruits*, is indispensable for the full appreciation of the *Affections*. Reference to these works might have given Professor Smith more confidence for the tentative conclusion he reaches concerning the actual unity there is between all of Edwards' signs.[593]

Eleventh, "Another great and very distinguishable difference between gracious affections and others is, that gracious affections, the higher they are raised, the more is a spiritual appetite and longing of the soul after spiritual attainments increased." This, Edwards asserts, is not the case with "false affections." "On the contrary, false affections rest satisfied in themselves."[594]

> The more a true saint loves God with a gracious love, the more he desires to love Him, and the more uneasy he is at his want of love to Him: the more he hates sin, the more he desires to hate it, and laments that he has so much remaining love to it ... the more he longs to long ... the kindling and raising of gracious affections is like kindling a flame; the higher it is raised, the more ardent it is ... The most eminent saints in this state are but children, compared with their future, which is their proper state of maturity and perfection ...[595]

---

593 Ibid., 24.
594 Ibid., 376. This, of course, is similar to the second sign of the *Distinguishing Marks*.
595 Ibid., 377.

A Christian does not rest upon his conversion. The more he receives from God's hand, the more he recognizes this own impoverishment and "the more does he become of an earnest beggar for grace and spiritual food, that he may grow; and the more earnestly does he pursue after it, in the use of proper means and endeavors ..."[596] He recognizes that his conversion is but a beginning – a birth – and he longs to grow to maturity. "And the Scriptures everywhere represent the seeking, striving and labor of a Christian, as being chiefly after his conversion, and his conversion as being but the beginning of the work."[597] Furthermore, this seeking of a Christian is distinguished from the seeking of an unconverted person, in that it is a seeking not after comfort but after holiness: "This is the meat and drink that is the object of the spiritual appetite ... John 4:34."[598]

Twelfth, "Gracious and holy affections have their exercise and fruit in Christian practice."[599] This, Edwards says, implies 1) that a Christian's conduct be "conformed to, and directed by Christian rules"; 2) that this be done as the chief endeavor of the Christian's life, in all that he does; and 3) "That he persists in it to the end of life," not just at certain times but at all times, "it being that business which he perseveres in through all changes, and under all trials, as long as he lives."[600]

This is the longest single section of *Religious Affections*, comprising almost eighty pages of the Yale edition and including more than four hundred references to Scripture. To Edwards' thinking, Christian *practice* was the most important single test of truly religious and saving affections, and provided the best provisional means by which a person might estimate his own relationship to God, and by which a congregation might be enabled to distinguish those who belonged in the fellowship from those who (apparently) did not. By endeavoring to render to God "universal" obedience (holding nothing back and cherishing no sin, but seeking to renounce all that God condemns), by giving one's heart to this task as the major endeavor of life, and by struggling to persevere in it through all the troubles of life – by this might persons

---

596 Ibid., 378.
597 Ibid., 381-382.
598 Ibid., 383.
599 Ibid.
600 Ibid., 383-384.

see what their hearts were made of, and by what principles and powers they are ruled.

> The tendency of grace in the heart to holy practice is very direct, and the connection most natural, close and necessary. True grace is not an unactive thing: there is nothing in the universe that in its nature has a greater tendency to fruit. Godliness in the heart has as direct a relation to practice, as a fountain has to a stream ... or as a habit of principle of action has to action: for 'tis the very nature and notion of grace, that tis a principle of holy action or practice. Regeneration, which is that work of God in which grace is infused, has a direct relation to practice; for 'tis the very end of it, with a view to which the whole work is wrought ... (Eph. 2:10) ... Yea, 'tis the very end of the redemption of Christ; 'Who gave Himself for us, that He might redeem us from all iniquity, and purify unto Himself a peculiar people, zealous of good works' (Titus 2:14) ... (Heb. 9:14) ... (Col. 1:21-22) ... (Lk. 1:74-75) ... Holy practice is as much the end of all that God does about His saints, as fruit is the end of all the husbandman does about the growth of his field or vineyard ... And therefore everything in a true Christian is calculated to reach this end. This fruit of holy practice, is what every grace, and every discovery, and every individual thing, which belongs to Christian experience, has a direct tendency to.[601]

Christian practice "is the chief of all the signs of grace,"[602] and there is nothing in Scripture more often insisted upon as the surest means of discerning such grace.[603]

> Christ, who knew best how to give us rules to judge of others, has repeated it ... that ... 'Ye shall know them by their fruits (Matt. 7:16 ... ver.20) ...' 'Either make the tree good and his fruit good ... (12:33) ... so' Luke 6:44: 'Every tree is known by his own fruit.'[604]

Furthermore, "the apostles do mention a Christian practice, as the principal ground of their esteem of persons as true Christians ... the sixth chapter of Hebrews ... Phil. 2:21-22 ... 3 John 3-6 ... Jas. 2:14, 18."[605]

---

601 Ibid., 398-399.
602 Ibid., 406.
603 Ibid., 407f.
604 Ibid.
605 Ibid., 408f.

Again, Edwards insists that no external signs are certain and infallible tests of grace in the soul,[606] but he insists also that the Scripture shows abundantly the role consistent Christian practice plays in this regard: "He that hath my commandments and keepeth them, he it is that loveth me" (John 14:21).[607] Such practice is thus a sign to the individual as well as to his Christian neighbors:

> ... 1 John 2:3: 'Hereby do we know that we know Him, if we keep His commandments' ... 'My little children, let us not love in word, neither in tongue, but in deed [in the Greek it is *ergo*, 'in work'] and in truth. And hereby we know that we are of the truth, and shall assure our own hearts before Him' (1 John 3:19) ... Heb. 6:9f ...[608]

Practice, of course, includes also the inner workings of the heart. Christian practice includes that love of God and man that expresses itself in appropriate action. The Final Judgment, where all mankind shall be "judged according to their works, and all shall receive according to the things done in the body," will examine also the inner "works" of the heart and mind and soul. God, therefore, is often spoken of as "searching the hearts and trying the reins," for the practice of the souls of men is more open to Him than their own neighbors' bodily actions.[609]

Christian practice, then, is to be preferred over one's conversion experience, "enlightenments and comforts," or feelings of grace, as a far more reliable guide for testing one's real relationship with God in Christ.[610] It is not he who feels that he has begun a race, but he that finds himself running it, who has grounds for believing that God's Spirit is working savingly in him. Scripture abounds with reference to "trials or proofs" by which gold is distinguished from stubble, and true faith from false.[611] God uses these trials abundantly to test His people, and Christians might well reflect on their own conduct and dispositions, to see whether they reveal loyalty or disloyalty to their Lord. For "there is no place in the New Testament," Edwards says, "where the declared design is to give signs of godliness, but that holy practice,

---

606 See the clear warning with which he begins the discussion of the positive signs, ibid., 193f, and 420.
607 Ibid., 410.
608 Ibid., 420f.
609 Ibid., 422f.
610 Ibid., 426f.
611 Ibid., 429f.

and keeping Christ's commandments, is the mark chosen out from all others to be insisted on."[612] Such Christian conduct testifies to persons' "sincerity," to their having "true and saving knowledge of God," to their real "repentance," their real belief in the "truth" of the gospel, their "true coming to Christ," their "true trusting in Christ for salvation," their real "humility," their "truly holy joy," and their "Christian fortitude" and "hope."[613]

There are two major objections to Edwards' position, and these he carefully examines. The first is that Christians should really "judge of their state, chiefly by their inward experiences," and not by the appeal to practice that Edwards continually made. He refutes this objection:

> To speak of Christian experience and practice, as if they were two things, properly and entirely distinct, is to make a distinction without consideration or reason. Indeed all Christian experience is not properly called practice; but all Christian practice is properly called experience ... Holy practice is one kind or part of Christian experience, and both reason and Scripture represent it as the chief, and most important, and most distinguishing part of it ... Jer. 22:15-16 ... 1 John 5:3 ... 'In all things approving ourselves as the ministers of God, in much patience, in afflictions, in necessities, in distresses ... in labors, in watchings, in fastings; by love unfeigned ... by the power of God' (2 Cor. 6:4-7) ... Phil 3:7-8 ... Col 1:29 ... 2 Tim. 4:6-7 ...[614]

It is clear, then, that "experience," if it is *Christian,* is the experience of the justifying and sanctifying power of Jesus Christ in the mind and heart and life of man. As such, this kind of experience, which issues in Christian love and behavior, is just what Edwards has discussed in this section, and the objection to it thus falls to the ground.[615]

On the other hand, those rationalists who shuddered at the very term "experience" revealed themselves as having a deficient knowledge of Scripture or of the actual working of God's Spirit:

> The witness or seal of the Spirit, that we read of, doubtless consists in the effect of the Spirit of God in the heart, in the implantation and exercises of grace there, and so consists in experience. And ... this seal of the Spirit, is the highest kind of evidence of the saints' adoption, that ever they obtain. But in

---

612 Ibid., 437.
613 Ibid., 443f.
614 Ibid., 450f.
615 Ibid., 451f.

these exercises of grace in practice, that have been spoken of, God gives witness, and sets to His seal, in the most conspicuous, eminent and evident manner. It has been abundantly found to be true in fact, by the experience of the Christian church; that Christ commonly gives, by His Spirit, the greatest, and most joyful exercises of grace, under trials ... as is manifest in the full assurance, and unspeakable joys of many of the martyrs ...[616]

The second objection to which Edwards replies, is the charge that "this is a legal doctrine; and that this making practice a thing of such great importance in religion, magnifies works, and tends to lead men to make too much of their own doings" and thus minimizes "the glory of free grace."[617]

Edwards' answer to this objection places him squarely within the Reformation tradition:

But this objection is altogether without reason. Which way is it inconsistent with the freeness of God's grace, that holy practice should be a sign of God's grace? *'Tis our works being the price of God's favor, and not their being the sure sign of it*, that is the thing which is inconsistent with the freeness of the favor.[618]

What contradicts free grace is the claiming that our works are deserving of God's favor. It is asserting that we possess inherent righteousness of our own, apart from Christ's righteousness and that these works illustrate the existence of that inherent righteousness within us.

"The notion of the freeness of the grace of God to sinners, as that is revealed and taught in the gospel, is not that no holy and amiable qualifications or actions in us will be a fruit, and so a sign of that grace; but that it is not the worthiness or loveliness of any qualification or action of ours that recommends us to that grace; that kindness is shown to the unworthy and unlovely; that there is great excellency in the benefit bestowed, and no excellency in the subject as the price of it; that goodness goes forth and flows out, from the fullness of God's nature, the fullness of the Fountain of Good, without any amiableness in the object to draw it ... Thus we are justified only by the righteousness of Christ, and not by our own righteousness."[619]

---

616 Ibid., 454.
617 Ibid., 455.
618 Ibid.
619 Ibid.

This was a very important point. Critics were using one central doctrine – that of Justification by Grace – to deny the reality of another – Sanctification. Once again, the whole of the Scriptural witness to God and His work was required, said Edwards, to find the truth in this controversy. "'Tis greatly to the hurt of religion," he said, "for persons to make light of, and insist little on, those things that the Scriptures insist most upon, as of the most importance in the evidence of our interest in Christ."[620] Scripture shows that the indwelling of the Holy Spirit brings men and women into new life, out of the living death of sin. Such persons are not perfect, but they are really being perfected. "True saints may be guilty of some kinds and degrees of backsliding – and may be soiled … and may fall into sin, yea great sins …"[621] They may fall, but they do not fall away. Their hearts having been changed, their prevailing dispositions altered, their minds given new objects and their hearts new loves, their lives now are lived for God in Christ by the power of His Spirit. They are led to grow in holiness, they "walk in newness of life, and continue to do so to the end of life."[622]

Conclusion

This present chapter "On Discerning the Spirit" has been an exposition, from Edwards' own writings, of the meaning of his statements concerning the doctrine of Regeneration. Such a presentation is required if his doctrine of Regeneration is to be understood, and that for several reasons. First, Edwards' doctrine of the New Birth in the Spirit was no idle appendage to his view of the other major *loci* of Christian teaching that he believed and preached but was integrally related to and dependent upon his doctrines of the Triune God, and of God's works *ad intra* and *ad extra*. As we have seen, Edwards was convinced that God revealed nothing less than Himself in His gracious, saving work among men. Specific, concrete observations had to be made, therefore, concerning the results of His saving work because what He does with us corresponds to who He is. As He expresses Himself in His eternal Word, and eternally comprehends all His love and joy in the Person of His Spirit, so has He revealed Himself to our minds in His Son (*Logos*, or Word), and comes into our hearts in the person of His Holy Spirit. He deals with us as He is in Himself. The *Distinguishing Marks* and the *Religious Affections* must be recognized not primarily as sociological or

---

620 Ibid., 459.
621 Ibid., 390.
622 Ibid., 391.

anthropological studies, but as doctrinal treatises that deal with man because they deal with the work of the Living God within him.[623]

Second, Edwards' doctrine of Regeneration did not arise from mere sociological or even doctrinal speculation, but rather from his attempt to exercise his specific theological and pastoral responsibility in the theological and social crises of his own time. He was thoroughly acquainted with the best Reformed and Puritan literature on this subject, and he used these rich storehouses of theological reflection for the construction of his own formulations, but it was in the exercise of his immediate responsibilities as a pastor and as a theologian that he forged the exposition of his doctrine. He did so in connection with the personal experience he and hundreds of men and women of his acquaintance had had and were having of the indwelling influences of the Spirit of Christ.

This point is important: Edwards wrote from the conviction that what the Scripture witnessed to concerning the regenerating work of the Spirit was an accurate characterization of the work of the Spirit in New England, Old England, and the Europe of his own day. The doctrine he felt was proclaimed in Scripture was being lived in his time, and it was the correspondence of Scripture with present facts that gave him such confidence in the Bible as a whole guide for the Christian life. In other words, the *doctrine* of Scripture concerning regeneration was, in fact, being *exposited* by the Spirit in the lives of his contemporaries, and for this reason, a concrete exposition of the doctrinal statement was not only possible but was demanded as a testimony to the present work of God in the world.

Finally, it was necessary for us to present his own explanation of this doctrine because, in fact, this is the form in which Edwards himself has given us his teaching! It was in the period before, during, and after the revival in Northampton and the Great Awakening in New England that the corpus of Edwards' writings dealing with this theme appeared. No significant changes in his thought are to be found, but the detailed exposition, and the increasingly fine discriminations and subtle clarifications in themselves represent his doctrine of the regenerating work of God among men. We have received his view in no other way. Perhaps that is best. It may help us to remember that this man's thought is no

---

623 See Paul Helms' excellent discussion in his editor's introduction to the *Treatise on Grace, op. cit.*, 5-17. The whole introduction is a brilliant brief introduction to Edwards' theology.

system dropped from heaven, but the strenuous formulations of an experienced pastor and theologian and writer, forged in the heat of battle, in the midst and in the aftermath of the greatest, most dramatic, and in every way exciting and confusing, "revival" of the Christian religion that the New England colonies had ever known.

Let us conclude this discussion of Edwards' doctrine of Regeneration by a final quotation from his treatment of the twelfth sign of "truly gracious affections:"

> ... gracious affections do arise from those operations and influences which are spiritual, and ... the inward principle from which they flow, is something divine, a communication of the divine nature, Christ living in the heart, the Holy Spirit dwelling there, in union with the faculties of the soul, as an internal vital principle, in the exercise of those faculties. This is sufficient to show us why grace should have such activity, power and efficacy ... If God dwells in the heart, and be vitally united to it, He will show that He is a God, by the efficacy of His operation. Christ is not in the heart of a saint, as in a sepulcher, or as a dead Saviour, that does nothing; but as in His temple, and as one that is alive from the dead. For in the heart where Christ savingly is, there He lives, and exerts Himself after the power of that endless life, that He received at His resurrection. Thus every saint that is the subject of the benefit of Christ's sufferings, is made to know and experience the power of His resurrection. The Spirit of Christ, which is the immediate spring of grace in the heart, is all life, all power, all act... (2 Cor. 2:4) ... And thus it is that holy affections may have a governing power in the course of a man's life.[624]

---

624 Ibid., 392-393.

About the Author

As a pastor and professor, Peter Reese Doyle has spent most of his adult life studying and teaching the writings of Christianity's great thinkers.

Peter studied at Virginia (Episcopal) Theological Seminary in Virginia and at Seabury-Western Seminary in Illinois, receiving the Bachelor of Divinity degree in 1957.

In 1963 Peter commenced doctoral studies at the University of Basel where he studied Jonathan Edwards' extensive writings on the work of God's Spirit in human lives under the guidance of Professor Karl Barth.

Peter and his wife, Sally Ann, served as Episcopal missionaries at Cuttington College and Divinity School in Liberia where he taught theology and she taught French.

Peter later served as a pastor in Virginia, South Carolina, Tennessee, and Alabama and taught theology at several seminaries.

Since retiring from the pastorate in 2006, Peter has continued his ministry of writing inspirational adventure stories for young readers (The Daring Family Adventures series and The Drums of War series).

Bibliography

Works of Jonathan Edwards Cited:

The History of Redemption. Evansville, IL: The Sovereign Grace Book Club, 1959.

Treatise on Grace and Other Posthumous Writings. Edited by Paul Helm. Cambridge: James Clarke & Co., 1971.

The Select Works of Jonathan Edwards. Edited by Iain H. Murray. 3 volumes. London: The Banner of Truth Trust.

Works of President Edwards (a reprint of the Worcester Edition). 4 volumes. New York, NY: Leavitt & Allen, 1858).

Works of President Edwards. Edited by Sereno E. Dwight. 10 volumes. New York, NY: S. Converse, 1829-30.

Charity and its Fruits. Edited by Tryon Edwards. New York, NY: Robert Carter & Bros., 1852.

Works of Jonathan Edwards. Perry Miller, General Editor. New Haven, CT: Yale University Press, 1957 – Vol. I, 1957; Vol. II, 1959; Vol. III, 1970; Vol. IV, 1972; Vol. V, 1977.

The Works of Jonathan Edwards. 2 volumes. Revised and corrected by Edward Hickman, 1834. Republished by The Banner of Truth Trust, London, 1974.

Jonathan Edwards on Evangelism. Edited by Carl J.C. Wolf. Grand Rapids, MI: William B. Eerdmans Publishing Co., 1958.

Secondary Sources:

Ames, William. *The Marrow of Divinity*. English translation by John Dykstra Eusden. Boston, MA: Pilgrim Press, 1968.

Barth, Karl. *Die Kirchliche Dogmatik*, I, 1. Zurich: Evangelischer Verlag, 1932. English translation by G.T. Thomson. *Church Dogmatics*, I, 1. Edinburgh: T&T Clark, 1936.

Beardslee, John W. (ed.). *Reformed Dogmatics*. New York, NY: Oxford University Press, 1965.

Book of Common Prayer.

Bridge, William. *A Lifting Up for the Downcast*. London: The Banner of Truth Trust, 1961.

Brooks, Thomas. *Heaven on Earth*. London: The Banner of Truth Trust, 1961.

Browne, Edward Harold. *An Exposition of the Thirty-Nine Articles*. London: Longmans, Green, & Co., 1894.

Burt, E.A. *The Metaphysical Foundations of Modern Science*. Garden City, NY: Doubleday & Co., 1932.

Butler, Bishop. *The Analogy of Religion*. Oxford: The University Press, 1848.

Chauncy, Charles. *Seasonable Thoughts*. Boston, MA: Rogers and Fowle, 1743.

Cherry, Conrad. *The Theology of Jonathan Edwards: A Reappraisal*. Garden City, NY: Doubleday & Co., 1966.

Clark, Francis. *Eucharistic Sacrifice and the Reformation*. London: Darton, Longman, & Todd, 1960.

Clarkson, John F., John F. Edwards, William J. Kelly, John J. Welch (eds.). *The Church Teaches*. Documents of the church in English translation. St. Louis: B. Herder Book Co., 1955.

Copleston, Frederick. *A History of Philosophy: Volume V, Hobbes to Hume*. Garden City, NY: Doubleday & Co., 1964.

Currock, Nehemiah (ed.). *The Journal of the Rev. John Wesley, A.M.* 8 volumes. London: The Epworth Press, 1938.

Dampier, William Cecil. *A History of Science, and its Relations with Philosophy and Religion*. Cambridge: University Press, 1948.

Denzinger, Henricus (ed.). *Enchiridion Symbolorum*. Edition XXXII. Freiburg im Breisgau: Verlag Herder K.G., 1963.

Elwood, Douglas J. *The Philosophical Theology of Jonathan Edwards.* New York, NY: Columbia University Press, 1961.

Ferm, Vergilius. *Puritan Sage.* New York, NY: Library Publishers, 1953.

Foster, F.H. *A History of New England Theology.* Chicago, IL: University of Chicago Press, 1907.

Gausted, E.A. *The Great Awakening in New England.* New York, NY: Harper & Brothers, 1957.

Gerstner, John H. *Steps to Salvation, the Evangelistic Message of Jonathan Edwards.* Philadelphia, PA: The Westminster Press, 1960.

Goen, C.C. *Revivalism and Separatism in New England.* New Haven, CT: Yale University Press, 1962.

Grosart, Alexander B., ed. *Selections from the Unpublished Writings of Jonathan Edwards.* Edinburgh: Ballantyne & Co., 1865.

Grosart, Alexander B., ed. *Works of Richard Sibbes.* Edinburgh: James Nichol, 1862-63.

Haller, William. *The Rise of Puritanism.* New York, NY: Harper & Brothers, 1957.

Heppe/Bizer. *Die Dogmatik der Evangelisch – reformierten Kirche.* Neukirchen: Neukerchen Verlag, 1958. English translation by G.T. Thomson, *Reformed Dogmatics.* Grand Rapids, MI: Baker Book House, 1978.

Hirsch, Emanuel. *Geschichte der neueren evangelischen Theologie.* Vol. I. Gutersloh: Gerd Mohn, 1960.

Hoekema, Anthony A. "A New Translation of the Canons of Dort." *Calvin Theological Journal,* 1968.

Stephen R. Holmes, *God of Grace & God of Glory: An Account of the Theology of Jonathan Edwards.* Grand Rapids, MI: Eerdmans, 2000.

Hughes, Philip Edgcumbe. *Theology of the English Reformers.* London: Hodder and Stoughton, 1965.

Jewel, John. *An Apology of the Church of England.* Edited by J.E. Booty. Ithaca, NY: Cornell University Press, 1963.

Lee, Sang Hyun, ed. *The Princeton Companion to Jonathan Edwards.* Princeton, NJ: Princeton University Press, 2005.

Lee, Sang Hyun, ed. *Jonathan Edwards: Writings on the Trinity, Grace, and Faith*. Volume 21 in *The Works of Jonathan Edwards*. New Haven, CT: Yale University Press, 2003.

Leith, John H. *Creeds of the Churches*. Garden City, NY: Doubleday & Co., 1963.

Litton, E.A. *Introduction to Dogmatic Theology*. Edited by Philip E. Hughes. London: James Clark & Co., 1960.

Locke, John. *Essay Concerning Human Understanding*. New York, NY: Dover, 1959.

Luther, Martin. *Commentary on St. Paul's Epistle to the Galatians*. Westwood, MI: Fleming H. Revell Co., 1953.

Luther, Martin. *Luther: Early Theological Works*. Vol. XVI of The Library of Christian Classics. Edited by James Atkinson. London: SCM Press, 1962.

Luther, Martin. *On the Bondage of the Will*. English translation by J.L. Packer & O.R. Johnston. London: James Clarke & Co., 1957.

Marsden, George A. *Jonathan Edwards: A Life*. New Haven, CT: Yale University Press, 2003.

McClymond, Michael J., and Gerald R. McDermott, *The Theology of Jonathan Edwards*. New York, NY: Oxford University Press, 2012.

McDermott, Gerald R., ed. *Understanding Jonathan Edwards: An Introduction to America's Theologian*. New York, NY: Oxford University Press, 2009.

McNeill, John T. *The History and Character of Calvinism*. New York, NY: Oxford University Press, 1954.

McGiffert, A.C., Jr. *Protestant Thought Before Kant*. New York, NY: Scribner, 1911.

McGiffert, A.C., Jr. *Jonathan Edwards*. New York, NY: Harper, 1932.

Miller, Perry (ed.). *Images or Shadows of Divine Things*. New Haven, CT: Yale University Press, 1948.

Miller, Perry. *Errand into the Wilderness*. New York, NY: Harper & Row, 1964.

Miller, Perry. *Jonathan Edwards*. New York, NY: Meridian, 1959.

Miller, Perry. *The American Puritans*. Garden City, NY: Doubleday & Co., 1956.

Miller, Samuel S. *The Younger Jonathan Edwards*. Unpublished book presented to the University of Chicago, 1955.

Moorman, J.R.H. *A History of the Church in England*. New York, NY: Morehouse-Gorham, 1954.

Moss, C.B. *The Christian Faith*. London: S.P.C.K., 1965.

Murray, Iain H., ed. *George Whitefield's Journals*. London: The Banner of Truth Trust, 1960.

Murray, Iain H. *Jonathan Edwards: A New Biography*. Carlisle, PA: The Banner of Truth Trust, 1987.

Neve, J.L. *A History of Christian Thought*. Philadelphia, PA: The Muhlenberg Press, 1946.

Nichols, Stephen J. *An Absolute Sort of Certainty: The Holy Spirit and the Apologetics of Jonathan Edwards*.Phillipsburg, NJ: P&R Publishing, 2003.

Noll, Mark A. *The Rise of Evangelicalism: The Age of Edwards, Whitefield, and the Wesleys*. Downers Grove, IL: InterVarsity Press, 2003.

Nuttall, Geoffrey F. *The Holy Spirit in Puritan Faith and Experience*. Oxford: B. Blackwell, 1947.

Orr, James. *The Progress of Dogma*. London: Hodder & Stoughton, 1901.

Ortlund, Dane C. *Edwards on the Christian Life: Alive to the Beauty of God*. Wheaton, IL: Crossway, 2014.

Ott, Ludwig. *Fundamentals of Catholic Dogma*. Edited by James Canon Bastible. Cork: The Mercier Press, 1963.

Owen, John. *The Death of Death in the Death of Christ*. London: The Banner of Truth Trust, 1959.

Owen, John. *Works of John Owen*. 16 volumes. Edinburgh: Johnstone & Hunter, 1851-52. Reprinted by The Banner of Truth Trust, London, 1965.

Parker, T.H.L., ed. *English Reformers*. Vol. XXVI of the Library of Christian Classics. Philadelphia, PA: The Westminster Press, 1966.

Parrington, V.L. *Main Currents of American Thought*. 2 volumes. New York, NY: Harcourt Brace, 1930.

Paul, Robert S. *The Lord Protector*. Grand Rapids, MI William B. Eerdmans Publishing Co., 1955.

Paul Robert S., ed. *An Apologetical Narration*. London: Robert Dawlman, 1643.

Pauw, Amy Plantinga. *The Supreme Harmony of All: The Trinitarian Theology of Jonathan Edwards.*Grand Rapids, MI: Eerdmans, 2002.

Ramsey, Paul, ed. *Jonathan Edwards: Ethical Writings. The Works of Jonathan Edwards*, Volume 8. New Haven: CT: Yale University Press, 1989.

Ridley, Jasper. *Thomas Cranmer*. Oxford: The University Press, 1967.

Rossiter, Clinton. *The First American Revolution*. New York, NY Harcourt, Brace, and Co., 1956.

Routley, Erik. *Creeds and Confessions*. London: Duckworth, 1962.

Sabine, G.H. *A History of Political Theory*. New York, NY: Henry Holt, 1958.

Schaff, Philip. *Creeds of Christendom*. Vol. III. New York and London: Harper & Brothers, 1877.

Schneider, H.W., ed. *Samuel Johnson: His Career and Writings*. New York, NY: Columbia University Press, 1929.

Simonson, Harold. *Jonathan Edwards: Theologian of the Heart*. Grand Rapids, MI: William B. Eerdmans, 1974.

Simpson, Alan. *Puritanism in Old and New England*. Chicago, IL: The University of Chicago Press, 1955.

Smith, Preserved. *The Enlightenment*. New York, NY: Collier Books, 1962.

Stein, Stephen J., ed. *The Cambridge Companion to Jonathan Edwards*. New York, NY: Cambridge University Press, 2007.

Storms, Sam. *Signs of the Spirit: An Interpretation of Jonathan Edwards' Religious Affections*. Wheaton, IL: Crossway Books, 2007.

Strobel, Kyle. *Formed for the Glory of God: Learning from the Spiritual Practices of Jonathan Edwards.* Downers Grove, IL: InterVarsity Press, 2013.

Sweeney, Douglas A.. *Jonathan Edwards and the Ministry of the Word.* Downers Grove, IL: Inter-Varsity press, 2009.

Sweeney, Douglas A., and Allen C. Guelzo, eds. *The New England Theology: From Jonathan Edwards to Edwards Amasa Park.* Grand Rapids, MI: Baker Academic, 2006.

Sweet, William W. *The Story of Religion in America.* New York & London: Harper & Brothers, 1950.

Taylor, John. *The Scripture Doctrine of Original Sin Proposed to Free and Candid Examination.* 3rd ed. Belfast: John Hay, 1746.

The New Schaff-Herzog Encyclopedia. New York & London: Funk & Wagnalls Co., 1908-14.

Thomas, G.F. *The Principles of Theology.* London: Church Book Room Press, 1956.

Thomas, W.A. Griffith. *The Principles of Theology.* London: Church Book Room Press, 1956.

Tillich, Paul. *Systematic Theology.* 3 volumes. Chicago, IL: The University of Chicago Press, 1951-63.

Toon, Peter. *God's Statesman: The Life and Work of John Owen.* Grand Rapids, MI: Zondervan Publishing House, 1973.

Torrance, T.F. *The School of Faith.* New York, NY: Harper & Brothers, 1959.

Townsend, H.G. (ed.). *The Philosophy of Jonathan Edwards from His Private Notebooks.* Eugene, OR: The University Press, 1955.

Watson, Thomas. *A Body of Divinity.* London: The Banner of Truth Trust, 1960.

Wendel, Francois. *Calvin: Origins and Development of His Religious Thought.* New York, NY: Harper & Row, 1963.

Wertenbaker, Jefferson. *The Puritan Oligarchy.* New York, NY: Grosset & Dunlap, 1947.

Whitefield, George. *George Whitefield's Journals.* London: The Banner of Truth Trust, 1960.

Willey, Basil. *The Seventeenth Century Background*. London: Penguin Books, 1962.

Willey, Basil. *The Eighteenth Century Background*. London: Penguin Books, 1962.

Williams, J. *An Exposition of the Thirty-Nine Articles*. New York, NY: E.P. Dutton & Co., 1895.

Windelband, Wilhelm. *A History of Philosophy*. New York, NY: Harper & Brothers, 1958.

Winslow, Ola Elizabeth. *Jonathan Edwards*. New York, NY: Collier Books, 1961.

Wood, A.S. *The Inextinguishable Blaze*. Grand Rapids, MI: Eerdmans, 1960.

Zurich Letters. Cambridge: The University Press, M.DCCC.XLV.